SONAR™ 5

IGNITE!

The Visual Guide for New Users

Brian Smithers

THOMSON

COURSE TECHNOLOGY™

Professional ■ Technical ■ Reference

ISBN: 1-59200-993-X
Library of Congress Catalog Card Number: 2005931882
Printed in the United States of America
06 07 08 09 10 PH 10 9 8 7 6 5 4 3 2 1

Publisher and General Manager, Thomson Course Technology PTR:
Stacy L. Hiquet

Associate Director of Marketing:
Sarah O'Donnell

Manager of Editorial Services:
Heather Talbot

Marketing Manager:
Mark Hughes

Senior Acquisitions Editor:
Todd Jensen

Senior Editor:
Mark Garvey

Marketing Coordinator:
Jordan Casey

Project Editor and Copy Editor:
Cathleen D. Snyder

Technical Reviewer:
Ryan Pietras at Cakewalk

Thomson Course Technology PTR Editorial Services Coordinator:
Elizabeth Furbish

Interior Layout Tech:
Shawn Morningstar

Cover Designers:
Mike Tanamachi and Nancy Goulet

Indexer:
Sharon Shock

Proofreader:
Anne Smith

THOMSON
COURSE TECHNOLOGY ™
Professional ■ Technical ■ Reference

Thomson Course Technology PTR, a division of Thomson Course Technology
25 Thomson Place ■ Boston, MA 02210 ■ http://www.courseptr.com

To Barb: You're my inspiration.

Acknowledgments

Thanks to Acquisitions Editor Todd Jensen for his confidence, enthusiasm, and guidance, and to the rest of the Thomson Course Technology PTR team, especially Cathleen Snyder for lending her expertise to the task of making me look good in print. I am indebted to Steve Thomas and the gang at Cakewalk for wading through my seemingly endless torrent of questions along the way, and in particular to Cakewalk's Ryan Pietras for the technical edit.

I would be remiss in not acknowledging David Battino, who gave me my first writing opportunity and who always makes me a better writer, along with my great friend Tony Hill, who prodded me to pick up the phone and call David in the first place. Steve Oppenheimer and his fantastic crew at *Electronic Musician*—Dennis Miller, Gino Robair, Len Sasso, Geary Yelton, and company—continually challenge and inspire me, and I am grateful to be part of the *EM* extended family. Thanks also to Neil Worley and *Music Tech Magazine* for giving me an ongoing outlet for SONAR tutorials.

On a personal note, I would like to thank God for blessing me with the greatest family and the most wonderful friends one could have. Thanks to my loving wife Barb for being my loving wife...and my best friend. Thanks, Mom and Dad, for unconditional love and support, even when I decided not to go into mathematics. Thanks to Andy Hagerman for "shifting my paradigm" and unleashing my inner geek. Finally, my love and gratitude go to Nermal, Hillary, and Leopold for making me laugh even in the middle of post-post-deadline panic and exhaustion.

About the Author

Brian Smithers is a classically trained musician, conductor, and composer who has been performing and teaching music for more than 20 years. Taking the concept of the "Renaissance man" to heart at an early age, he has always maintained a diverse professional and artistic life, performing in everything from jazz combos to symphony orchestras while composing and arranging commercial music. The culmination of this ironic juxtaposition saw him spend several years as conductor of a traditional all-acoustic wind band—the world-famous Walt Disney World Band—by day and as a music technology writer for *Electronic Musician*, *Music & Computers*, and *Keyboard* by night. An accomplished recording engineer, Mr. Smithers was at the vanguard of the movement to use notebook computers for live remote recording, performance, and production. He founded a Web site that for several years was the only sustaining Internet resource on laptop-based music production. As Course Director of Audio Workstations and Advanced Audio Workstations at Full Sail Real World Education in Winter Park, Florida, Mr. Smithers coordinates and guides the curriculum of what is arguably the largest digital audio workstation lab environment in the world. He teaches Music Technology at Stetson University in DeLand, Florida, where he also trains the student recording staff and engineers the School of Music's recordings. He has been a SONAR user since it was Cakewalk 3.0.

Contents

Introduction xv

PART I   A TOUR OF THE STUDIO 1

CHAPTER 1   Working with Projects and Files 3

Creating a New Project 4

Opening an Existing Project 6

Importing Audio 7

Documenting Project Information 9

Saving a Project 11

Closing a Project 12

CHAPTER 2   Playing and Listening to SONAR Songs 13

Adjusting Playback Volume 14

Playing a Song 15

Moving Forward and Backward 17

   Fast Forward and Rewind 17

Understanding the Now Time and the Now Slider 18

Using the Project Navigator 19

Looping Playback 21

Muting and Soloing Parts 23

CHAPTER 3   Working with Audio and MIDI Clips 25

Selecting a Clip 26

Setting Drag and Drop Options 27

Moving a Clip 29

CONTENTS }

Copying and Pasting a Clip 30

Deleting a Clip 34

Working with Linked Clips 36

    Pasting Clips as Linked Clips 36

    Selecting Linked Clips 38

    Unlinking Linked Clips 39

CHAPTER 4   Managing SONAR's Views. 41

Showing and Hiding Toolbars 42

Customizing the Track View 43

    Creating and Naming Tracks 43

    Deleting Tracks 45

    Changing the Order of Tracks 45

    Fitting Tracks to the Window 47

    Setting Track View Options 48

    Resizing the Track and Clips Panes 49

    Showing Track Icons .50

Using the Zoom Controls 51

PART II   **USING AUDIO LOOPS** **53**

CHAPTER 5   Importing and Using Audio Loops. 55

Using the Loop Explorer View 56

    Opening the Loop Explorer View 56

    Customizing the Loop Explorer View 57

    Locating and Auditioning a Loop 58

    Bringing a Loop into a Project 59

Working with Loops 60

Making a Clip into a Loop 62

CHAPTER 6   Using Groove Clips 65

Working with Groove Clips 66

Setting the Tempo 68

Working with Project Pitch 70

CONTENTS }

CHAPTER 7 Creating and Editing Groove Clips 73

Opening the Loop Construction View 74

Following Project Pitch (or Not!) .75

Creating Groove Clips 76

    Enabling Looping 77

    Enabling Stretching 79

    Setting a Clip's Root Note .80

Changing the Sound of a Groove Clip 81

Fine-Tuning a Groove Clip's Timing 81

PART III **CREATING YOUR OWN AUDIO** **87**

CHAPTER 8 Recording Your Own Audio 89

Choosing Audio Inputs and Outputs 90

Preparing an Audio Track for Recording 93

    Arming a Track for Recording 93

    Starting and Stopping SONAR's Audio Engine 94

    Enabling Input Echo 95

Making Your First Audio Recording 96

Using Punch Record 97

Loop Recording 100

CHAPTER 9 Editing Audio. 103

Using Snap to Grid 104

Splitting Audio Clips 106

Selecting Partial Clips 108

Slip-Editing a Clip 109

Using Fades and Crossfades 110

    Fading In and Out 110

    Creating Crossfades 112

    Setting Default Fade Curves 113

Processing Audio 114

    Normalizing Audio 114

    Reversing Audio 115

    Removing Silence 116

CHAPTER 10 Managing Audio 119

Archiving Audio Tracks .120

Cloning a Track 121

Wiping a Track 123

Consolidating Project Audio 124

Applying Clip Trimming 125

Cleaning Audio Folders .126

PART IV **WORKING WITH MIDI** **129**

CHAPTER 11 Using the Cakewalk TTS-1 131

Opening the Tutorial Project 132

Using the Synth Rack 134

Starting the TTS-1 134

Assigning MIDI Track Outputs 136

Playing the Tutorial Project 137

Changing Patches 137

Setting the Default Bank and Patch 137

Inserting a Patch Change 139

Changing Tempo Gradually 140

CHAPTER 12 Editing MIDI 143

Using MIDI Clips 144

Slip-Editing MIDI Clips 144

Transposing Clips 146

Reversing MIDI Clips 147

Changing the Length of MIDI Notes 148

Editing MIDI in the Piano Roll View 150

Moving and Copying Notes 150

Changing a Note's Length 152

Adding and Deleting Notes 153

Editing Note Velocities 154

Drawing Controllers and Other Events 155

CONTENTS }

CHAPTER 13 Recording MIDI Tracks 159

Choosing MIDI Inputs and Outputs 160

Configuring the Metronome 161

Setting Up for Recording 163

   Assigning the MIDI Track Input and Output 163

   Getting Ready to Record 166

Recording Your First MIDI Part 168

Punch-Recording MIDI 169

Loop Recording 171

CHAPTER 14 Cleaning Up Your MIDI Act. 175

Fixing Timing with Quantize 176

Better Timing with Groove Quantize .179

Using Logical MIDI Processes 182

   Scaling Velocity 182

   Sliding MIDI Data 183

Using Track Parameters 185

   Using Velocity Trim (Vel+) 185

   Using Time Offset (Time+) 186

   Using Key Offset (Key+) 187

CHAPTER 15 Mastering MIDI's Ins and Outs 189

Using Instrument Definitions 190

   Assigning Instruments 190

   Importing Instrument Definitions 193

Recording Multiple Inputs 197

Filtering MIDI Input 198

PART V EFFECTS AND MIXING 201

CHAPTER 16 Using Audio Effects. 203

Using Real-Time Audio Effects 204

   Using Cakewalk FxChorus 204

   Using Sonitus:fx Equalizer 207

   Using Sonitus:fx Compressor 210

Creating Effects Presets 211

Bypassing an Effect 212

Changing the Order of Effects 213

Using Clip-Based Audio Effects 214

Freezing Audio Tracks 216

CHAPTER 17   Mastering Audio's Ins and Outs 217

Using the Bus Pane 218

Creating a Headphone Mix 221

Creating an Interface Send 221

Creating a Bus Send 223

Using a Send to Apply Reverb 224

Creating Subgroups, Submixes, and Stems 227

Creating a Subgroup 227

Creating a Submix or Stem 229

Surround Mixing 231

Setting SONAR's Surround Format 231

Using Surround Tracks and Buses 233

Using Surround Effects 236

CHAPTER 18   Using the Console View 239

Assigning Inputs and Outputs 240

Adjusting Level and Pan 242

Creating Tracks, Sends, and Buses 243

Using the Channel EQ (Producer Edition) 245

Configuring the Console View's Appearance 247

CHAPTER 19   Capturing Your Mix for CD and the Internet 251

Recording External Synth Parts 252

Exporting Audio 254

Exporting as a WAV File 254

Exporting an MP3 File 257

PART VI   **HIDDEN MAGIC** **261**

CHAPTER 20   Working with Notes and Lyrics 263

Using the Staff View 264

Configuring the Staff View 264

Working with Notes 266

Changing How Notes Are Displayed 268

Using the Fret View 269

Adding Expression Marks 272

Using Lyrics 274

CHAPTER 21   Using Drum Maps and the Drum Grid 277

Assigning a Track to a Drum Map 278

Viewing the Drum Grid 279

Editing in the Drum Grid 281

Painting MIDI Note Patterns 283

Editing Drum Maps 284

CHAPTER 22   Getting More Efficient 289

Using Templates 290

Creating Your Own Templates 290

Creating a New Default Template 292

Using Key Bindings 294

Using the Patch Browser 297

Using the Track/Bus Inspector .299

Assigning I/O from the Track Menu 300

PART VII   **APPENDIXES** **303**

APPENDIX A   Setup and Troubleshooting 305

Audio Drivers 306

Wave Profiler 309

Managing Audio Latency 311

APPENDIX B Understanding Audio and MIDI 313

What Is MIDI? 313

What Is Digital Audio? 314

Comparing MIDI and Digital Audio 315

APPENDIX C Managing Your CPU Resources 317

The CPU and Disk Meters 317

Lightening the Load 318

Using Group Effects 318

Submixing Audio Tracks 319

Freezing Tracks and Synths 319

Index 321

} Introduction

This book will get you started making music with one of the most powerful Windows-based music production programs available—Cakewalk's SONAR 5 Producer Edition. It is an equally useful guide to SONAR 5 Studio Edition, Cakewalk's less-expensive but still feature-rich offering. In these pages you will find everything you need to demystify the deep and powerful functions of this popular program, regardless of your prior experience.

SONAR 5 Ignite!: The Visual Guide for New Users takes you step by step through MIDI sequencing, digital audio recording, and mixing your song into a finished product. You'll learn how to set up your project, create tracks, edit MIDI and digital audio clips, and utilize virtual instruments. Finally, you'll see how SONAR's effects plug-ins and exciting surround-sound capabilities enable you to realize a great-sounding mix that's ready for CD or Web distribution.

If you want to make music and you're looking for maximum-strength tools with a minimal learning curve, SONAR 5 Producer Edition and this book will have you jamming in no time. In addition, you'll find extra material on the book's companion Web site, located at http://www.courseptr.com/downloads.

Who Should Read This Book?

This book is intended for novices who are new to music-production software or new to SONAR. Some basic computer knowledge is assumed—such as the ability to navigate drives and folders and use icons, menus, and dialog boxes—as is a basic grasp of music terminology.

Because its capabilities are so vast, SONAR can seem pretty daunting at first, so each chapter deals with a manageable chunk of technology. Each successive chapter builds on the previous ones, taking you to the summit one sure-footed step at a time.

Nearly every step in this book is accompanied by a clear illustration, so you'll never have any doubts about whether you're looking at the right screen or choosing the right tool. The non-technical language helps move you gradually from neophyte to seasoned user with a minimum of trauma; if you're looking for techno-babble you can use to impress your friends, you won't find any here!

Each task is clearly identified by heading, so you can easily find what you need by checking the Table of Contents. Although the materials are intended to be read and practiced in order, if you're inclined to skip around or jump straight to what you need, this book will suit your working style and help you find what you're after.

Added Advice to Make You a Pro

You'll soon see that everything in this book is distilled to the essentials that will help you get results, going step by step without lengthy explanations. Be aware, however, that you're jumping into some sophisticated technology, so here and there you'll find special boxes to fill you in on important details.

At the end of the book are three appendixes that delve more deeply into the technology behind SONAR's sequencing and recording capabilities. Discover ways to manage your system's audio setup, learn the ins and outs of MIDI and digital audio and why they're such a complementary team, and find ways to get the best performance out of your computer.

It doesn't matter whether you're into classical recording, hip-hop production, or becoming a member of the next Beatles—you've got the power in your hands, so let's get started!

PART I

A Tour of
the Studio

Chapter 1: Working with Projects and Files

Chapter 2: Playing and Listening to SONAR Songs

Chapter 3: Working with Audio and MIDI Clips

Chapter 4: Managing SONAR's Views

1 } Working with Projects and Files

As you create music in SONAR 5, you will gradually accumulate numerous files of various types. By knowing what sort of information is contained within each file and how the files work together, you will always be in command of your creative efforts. In this chapter, you'll learn how to:

※ Create and open a project

※ Import audio into a project

※ Document project information

※ Save your project

※ Close a project

Creating a New Project

A new song idea usually starts with a new SONAR project. A new project is the musical equivalent of a painter's blank canvas. The project file will eventually hold a complete description of your song—everything from tempo to number of bars, lyrics, effects, MIDI data, and links to external audio and video files. Here's how to create that blank canvas.

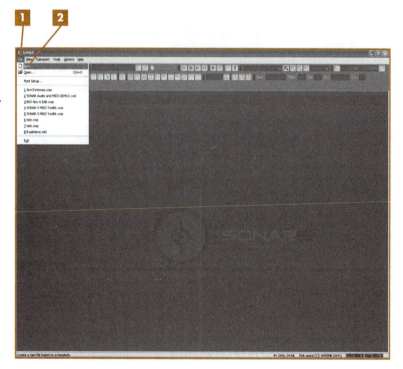

1 Click on File. The File menu will appear.

2 Click on New. The New Project File dialog box will open.

3 Type a meaningful name in the Name text box.

4 Click on the desired template. The template name will be highlighted.

5 Click on OK. The new project file will appear onscreen.

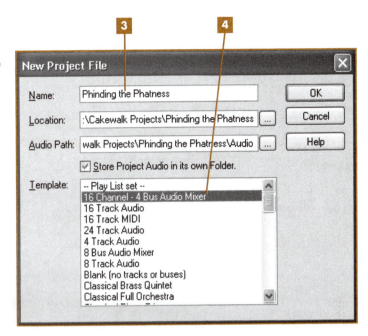

3 **4**

New Project File

Name: Phinding the Phatness

Location: :\Cakewalk Projects\Phinding the Phatness ...

Audio Path: walk Projects\Phinding the Phatness\Audio ...

☑ Store Project Audio in its own Folder.

Template:
-- Play List set --
16 Channel - 4 Bus Audio Mixer
16 Track Audio
16 Track MIDI
24 Track Audio
4 Track Audio
8 Bus Audio Mixer
8 Track Audio
Blank (no tracks or buses)
Classical Brass Quintet
Classical Full Orchestra

OK

Cancel

Help

❋ **Templates**

SONAR 5's templates allow you to choose how you want your new project to look and act, so you can get started making music more quickly. For now, accept the default selection, the Normal template.

Opening an Existing Project

When you want to do further work on a project you created previously, you simply open the project and pick up where you left off.

1 Click on File. The File menu will appear.

2 Click on Open. The Open dialog box will open.

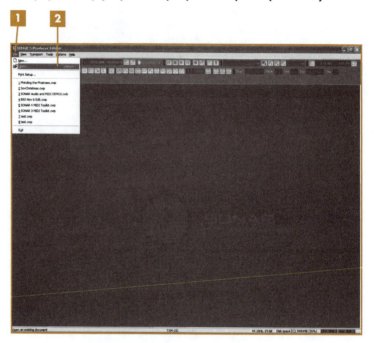

❖ **Recent Files**

SONAR 5 keeps track of the files you've had open recently, listing them as numbered items at the bottom of the File menu. To open a recently used file, click on the File menu, point to the file you want to open, and click on the file's name.

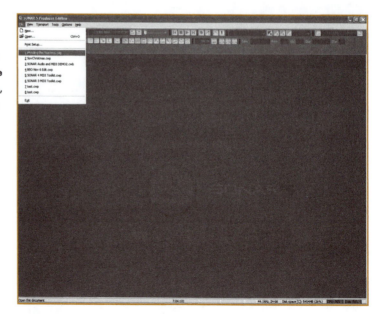

❖❖❖

3 Navigate to the file's location.

4 Click on the file you want to open. The name of the file will appear in the File name box.

5 Click on Open. The file will appear onscreen.

Importing Audio

Once you've got a SONAR project open, you can begin to add audio and MIDI information to start building your song. One way to get audio into SONAR is to import existing audio files. Here's how to do that.

1 Click on File. The File menu will appear.

2 Point to Import. The Import submenu will appear.

3 Click on Audio. The Import Audio dialog box will open.

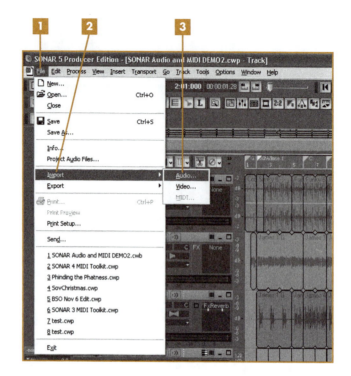

4 Navigate to the file's location.

5 Click on the file you want to open. The name of the file will appear in the File name box.

6 Optionally, click on the Play button to audition the audio file. The audio file will play.

7 Click on Open. One of two things will occur:

* If no audio track is selected, the audio file will be imported into a new audio track.

* If an audio track is selected, the audio file will be imported into that track.

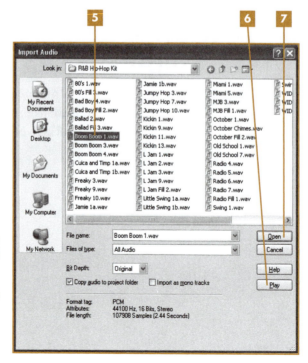

❋ Auditioning Audio Clips

The Import Audio dialog box will play the selected clip through whatever is designated as your default sound playback device in Windows's Sounds and Audio Devices Control Panel. If you have an audio interface separate from your computer's built-in soundcard, you will probably hear the clip through your soundcard, not the interface.

Documenting Project Information

One of the powerful things about working in a computer-based DAW such as SONAR 5 is the ability to keep notes about a project within the project itself. SONAR calls this File Info. Here's how to view and use it.

1 Click on File. The File menu will appear.

2 Click on Info. The File Info dialog box will open.

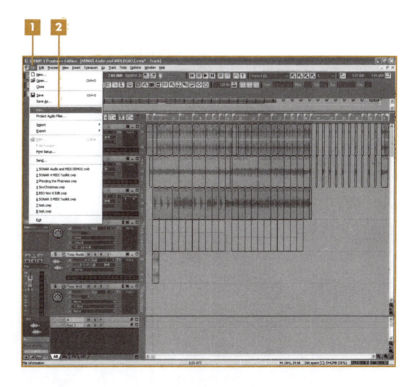

3 Click in any field and type some text to enter.

4 Click on the Close button when you are finished. The dialog box will close, and the infor-mation will be remembered.

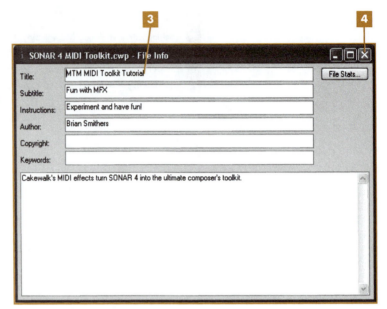

File Info

The File Info dialog box is a great place to store information, such as who wrote the song, who played on it, when it was created, and which version this file represents.

Saving a Project

Of course, there would be no point in slaving over a hot tune just to have it disappear when you turn off the computer, so SONAR 5 makes it easy for you to save your work. Saving your work means preserving all the changes you have made to a project—editing, recording, mixing, and so on—by updating the project file.

1 Click on File. The File menu will appear.

2a Click on Save. The current project will be saved with the current filename.

OR

2b Click on Save As to save the file with a different filename.

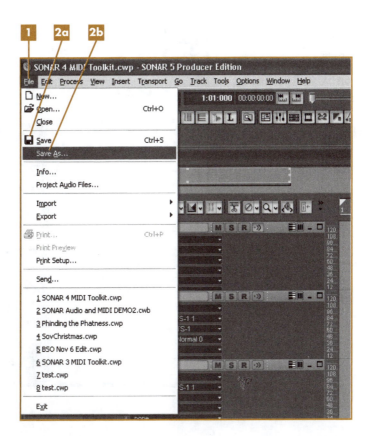

❀ Save As

Save As creates a copy of the project file, allowing you to do additional work on a project without changing the original project file. The copy uses the same audio files as the original, so you don't waste disk space.

Closing a Project

Sometimes you might want to stop working on one project and start working on another. Although SONAR allows you to have multiple projects open at one time, this can create clutter and potential confusion, so it's usually best to close one project before opening another.

1. Click on File. The File menu will appear.

2. Click on Close. If you have saved the project, it will close immediately. Otherwise, SONAR will prompt you to save the project before closing it.

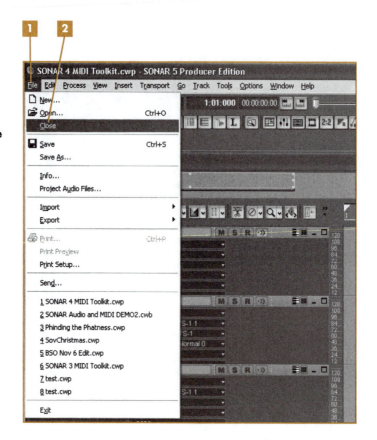

2 Playing and Listening to SONAR Songs

Before you get too involved in creating new songs, I want to explore how SONAR 5 handles playback of a song. After all, what's the point in making a song if you can't listen to it? In this chapter, you'll learn how to:

* Adjust the volume for playback
* Start and stop playback of a song
* Move forward and backward through a song
* Loop (repeat) a section of a song
* Mute and solo parts of a song

Adjusting Playback Volume

It's extremely important to know how to control the volume of your music. If it's too quiet, you won't be able to make good judgments about how to make the music better, especially when you get into mixing in Part V, "Effects and Mixing." If the music is too loud, it can damage your ears. Your ears are the whole reason you're making music, so protect them!

❋ Adjusting Volume

The steps for adjusting volume may vary according to what audio interface or soundcard you are using. The following procedure will cover the majority of built-in soundcards, but some may have their own mixers or control panels. Such applets are usually found within the Windows Control Panel, which you can access via the Start menu.

1 Click on the speaker icon in the System Tray section of the Taskbar. The volume control slider will appear.

2a Drag the volume slider up or down. The volume will increase or decrease, respectively.

OR

2b Click on the Mute check box. A ☑ will appear in the box and all audio playback will be silenced. Click again to un-mute the audio.

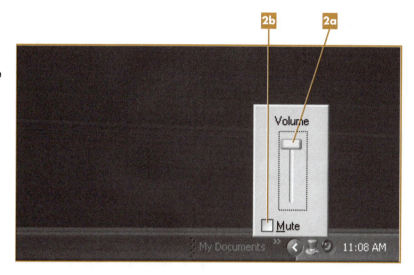

Playing a Song

Now it's time to listen to a song playing back through SONAR. You'll notice that SONAR's basic playback controls resemble those of a tape deck or CD player. These familiar controls are part of what makes SONAR so user-friendly, but there are also some important differences, as you'll see.

1 Open a SONAR project following the procedure from Chapter 1.

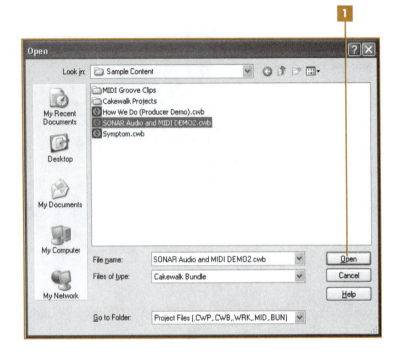

2 Click on the Play button. The song will start to play.

3 If necessary, adjust the playback volume as described in the preceding section.

4 Click on the Stop button. The song will stop playing.

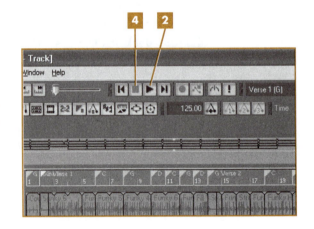

✱ Play/Stop Shortcut

Instead of clicking on the Play and Stop buttons, you can simply press the spacebar to start and stop playback.

Moving Forward and Backward

In music creation, there is rarely a time when you'll simply want to listen to a song from beginning to end. That's what you want your listeners to do! While you're creating, you need to be able to move from verse to verse to chorus to intro efficiently. Here's how.

Fast Forward and Rewind

Surrounding the Stop and Play buttons on the Transport toolbar are two icons that look very much like the Fast Forward and Rewind buttons on a tape deck or CD player. They are indeed similar, but instead of moving gradually forward and backward they jump directly to the beginning and end of the song.

1 Click on the Rewind button. SONAR will jump to the beginning of the song.

2 Click on the Go to end button. SONAR will jump to the end of the song.

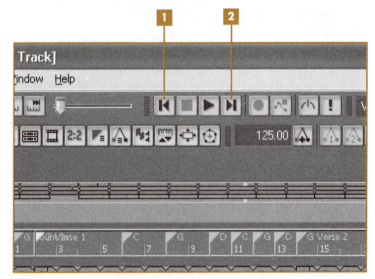

❈ **More Shortcuts**

It's often more efficient to navigate using the computer keyboard instead of the mouse. You can press the W key or Ctrl+Home to rewind, and press Ctrl+End to go to the end of the song.

Understanding the Now Time and the Now Slider

SONAR defines the current location within a song by what it calls the *Now time*. When you start playback, SONAR always starts from Now. The Now time is indicated by a vertical cursor that stretches across the Track pane, and it moves to indicate song position during playback. You can set the Now time directly, either by clicking at the position you want or by moving a slider to the desired point in the song.

1a Drag the Now slider to the left or right. The Now time will move earlier or later, respectively.

OR

1b Click in the Time Ruler. The Now time will move to wherever you clicked.

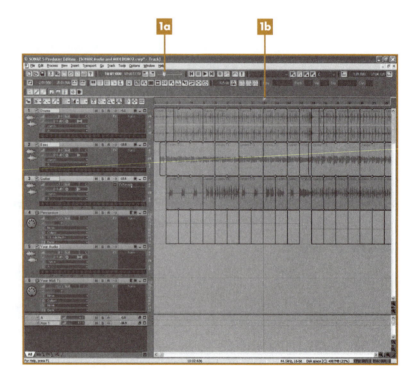

✻ Still More Shortcuts

You can move the Now time later one bar at a time by pressing Ctrl+PageDown. Pressing Ctrl+PageUp moves the Now time earlier one bar at a time.

Using the Project Navigator

The Project Navigator gives you a sort of bird's-eye view of your entire project. A green rectangle indicates what part of the project is currently displayed in the Clips pane, and you can view a different part of the project simply by dragging the rectangle to a new location. You can display the Project Navigator in the Track view above the Track and Clips panes, or you can open it in its own window.

By default, the Project Navigator shows the entire duration of your project (you can customize this if you choose to), but it will not show tracks that are hidden. DXi (virtual instrument) tracks are shown as blank spaces. You can resize the rectangle, effectively zooming the Clips pane in or out, by dragging on its handles. You can even Alt+drag around a segment to make it fill the Clips pane.

Note that repositioning the current Clips pane view does not move the Now time. If you want to start playback from the new position you will need to click in the Time Ruler or use another one of the methods outlined previously to set the Now time.

1a Click on the Views toolbar's Project Navigator button. The Project Navigator will appear in a separate window.

OR

1b Click on the Track view's Project Navigator button. The Project Navigator will appear at the top of the Track view.

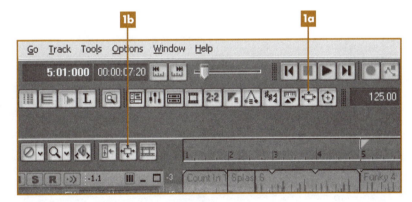

2 Drag the green rectangle within the Project Navigator. The Clips pane will show whatever is within the rectangle.

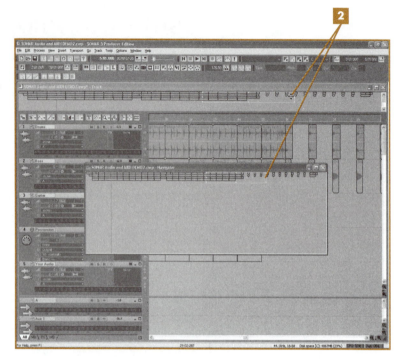

3 Drag one of the handles on the green rectangle. The Clips pane will zoom in or out as you resize the rectangle.

4 Alt+drag anywhere within the Project Navigator. When you release the mouse button, the Clips pane will relocate and zoom to show exactly what you selected.

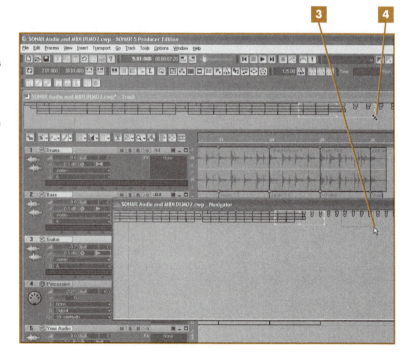

5 Right-click anywhere in the Project Navigator. The context menu will appear.

6 Choose a different horizontal zoom. Horz Zoom to Project will show the entire project timeline. The other selections will zoom in, with Level 1 providing the greatest detail.

7 Choose a different track height. Track Height Medium is the default.

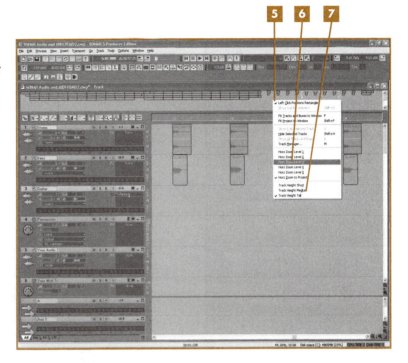

Looping Playback

As you're working on a song, you may want to have a passage repeat indefinitely so you can practice a part or tweak the mix. Doing this is a simple three-step process—define the beginning and ending points of the loop, engage Loop playback mode, and hit Play. The following steps show you how to do this.

1 Drag in the Time Ruler from the start of the loop to the end of the loop. The selection will be highlighted.

2 Click on the Set Loop to Selection button. The selection will be bracketed by yellow loop markers, and the Loop On/Off button will be turned on.

3 Click on the Play button. The selection will play, looping back to the beginning whenever it reaches the end.

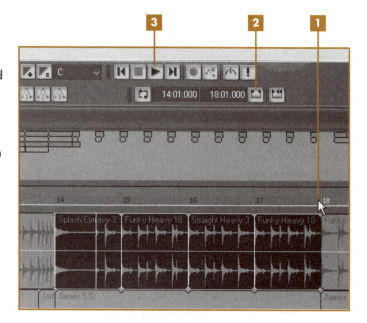

4 Drag a yellow loop marker. The Start or End time of the loop will change accordingly.

5 Click on the Loop On/Off button. SONAR will return to normal playback mode.

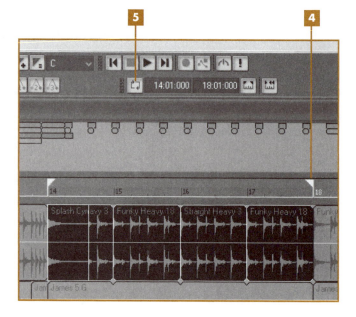

Muting and Soloing Parts

There will be times when you want to hear a particular track by itself, and other times when you want to hear the song temporarily without a part. Here's how to mute or solo a part.

1. Click on a track's Mute button. That track will not play back with the other tracks. Click on the Mute button again to hear the track.

2. Click on a track's Solo button. The track will play back by itself. Click on the Solo button again to hear the track in context.

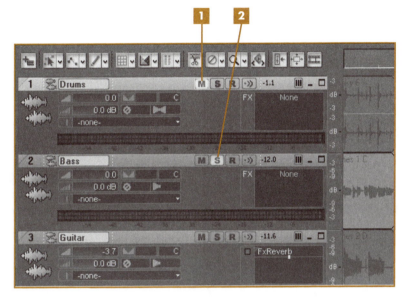

3 } Working with Audio and MIDI Clips

The key to mastering a powerful music production program like SONAR 5 is understanding how it organizes musical data. You've already looked at some of the different views SONAR provides of your music; now you'll look more closely at a data structure called a *clip*. A clip is a portion of recorded audio or MIDI that can be edited as a single unit. It appears as a rectangle in the right side of the Track view. In this chapter, you'll learn how to:

❊ Select clips

❊ Move and arrange clips

❊ Copy, paste, and delete clips

❊ Link clips

❊ ❊ ❊

Selecting a Clip

You'll find that working with clips is very intuitive and familiar. This is by design—clips are intended to allow you to manage your musical ideas with many of the same functions you use in a word processor. Of course, just as with your word processor, you have to select data before you can do anything with it. The following steps show you how to select one or more clips.

1 Click on the middle of a clip. The clip will turn a darker color to indicate that it is now selected.

2 Ctrl+click on another clip. Both clips will be selected.

3 Ctrl+click on either selected clip. That clip will no longer be selected.

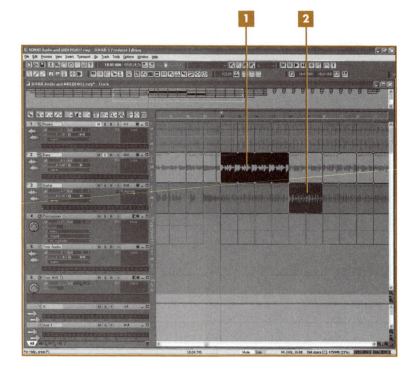

4 Click on a track number. All of the clips in that track will be selected.

5 Drag around several clips. Those clips will be selected.

6 Ctrl+drag around several other clips. Those clips will be added to the previous selection.

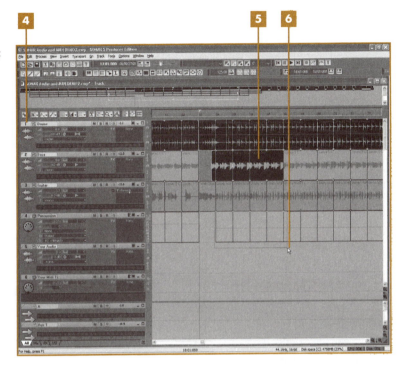

Setting Drag and Drop Options

SONAR 5 lets you define exactly what happens when you move and copy clips. Although you can change your mind at any time, the default behavior is defined in the Drag and Drop Options. Here's how to set them the way you want them.

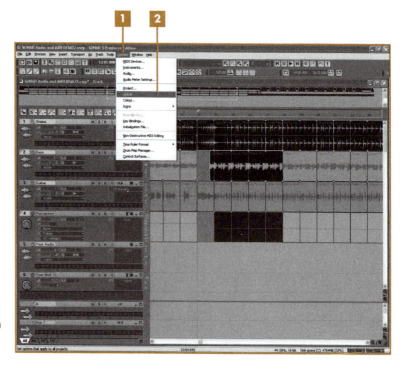

1. Click on Options. The Options menu will appear.

2. Click on Global. The Global Options dialog box will open.

3. Click on the Editing tab. The tab will come to the front.

4. Click on a check box or option button to choose the desired properties. The options work as follows:

   ❋ Blend Old and New. This will cause the clip you are moving to merge with any data at the location to which you've moved it, so both will be heard.

   ❋ Replace Old with New. This will cause any data at the destination to be deleted, leaving only the clip you moved there.

   ❋ Delete Whole Measures. When you choose to Replace Old with New, this option will cause the destination data to be deleted all the way to the next bar line, rather than deleting just enough to fit the moved clip.

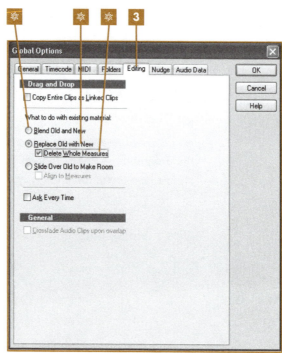

❋ **Slide Over Old to Make Room.** This will cause all data at the destination *and all data from there to the end of the track* to move to the right (later in time) far enough for the moved clip to fit in.

❋ **Align to Measures.** When you choose the Slide Over Old to Make Room option, this option causes the old data to slide later in whole-measure amounts, rather than just enough to squeeze in the moved clip.

❋ **Ask Every Time.** If you ordinarily prefer one of the aforementioned options, you can save yourself time by unchecking this box, preventing the Drag and Drop Options dialog box from opening when you move a clip.

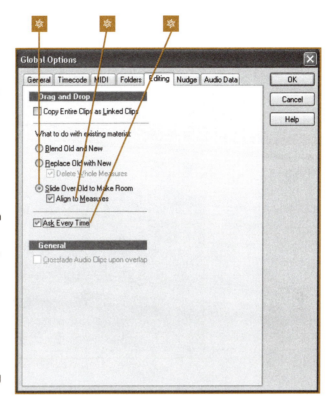

Moving a Clip

When you've selected a clip or clips, you can easily move them to a new location using the same drag-and-drop technique you would use in almost any Windows application. The following steps show you how to do this, along with how to choose the way in which clips will be moved.

1 Select a clip or clips as described earlier. The clips will be highlighted.

2 Drag the selected clip(s) to a point earlier or later in a track or to a different track. The clip(s) will be moved to the new location. Anything at the destination will be moved, replaced, or blended according to the Drag and Drop Options you set earlier.

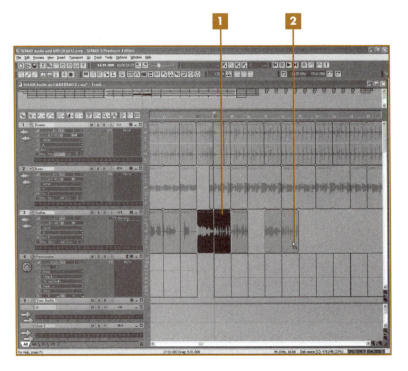

Ask Every Time

If you chose Ask Every Time in the Drag and Drop Options dialog box, you will see the Drag and Drop Options dialog box before the clip is moved. Choose the appropriate options for your current edit and then click on OK to complete the move.

Copying and Pasting a Clip

In music, as in life, one can never get too much of a good thing. It stands to reason, then, that you will often want to use a musical idea more than once in your song. SONAR 5 lets you copy and paste a clip or a selection of multiple clips, and it even lets you paste a selection repeatedly, saving you time and effort in the production process. Just follow these steps.

1 Select a clip or clips as described earlier.

2 Click on Edit. The Edit menu will appear.

3 Click on Copy. The Copy dialog box will open.

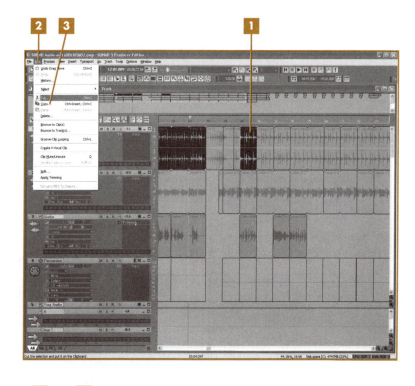

4 If Events in Tracks is not already checked, click in the check box. A ☑ will appear, indicating that events in the track or tracks will be copied.

5 Click in other check boxes to choose other options as needed. A ☑ will appear for each option you have chosen.

6 Click on OK. The dialog box will close, and the selected clips will be copied.

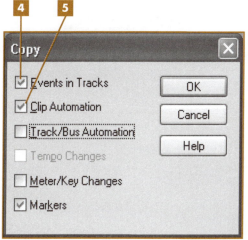

❋ Why Doesn't Anything Happen?

You won't actually see any result from simply copying a clip. The clip is copied to the Windows *clipboard,* where it remains available to be pasted once or several times. If you want to remove a clip from its current location and load it into the clipboard to be pasted, follow the aforementioned procedure using the Cut command instead of the Copy command.

7 Click in the Time Ruler to place the Now time where you want to paste the selection. The cursor will indicate the Now time's new position.

8 Click on Edit. The Edit menu will appear.

9 Click on Paste. The Paste dialog box will open.

10 If necessary, click in the Starting at Time field and type a new time to change where the clips are to be pasted.

11 Type the number of times you want to paste the selection in the Repetitions field.

12 Click on the down arrow at the right of the Starting Track field.

13 Click on the number of the track into which you want to paste the clips.

14 Click on Advanced. The Paste dialog box will expand to display the advanced options.

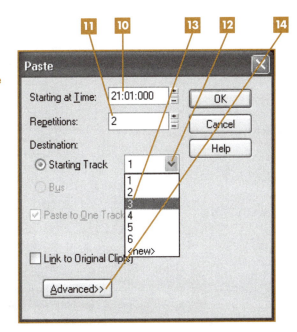

15 Choose the appropriate advanced options. These options include:

❀ **Align to Measures.** Each repetition of the pasted clips will start on a bar line.

❀ **Interval.** Each repetition of the pasted clips will start this far after the previous one started. This value always starts at the length of the selection currently on the clipboard.

❀ **What to do with existing material.** These options mean exactly what they did in the Drag and Drop Options dialog box discussed earlier.

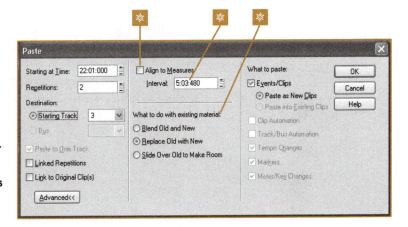

33

❀❀❀

❋ **Paste as New Clips.** The data will be pasted as distinct clips.

❋ **Paste into Existing Clips.** The pasted data will be incorporated into any clips that exist at the destination.

16 Click on OK. The dialog box will close, and the selection will appear where you pasted it.

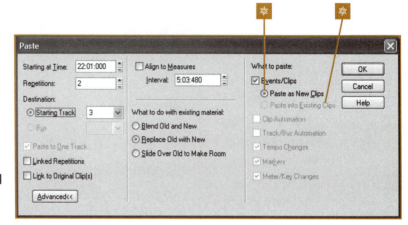

❋ **Drag and Drop**

You can also copy a clip once using drag and drop. Just hold down the Ctrl key as you move a clip, and SONAR will make a copy of the clip and leave the original in place.

Deleting a Clip

Even Beethoven needed an eraser; fortunately, SONAR 5 allows you to delete clips easily. Of course, you'll want to be sure you're deleting exactly what you want—nothing more and nothing less—so follow these steps.

1 Select any clip or clips you want to delete.

2 Right-click on a selected clip. The context menu will appear

3 Click on Delete. The Delete dialog box will open.

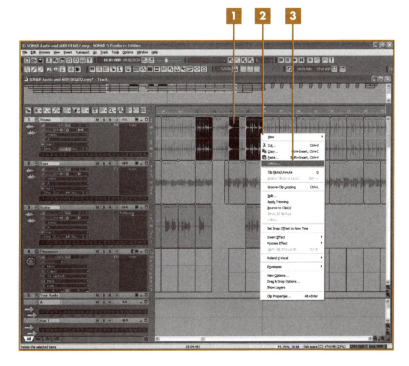

4 If necessary, click on the Events in Tracks check box. A ✓ will appear.

5 Click to choose additional options as appropriate. A ✓ will appear for each chosen option.

6 Click on OK. The dialog box will close, and the selected clips will be removed from the tracks.

35
❁❁❁

Working with Linked Clips

Wouldn't it be terrible to copy and paste a cool bass clip about a million times and later decide you want to change one note of the clip...and have to re-paste it a million times? SONAR 5 can save you from this kind of heartache! All you need to do is create *linked clips*. Linked clips are automatically updated with any changes you make to any one of them. Had you done that with your bass clip, you could change that one note in any of the linked copies, and the note would be changed throughout the entire song. If this sounds cool and powerful, read on and see how to make it happen.

Pasting Clips as Linked Clips

You create linked clips during the pasting process. You can choose to have the new copies linked only to each other (and not to the original), or you can choose to have the original and the new copies all be interdependent.

❄ **Delete Hole**

Choose Delete Hole to make everything that follows the deleted data move to the left (earlier) to fill in the gap. Specify Shift by Whole Measures to fill in the gap while maintaining the same bar and beat relationships within the moved data.

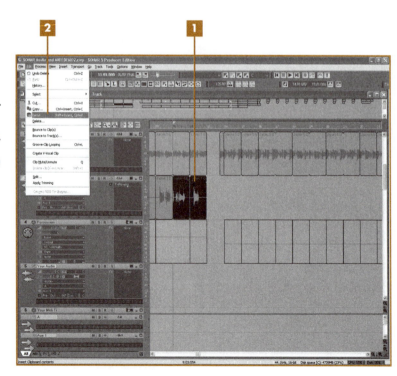

1 Select and copy one or more clips as described previously or by using the shortcut Ctrl+C. The clips will be held in the clipboard, ready to be pasted.

2 Click on Paste in the Edit menu or use the shortcut Ctrl+V. The Paste dialog box will open.

3 Type a number of repetitions in the Repetitions box and then choose from the following advanced options:

- ❀ Linked Repetitions. Check this option to make the copied clips interdependent without affecting the original.

- ❀ Link to Original Clip(s). Check this option *in addition to Linked Repetitions* to make all of the copied clips and the original interdependent.

4 Click on OK. The dialog box will close, and the linked clips will be pasted.

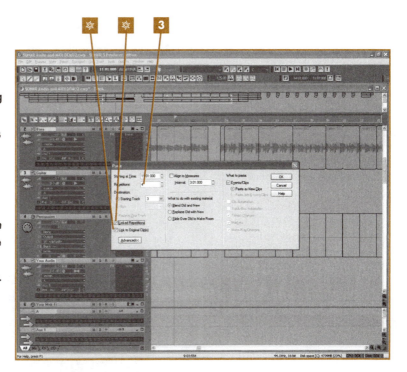

❀ **Dragging, Dropping, and Linking**

You can link clips using drag-and-drop copying by checking the Copy Entire Clips as Linked Clips option in the Drag and Drop Options dialog box.

Selecting Linked Clips

It's easy and convenient to select a group of linked clips so they can be copied, moved, or deleted as a unit. Here's how.

1. Right-click on any one of a group of linked clips. The context menu will appear.

2. Click on Select All Siblings. All of the linked clips will be selected and ready to be copied, moved, or deleted.

Unlinking Linked Clips

SONAR 5 knows that we all change our minds sometimes, so linking clips is not necessarily a permanent arrangement. Follow these steps to break the link between clips.

1 Select one or more of a group of linked clips. The clips will be highlighted.

2 Right-click on any one of the selected clips. The context menu will appear.

3 Click on Unlink. The Unlink Clips dialog box will open.

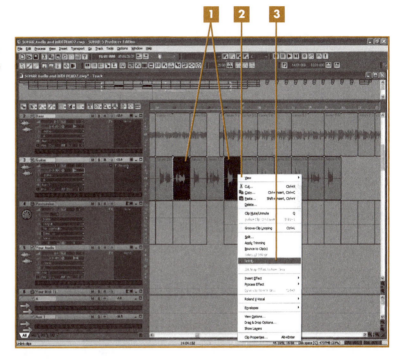

4 Click on the desired option. The option will be selected. The options are:

❁ New Linked Group. The selected clips will no longer be linked to the original group, but they will be linked to each other.

❁ Independent, Not Linked At All. The selected clips will not be linked to each other or to the original group.

5 Click on OK. The dialog box will close, and the clips will be unlinked.

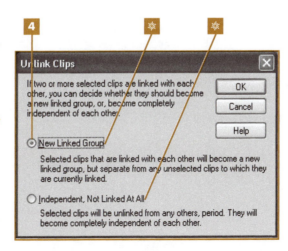

4 } Managing SONAR's Views

Call it computer *feng shui*. Being efficient and productive means making SONAR's user interface work for you. Cakewalk has thoughtfully provided ways for you to customize SONAR's work environment so it looks and acts the way you want it to. In this chapter, you'll learn how to:

* Show and hide various toolbars
* Create, resize, rename, and sort tracks
* Customize the appearance of the Track view
* Zoom in and out

Showing and Hiding Toolbars

SONAR 5 features a variety of toolbars, each one providing important one-click functions for specific situations. You already worked with the Transport toolbar in Chapter 2. If you display all of the toolbars all of the time, your screen will be quite cluttered, so here's how to pick and choose only the ones you need.

1 Click on View. The View menu will appear.

2 Click on Toolbars. The Toolbars dialog box will open.

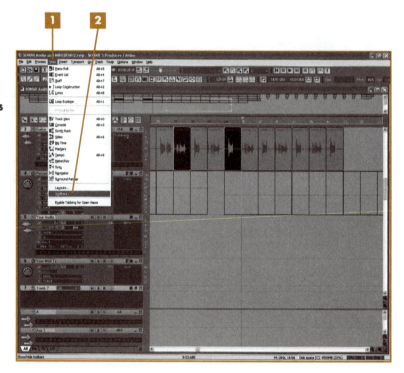

3 Click in a check box to show a toolbar. Some of the most common toolbars are:

✷ **Standard.** Includes basic Windows functions, such as Open, Save, Cut, Copy, and so on.

✷ **Transport.** Includes Start, Stop, Rewind, Record, and so on.

✷ **Position.** Displays the Now time and the Now time slider.

✷ **Views.** Lets you open different views.

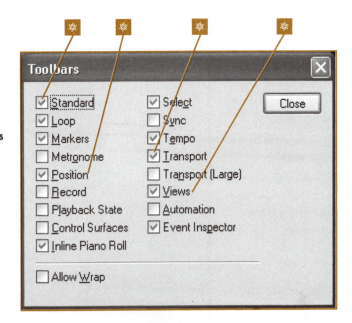

Customizing the Track View

SONAR 5's Track view is the default view of your music and is your primary workspace. It is the one view that cannot be closed without closing the current project, although it can be modified in numerous ways or minimized. You'll notice that the Track view is divided into two spaces: the Track pane on the left and the Clips pane on the right. Next, you'll explore ways to make the Track view display exactly what you need to see as you work—no more and no less.

Creating and Naming Tracks

As is typical of recording/sequencing programs, SONAR 5 organizes your musical ideas into *tracks*. As you saw while playing songs in Chapter 2, tracks represent sequences of audio or MIDI information arranged along a timeline. Events that are displayed parallel in tracks take place simultaneously at playback. SONAR lets you create as many tracks as you need to hold and coordinate your musical ideas. When you need another track, here's how to make one.

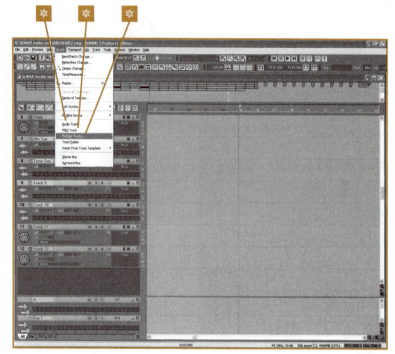

1 Click on the Insert menu and choose from the following:

* Audio Track. Creates a new blank audio track.

* MIDI Track. Creates a new blank MIDI track.

* Multiple Tracks. Opens a dialog box that allows you to create multiple audio and MIDI tracks.

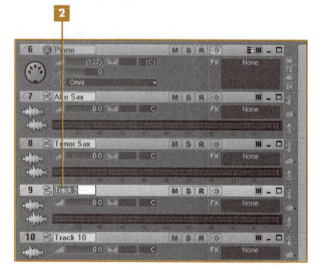

2 Double-click on any track name. The existing name will be highlighted.

3 Type a new name for the track.

4 Press Enter to confirm the name.

Deleting Tracks

In your efforts to keep your Track view neat and tidy, you'll want to get rid of any unused tracks. Here's how to delete them.

1 Click on a track number to select a track for deletion. As with clips, you can Ctrl+click to select multiple tracks. You can also Shift+click to select several adjacent tracks.

2 Right-click on the track number of any selected track. The context menu will appear.

3 Click on Delete Track. The selected tracks will be deleted.

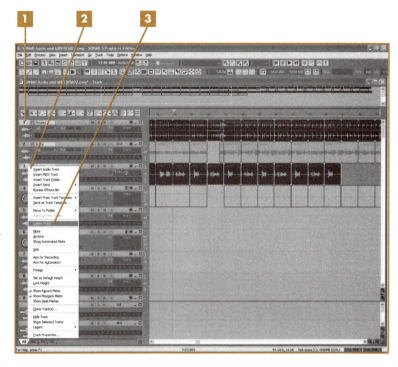

Changing the Order of Tracks

Once you've got a complex arrangement going, you will want to bring some order to the chaos. Fortunately, SONAR 5 lets you reorganize your tracks whenever the whim strikes you. For example, you might want your keyboard parts all to be next to each other for ease of editing. Here's how to rearrange the Track view.

1 Click on a track's track type icon. The cursor will appear as a two-headed vertical arrow.

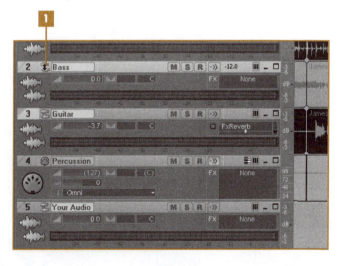

45
❈❈❈

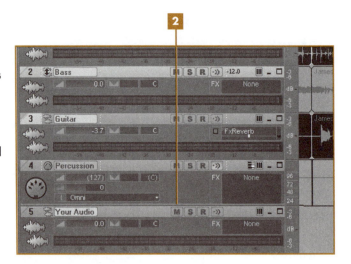

2 Drag the track up or down. A red line will show the track's new position.

3 Drop the track at its new position. The track will appear at that position, and all tracks will be renumbered accordingly.

✳ Track Numbers

Notice that the track numbers always start at 1 and run in sequence down the Track pane. The numbers are for reference only and do not travel with individual tracks.

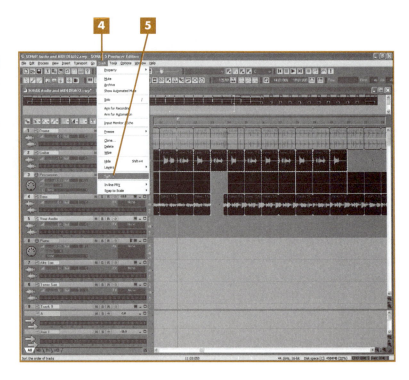

4 Select two or more tracks and then click on Track. The Track menu will appear.

5 Click on Sort. The Sort Tracks dialog box will open.

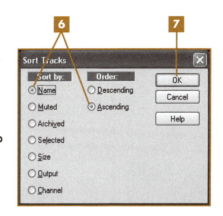

6 Click to select the desired sort options.

7 Click on OK. The dialog box will close, and the selected tracks will be moved to the top of the Track pane.

Fitting Tracks to the Window

SONAR 5 has a couple of really cool display functions that provide you with a clear overview of your song quickly. The following steps show you how to get all of your tracks to fit neatly into the available vertical window space and how to get your whole song to fit neatly from beginning to end into the available horizontal window space.

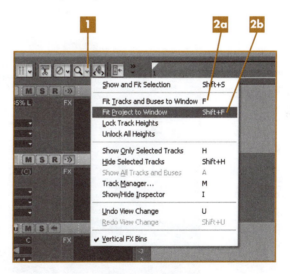

1 Click on the down arrow at the right of the Zoom tool. The View Options menu will open.

2a Click on Fit Tracks and Buses to Window. All tracks will be resized vertically so they fit in the window.

OR

2b Click on Fit Project to Window. All tracks will be resized vertically and horizontally so the entire project fits in the window.

3 Click on Undo View Change. Tracks will return to their previous sizes.

❄ **Maximum Zoom**

Sometimes a project will have enough tracks or be long enough that SONAR can't fit it all into the window. In this case, all tracks will be minimized and zoomed out as far as possible.

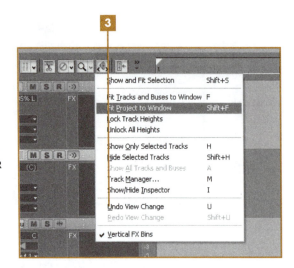

Setting Track View Options

The Clips pane has a number of visual cues to help you sort through the information presented there efficiently and accurately. By following these steps you can choose which options you need and want.

1 Right-click anywhere in the Clips pane. The context menu will appear.

2 Click on View Options. The Clip View Options dialog box will open.

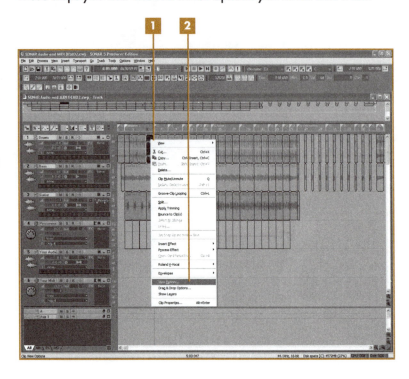

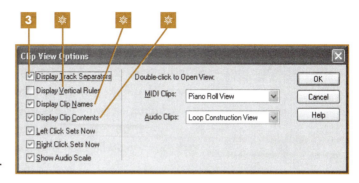

3 Click on a check box to choose an option. The most important options include:

- ❋ Display Vertical Rules. These vertical lines show the beginnings of measures so you can place clips accurately in time.

- ❋ Display Clip Names. If a clip has a name, it will be visible within the clip.

- ❋ Display Clip Contents. Audio clips will show waveforms, and MIDI clips will show MIDI notes.

Resizing the Track and Clips Panes

Sometimes you just need to see more of your clips, and other times you need to have a clear view of every track parameter. Luckily, SONAR 5 lets you decide how the Track and Clips panes share the available screen space.

1 Click and hold anywhere along the left or right edge of the pane divider. The cursor will appear as a two-headed arrow.

2 Drag the divider to the left or to the right. The Track and Clips panes will resize accordingly.

3 Click on the Show/Hide Inspector button. The Inspector pane will close, leaving more horizontal space for the Clips pane.

Showing Track Icons

SONAR 5 introduces customizable track icons, allowing you to distinguish one track from another at a glance. Numerous icons are included, or you can use any 24-bit .bmp file as a track icon. If you prefer an extremely spartan interface, you can opt to hide track icons, including the small track icon in the track header.

1 Click on Options. The Options menu will appear.

2 Point to Icons. The Icons submenu will appear.

3 Click on Show Icons. By default, each track will now display a large icon indicating its track type.

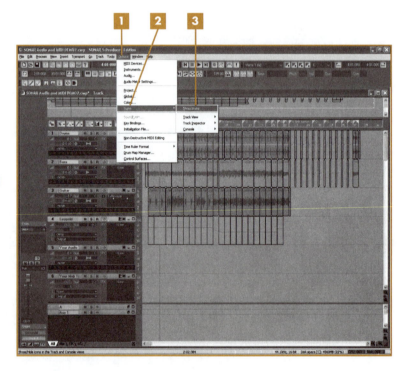

4 Right-click on a track icon. The context menu will appear.

5 Click on Load Track Icon to choose a different icon.

6 Click to choose track icon display options.

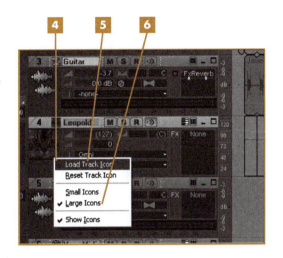

Using the Zoom Controls

One of the most common functions you'll use while working in SONAR is zooming in and out between a close-up view and a bird's-eye view of your song. The lower-right corner of the Track view holds the vertical and horizontal zoom controls, but it's usually quicker to zoom using the mouse.

1 Press and hold the Z key. The mouse pointer will appear as the Zoom tool.

2 Drag around an area in the Clips pane. When you release the mouse, the Clips pane will zoom to show only the area you selected.

3 Press the U key to return to the previous zoom level.

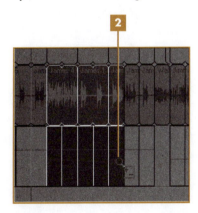

PART II

Using Audio Loops

Chapter 5: Importing and Using Audio Loops

Chapter 6: Using Groove Clips

Chapter 7: Creating and Editing Groove Clips

5 } Importing and Using Audio Loops

A lot of modern music production involves the use of musical elements that repeat anywhere from a few times in a row to throughout the duration of a song. A classical musician might call such a repetitive figure an *ostinato*, but in the contemporary vernacular it's called a *loop*. There are whole libraries of loops you can purchase for use in your own projects. SONAR 5 Producer and Studio Editions give you the tools necessary to work with loops efficiently and creatively. In this chapter, you'll learn how to:

* Use the Loop Explorer view
* Find and audition loops
* Bring loops into your project
* Repeat loops
* Turn clips into loops

Using the Loop Explorer View

A *loop* is simply a clip that is designed to be repeated over and over. The Loop Explorer view is your window into your collection of loops and the tool you will use to find the ones you want and import them into your project.

Opening the Loop Explorer View

If the Loop Explorer view looks suspiciously like Windows Explorer, that's no coincidence. The window is designed to take advantage of what you already know about navigating through your files and folders.

1 Click on View. The View menu will appear.

2a Click on Loop Explorer. The Loop Explorer view will appear.

OR

2b Click on the Loop Explorer icon on the Views toolbar. The Loop Explorer view will appear.

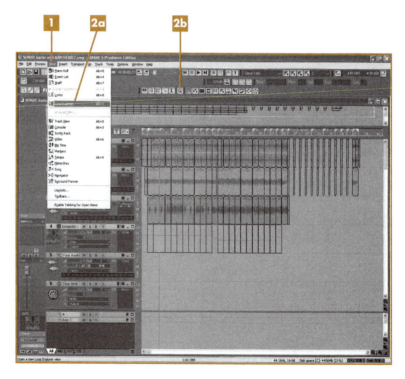

Customizing the Loop Explorer View

The default view of the Loop Explorer might not include all the information you need to pick out the loops you want, so here's how to tweak it to your way of thinking.

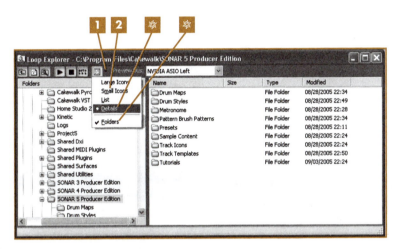

1 Click on the down arrow to the right of the Views button. The Views drop-down list will appear.

2 Click on a view option. The window will show that view. The most useful options are:

❋ Details. Presents a text-based list of files with information such as file date, file size, and file type.

❋ Folders. Causes the left-hand pane (Tree view) to be hidden or displayed.

❋ **Details, Details**

You can sort the Details view by any displayed attribute, making it easy to find a loop you created last month, the most recent version of a loop, or a particularly large loop. Simply click at the top of a column to sort by that attribute. Click again to reverse the order of the list.

Locating and Auditioning a Loop

Although the Loop Explorer might look like Windows Explorer, it's got a couple of tricks up its sleeve for picking out your loops. It lets you navigate files and folders using standard Windows techniques, and then it lets you listen to a loop to be sure it's the one you want. The following steps show you how to take advantage of this.

❄ **Preview Output**

The Loop Explorer plays through the output listed in the Preview Bus drop-down list. You will ordinarily want to choose your soundcard's main stereo output, the one through which you listen to SONAR songs. This is usually the default selection, so you might not need to change this setting.

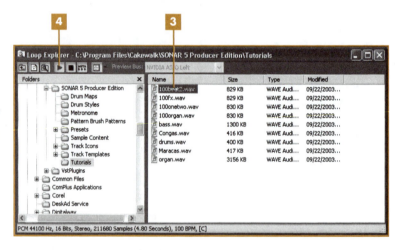

1 Click on a folder in the Tree view (left) pane. The folder's contents will be displayed in the Contents view (right) pane.

2 Click on the plus (+) to the left of a folder in the Tree view pane. The Tree view will expand to show the folder's subfolders

3 Click on the filename of the loop you want to audition. The loop will be selected.

4 Click on the Play button to audition the loop.

❄ **How Long Is My Loop?**

Because you are, after all, in the Loop Explorer view, any file you audition will loop indefinitely as it plays back, allowing you to hear what it sounds like when it repeats. Sometimes this can make it difficult to tell how long the loop actually is, but at the bottom of the Loop Explorer view the Status Bar shows you the length of the selected loop in seconds.

When Is a Loop Not a Loop?

Unfortunately, there's no way to tell in the Loop Explorer view whether a particular audio file is a loop or a plain old clip. Don't worry—in a few pages you'll learn how to make *any* clip into a loop.

Bringing a Loop into a Project

Okay, so you've found one or more loops you want to use in your song. Now you need to get them into your project. SONAR uses a simple drag-and-drop procedure for importing loops, as outlined in the following steps.

❋ **Sample Files**

The rest of this chapter uses a set of loops that are included with SONAR 5 as examples. Although the steps will work with any loops you might want to use, you will probably want to follow along with the sample files the first time through and then apply what you learn to other materials. The sample loops are installed within your SONAR 5 Producer Edition's Tutorials folder, which is ordinarily found at C:\Program Files\ Cakewalk\SONAR 5 Producer Edition\Tutorials.

1 Click on the filename of one or more loops.

2 Drag the loops into the Clips pane and drop them. The loops will be placed in existing or newly created audio tracks at the time position where you dropped them.

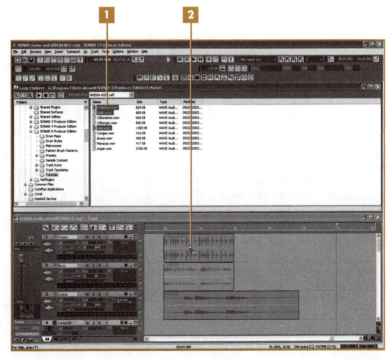

※ **Saving a Step**

If you drop a loop into any part of the Clips pane other than an audio track, an audio track will be automatically created to hold the loop. Knowing this can save you from having to create audio tracks manually!

※ **Order, Order!**

The loops will always be placed into tracks in the order in which they were listed in the Loop Explorer, whether you have sorted them by name, date, type, or size. Of course, once you've imported them, you can always rearrange them using the techniques discussed in Chapter 3.

Working with Loops

Because a loop is a special kind of clip, everything you learned in Chapter 3 about working with clips applies to loops as well, with the exception of linking. Additionally, loops make it ultra-simple to repeat musical ideas through a process that's almost like painting loops!

1 Drag the loop Maracas.wav from the Loop Explorer into an audio track. The loop will be added to the project and will appear wherever you dropped it in the track.

2 Drag the loop to the very beginning of a different audio track. The loop will be moved to measure 1 of the second track.

3 Ctrl+drag the loop to measure 5. The loop will be copied.

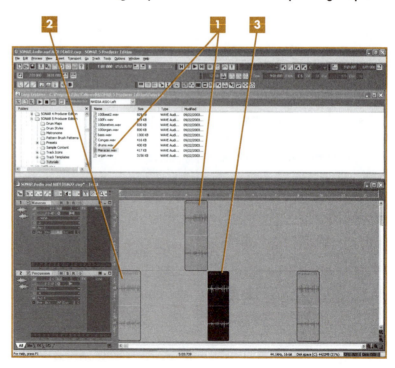

※ ※ ※

4 Copy the loop to measure 9. You will now have three copies of the loop, at measures 1, 5, and 9.

5 Select and delete the loop in measure 5. You will now have only two copies of the loop.

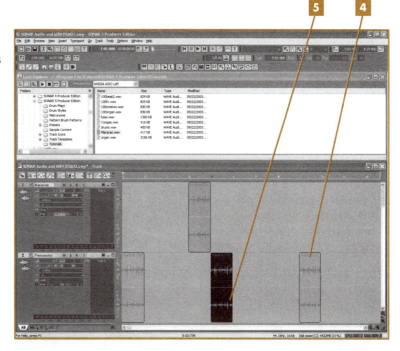

6 Point to the right edge of the loop. The cursor will turn into a little rectangle with a double-headed arrow, indicating that it is ready to adjust the right edge of the loop.

7 Drag the right edge of the loop to the right. The loop will "roll out" as far as you drag it.

8 Play the song from the beginning. You will hear the maracas loop repeat several times in perfect rhythm.

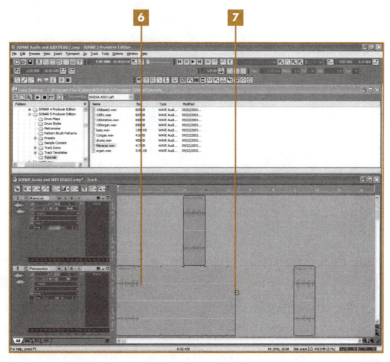

Making a Clip into a Loop

So by now you're asking yourself, "If a loop is a special type of clip, can I turn any clip into a loop?" The answer is yes! Any clip can be made into a loop by following the steps outlined here.

1 Drag the drums.wav clip from the Loop Explorer view into any audio track. The clip will be added to the project, and it will appear wherever you dropped it in the track.

2 Grab the right edge of the clip and drag it to the right. The clip will be extended.

3 Play the song. The clip will not repeat during playback because it is not yet a loop.

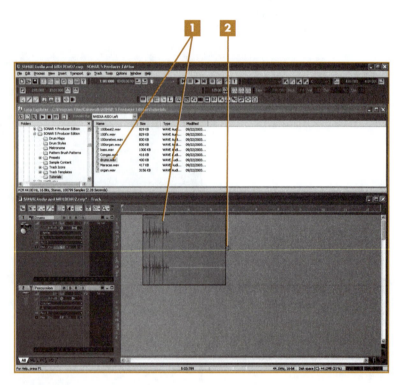

A Clip, Not a Loop

Unlike Maracas.wav, drums.wav is a plain, ordinary clip and not yet a loop. Two visual clues give this away. First, notice that the corners of the maracas clip are angled to indicate that it is a loop. Second, when you roll out a clip that isn't a loop, the waveform pattern doesn't repeat itself—in most cases, you will only see straight lines (indicating silence) extending to the right.

4 Press Ctrl+Z. The last edit (rolling out the drums clip) will be undone.

5 Right-click on the drums clip. The context menu will appear.

6 Click on Groove-Clip Looping. The clip's corners will be angled, indicating that it is now enabled for looping.

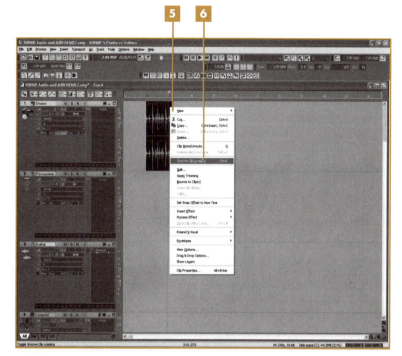

7 Roll out the drums loop.

8 Play the loop. This time it will repeat itself for as long as you rolled it.

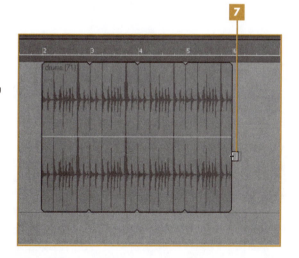

❈ **Loop Shortcut**

You can also enable Groove-Clip Looping by selecting a clip and pressing Ctrl+L. What's "groove-clip looping?" That's what the next chapter is all about!

6 } Using Groove Clips

As if loops weren't already cool enough, SONAR 5 also supports *groove clips*, a type of clip that takes looping even further. A groove clip knows its own tempo and pitch, enabling it to adapt to the tempo and pitch of your songs. This allows you to manipulate audio clips in ways that were unheard of even in megabucks studios just a couple of years ago. In this chapter, you'll learn how to:

* Work with groove clips
* Set and change tempos
* Set and change project pitch

Working with Groove Clips

SONAR 5 includes a variety of different groove clips for you to use in your songs. Additionally, SONAR allows you to import Sony Media Software ACID®-style loops, opening up dozens of commercial loop libraries for your use.

You can import groove clips as you did regular audio clips in Chapter 1, or you can drag groove clips into the Clips pane directly from the Loop Explorer view, as you did with loops in Chapter 5. The advantage of dragging them in is that you can drag them directly to whatever track and time you want without having to designate the location ahead of time.

Because groove clips are special loops and loops are special clips, it stands to reason that everything you know about arranging clips and loops applies to groove clips, doesn't it? Of course, groove clips give you a bit more than simple clips or loops, and you'll get to that soon. Before you get too fancy, though, you need to get some groove clips arranged in the Clips pane.

❄ Sample Groove Clips

The following steps use several groove clips from the SONAR 5 Producer Edition\Tutorials folder as examples. The steps apply equally to any groove clips, but you might want to follow along with these same clips the first time through.

1 Import one or more groove clips as described previously. In this example, I have imported the clips 100beat2.wav, 100fx.wav, and 100organ.wav to measure 1.

2 Copy the clips using either the Copy/Paste or drag-and-drop techniques discussed in Chapter 3. In this example, I have copied the three clips to measure 6.

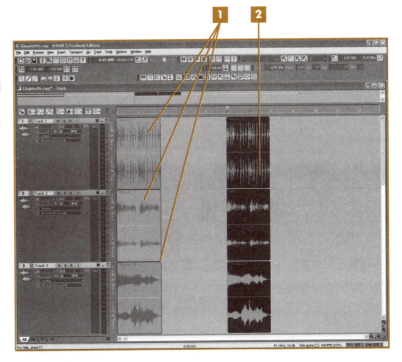

3 Roll out one or more groove clips as discussed in Chapter 5. In this example, I have rolled both copies of all three clips by two bars.

4 Click on Play. The groove clips will play back, looping where you rolled them and matching each other perfectly in time. If you have followed the example, you will hear four bars of the three loops playing together, followed by one bar of silence and four more bars of all three loops.

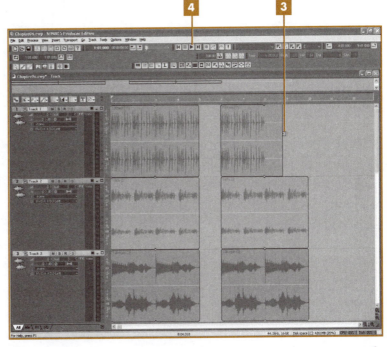

> ✳ **Bad Timing?**
>
> If you chose your own clips and any one of them doesn't match the timing of the others, it is probably not a real groove clip. You'll learn how to fix this in Chapter 7, "Creating and Editing Groove Clips," but for now you should simply replace it with a different clip.

Setting the Tempo

If one of the cool things about groove clips is that they are smart enough to follow your song's tempo, you should probably know how to set your song's tempo, right? In fact, SONAR 5 allows you to change tempo as often as you want, and no matter how crazy you get, your groove clips will follow along. Here's how to map out your tempos.

1. If necessary, display the Tempo toolbar by right-clicking on any empty space in the toolbars area and checking Tempo.

2. Click on the Tempo number box. The current tempo field will be highlighted.

3. Type a new tempo and press Enter. The project's tempo will change.

4. Click on Play. The song will play at the new tempo.

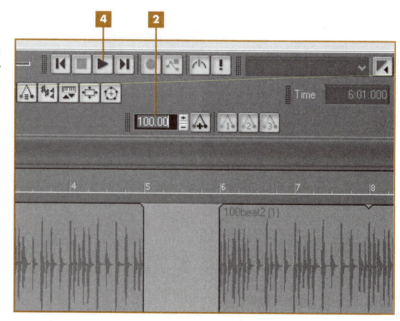

✳✳✳

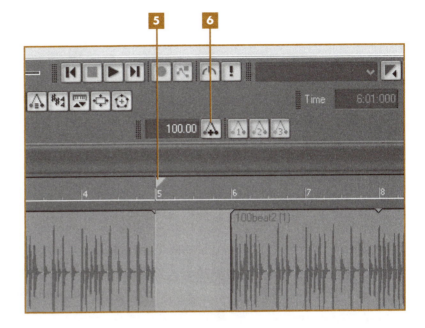

5 Click in the Time Ruler at measure 5. The Now time will move to measure 5.

6 Click on the Insert Tempo button. The Insert Tempo dialog box will open.

7 Type a new tempo in the Tempo box or click on the Click here to tap tempo button at your desired tempo. If you choose the latter option, SONAR will calculate the tempo of your mouse clicks and enter the time in the Tempo box.

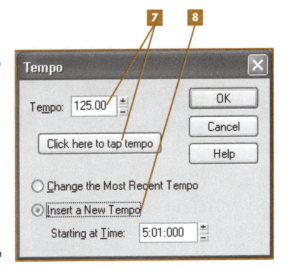

8 Click on the Insert a New Tempo option button.

9 Click on OK. The tempo change will be inserted at the time you chose.

10 Click on Play. The groove clips will play back at the original tempo for four bars, and after the measure of silence they will play back at the new tempo.

Working with Project Pitch

You've successfully dealt with the tempo coolness of groove clips—
now it's time to take advantage of their ability to follow your
project's pitch changes. This means that even though a groove clip
contains a nasty bass line in D, SONAR will make it a nasty bass
line in F-sharp and then a nasty bass line in E-flat if that's what your
song requires. How do you communicate all this pitch information?
By following these steps, naturally!

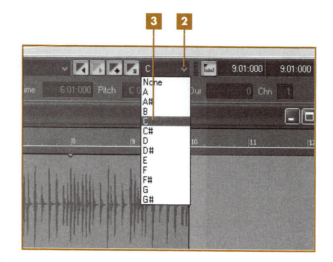

1 If necessary, display the
Markers toolbar by right-
clicking on any empty space
in the toolbars area and
checking Markers.

2 Click on the down arrow at
the right of the Default
Groove-Clip Pitch drop-down
list. The Default Groove-Clip
Pitch list will appear.

3 Click on a default pitch. The
list will close and the box will
display your choice. In the
example, I have chosen C.

❈ Key and Pitch

When dealing with groove clips, there is an important difference between the terms *key* and *pitch*. Although a musician considers them related terms, in SONAR you can choose a key signature for your song, and it will have no effect on your groove clips. The pitch of a groove clip is set by comparing its *reference note* to the project's default pitch (which you just set) and any pitch markers (which you are about to create), regardless of key signature.

4 Right-click in the Time Ruler. The Now time will be set to wherever you clicked, and the context menu will open. In the example, I have set the Now time to measure 3.

5 Click on Insert Marker. The Marker dialog box will open.

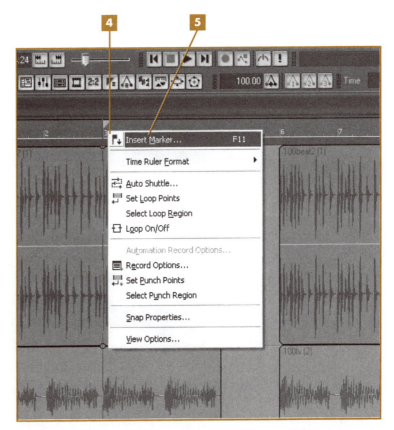

6 Click on the Groove-Clip Pitch down arrow. The Groove-Clip Pitch list will open.

7 Click on the new pitch. In the example, I have chosen A-sharp.

8 Click on OK. A pitch marker will be placed at the location you specified.

9 Click on Play. The groove clips will play back, changing pitch at the marker you created.

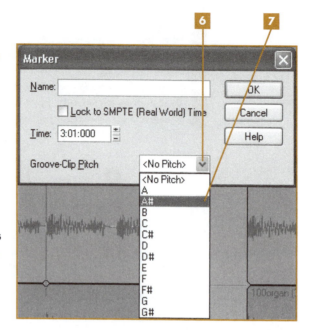

10 Ctrl+drag to copy the pitch marker to a new location. The Marker dialog box will open.

11 Change the Groove-Clip Pitch setting to a new value. In the example, I have chosen C.

12 Click on OK. A new marker will appear at the location to which you dragged the copy of the original marker.

13 Click on Play. The song will play back, changing pitch at each marker.

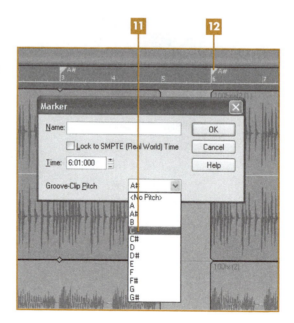

7 } Creating and Editing Groove Clips

SONAR 5 does more than simply let you use ACID-ized groove clips—it lets you fine-tune them and even create them from scratch. The key to this power is found in the Loop Construction view, so that's where you'll spend time next. In this chapter, you'll learn how to:

* ✳ Use the Loop Construction view
* ✳ Set and change groove clip parameters
* ✳ Turn a clip into a groove clip
* ✳ Manipulate the sound of a groove clip
* ✳ Fine-tune the time-stretching of a groove clip

Opening the Loop Construction View

The Loop Construction view lets you control all of a groove clip's parameters, from whether and how it changes key to how it changes tempo. Note that the Loop Construction view can only be opened when you already have audio selected. Unlike the Loop Explorer view, it doesn't include any provision for finding and opening a file—it only works with the clip you have selected when you open it.

❋ Sample Loops

Once again, I turn to the sample loops Cakewalk thoughtfully provided with SONAR 5 in the Tutorials folder. For this example, it's highly recommended that you follow along with the sample loop once before you start experimenting.

1 Import a percussion-based groove clip, such as 100beat2.wav, as discussed in Chapter 5.

2a Select the groove clip and click on the Loop Construction view button. The Loop Construction view will appear with the selected clip displayed.

OR

2b Double-click on the groove clip. The Loop Construction view will appear with the selected clip displayed.

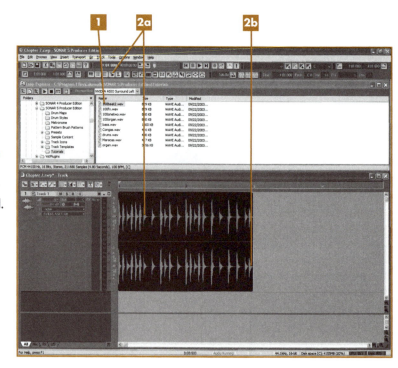

Following Project Pitch (or Not!)

In Chapter 6 you saw how to create pitch markers within your song so that groove clips could transpose themselves automatically and follow your song's harmonic progression. The Loop Construction view lets you enable this ability within a groove clip. As you'll see, sometimes this isn't desirable, so you can also disable pitch following. The following steps show you how to turn this ability on or off.

1 Set the default project pitch as previously discussed. The chosen default pitch will be displayed in the Default Project Pitch field.

2 Insert a pitch marker halfway through the percussion clip you just imported. The marker will appear where you created it.

3 Play the song and listen to what happens. The percussion will change pitch when it reaches the pitch marker.

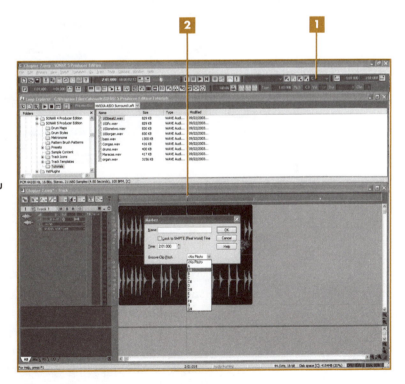

❄ What's Wrong?

That doesn't sound very natural, does it? We expect pitched instruments to follow the song's harmonic progression, but your drummer doesn't retune her drums every time you play a different chord, does she? In general, you will want the Follow Project Pitch option to be enabled for pitched instruments and disabled for non-pitched percussion instruments and special effects.

4 Double-click on the groove clip to open it in the Loop Construction view.

5 Click on the Follow Project Pitch button. The button will no longer be highlighted, and the Root Note field will be grayed out.

6 Play the song. The groove clip will no longer change pitch at the pitch marker. Should you want to hear the pitch change, click on the Follow Project Pitch button again.

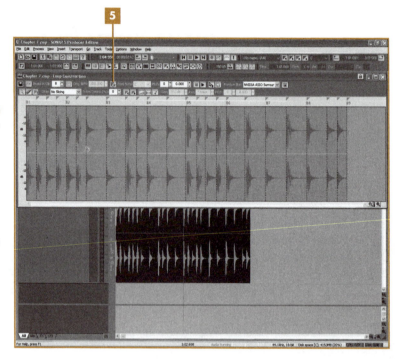

Creating Groove Clips

As if it weren't enough that SONAR 5 lets you manipulate the space-time continuum, the Loop Construction view also lets you turn ordinary, run-of-the-mill audio clips into groove clips. (Okay Einstein, that bit about space-time is a little overstated, but the control SONAR gives you over pitch and time is nothing short of magic!) In the steps that follow, you'll take a regular audio clip and enable it to follow your project's tempo and pitch changes.

Enabling Looping

When you enable looping in a clip, SONAR does two things. First, it allows you to roll out the clip in a track so it repeats itself, as you did in Chapter 5. Second, it uses information you provide about the number of beats in the clip to adjust the playback speed of the clip to the project tempo. The following steps show you how to turn looping on and provide the info SONAR needs to change the clip's tempo.

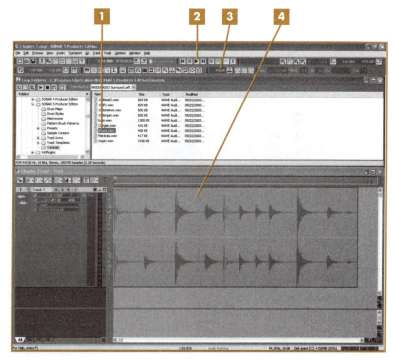

1 Drag a regular non-looping clip, such as drums.wav, into an audio track. These clips have square corners, indicating that they are not loops...yet.

2 Click on Play to hear the loop.

3 Change the tempo and play the clip again. The clip will play back exactly as it did before because, again, it's not yet a groove clip.

4 Double-click on the clip to open it in the Loop Construction view.

5 Click on the Enable Looping button. Beat-slicing markers will appear in the waveform, and the corners of the clip itself will be angled instead of square.

6 Click on Preview Loop. The loop will now play at the project tempo.

7 Click on Stop Preview.

8 Enter a new number in the Beats in Clip field and press Enter. The number of beat-slice markers will change to reflect the new number of beats.

9 Preview the loop. It will play back faster or slower, depending on the number you entered.

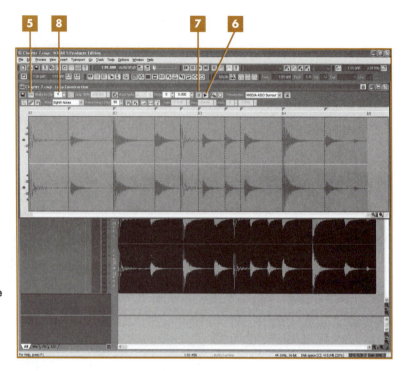

❄ Beats Me

SONAR uses the Beats in Clip value to calculate the playback speed of the loop. For example, if you tell SONAR the clip represents eight beats, it will play the clip at one speed, and if you say the clip represents four beats, it will play the clip twice as fast because four beats take half as long to play as eight beats at the same tempo. When you enable looping for a clip, SONAR makes a really good guess as to how many beats are in the clip, so if the numbers make your head hurt, relax and let SONAR do the work!

Enabling Stretching

Stretching a clip is similar to looping it, except that you can't roll the clip out as you can with a loop. A stretched clip does adapt to the project tempo, although it does so by comparing its original tempo with the project tempo, rather than basing the calculation on the Beats in Clip value. This would be a better way to stretch something that's not clearly rhythmic but needs to cover a specific musical time. Here's how to set this up.

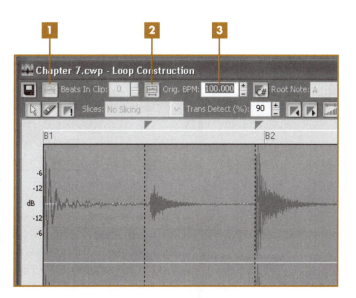

1 If necessary, click on the Enable Looping button to turn looping off. The button will not be highlighted, and the clip itself will have square corners.

2 Click on the Enable Stretching button. The button will be highlighted.

3 Enter a new tempo in the Original (Orig.) BPM field and preview the clip. The clip will play at a tempo that depends on the relationship between the original BPM setting and the project tempo.

❋ Faster and Slower

If the value in the Orig. BPM field is higher than the project tempo, the clip will play back slower than normal speed. If the value in the Orig. BPM field is lower than the project tempo, the clip will play back faster than normal speed. If the original BPM value is the same as the project tempo, the clip will play back at its natural speed.

Setting a Clip's Root Note

SONAR transposes groove clips by comparing a clip's root note with the default project pitch and any pitch markers. You can change this behavior by changing the clip's root note value as follows.

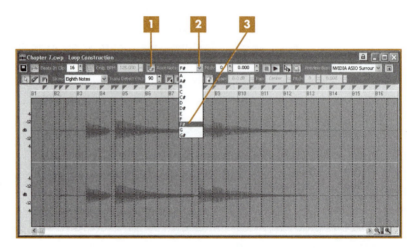

1 If necessary, click on Follow Project Pitch. The button will be highlighted.

2 Click on the Root Note down arrow. The Root Note drop-down list will appear.

3 Click on the desired root note.

❄ **Root Notes**

It's not really necessary to identify a groove clip's root note accurately, but it is a good idea. In the short run, all you need to know is the relationship between a clip's root note and the current pitch marker. If they're the same, the clip will play back at its original pitch, and everything else is relative. In the long run, however, you'll be much happier and more efficient if you take the time to label your groove clips according to their true original root notes.

Changing the Sound of a Groove Clip

SONAR is able to change the sound of a groove clip on a slice-by-slice basis. You can change the pitch, volume, or pan of each slice individually to create your own personal sound.

1 Click on the Enable Slice Auto-preview button.

2 Click on the Show/Hide Pitch Envelope button. The Pitch Envelope will be displayed.

3 Click on slices one by one until you find one you want to transpose.

4 Drag the Pitch Envelope for that slice up or down to transpose it.

5 Optionally, repeat the process to change the gain or pan of a slice.

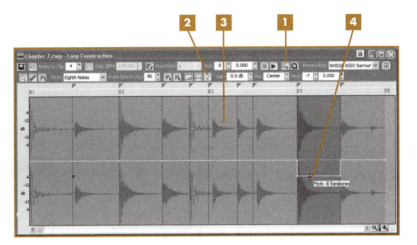

Fine-Tuning a Groove Clip's Timing

According to the laws of nature, the tempo and pitch of an audio sample are intertwined—when one goes up, so does the other. That's why when SONAR lets you manipulate groove clips, you sometimes hear odd artifacts and sonic misbehaviors, especially at extreme tempo changes. The Loop Construction view lets you fine-tune the beat slices so that this misbehavior is minimized.

You will still find that doubling the tempo of a groove clip makes it sound different, but following these steps will help you achieve the best-sounding results.

1 Import the clip drums.wav to the beginning of an audio track.

2 Play the clip. The clip will play once and stop.

3 Change the tempo to 90 BPM and play the clip again. The clip will sound exactly the same because it is not a loop or a groove clip.

4 Double-click on the clip to open it in the Loop Construction view.

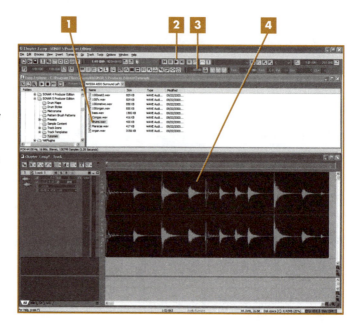

5 Preview the clip in the Loop Construction view. The clip will play repeatedly because the Loop Construction view loops clips when it previews them, regardless of whether looping is enabled.

6 Click on Enable Looping. A series of slicing markers will appear within the clip.

7 Preview the looped clip. The clip will play back slower, at the project tempo of 90 BPM.

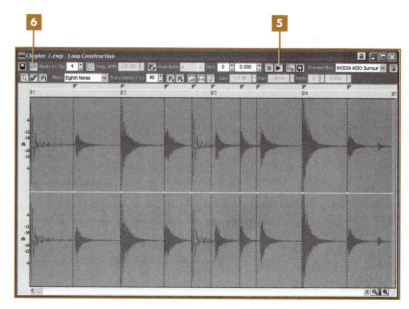

❋ Not Bad—Yet

The clip—now a loop—does a pretty good job of adapting to the project's tempo, which is a good deal slower than the clip was to begin with. SONAR usually does a good job of automatically determining the right way to change a clip's tempo. No doubt you notice a couple of telltale signs, though, especially at the very end of the clip, right before it loops. It sounds almost as if the drummer knocked over the hi-hat, doesn't it? We'll fix it, but to illustrate how the slicing process works, the first thing we're going to do is make it sound *worse!* Have faith—it will get better.

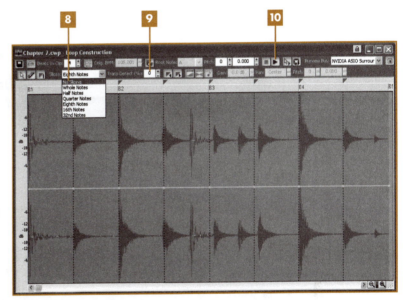

8 Click on the Slices down arrow and choose No Slicing.

9 Click in the Transient Detection (Trans Detect %) box, type 0 (zero), and then press Enter. All of the slicing markers will disappear.

10 Preview the clip. It will sound awful due to the complete lack of slicing markers.

11 Set the Slices value to Quarter Notes. Slicing markers will appear at beats 2, 3, and 4 (B2, B3, and B4).

12 Preview the clip. It will sound a little better, but not great.

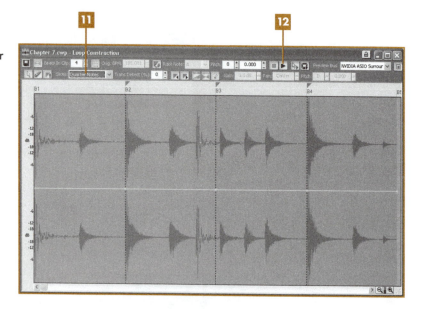

❋ Slices

The Slices value places slicing markers exactly at musical subdivisions, from whole notes to sixty-fourth notes. This is a good starting point for slicing a rhythmic loop such as this one.

13 Set the Slices value to Eighth Notes. Four more slicing markers will appear at eighth-note subdivisions.

14 Preview the clip. It will sound better still, but some glitches will remain.

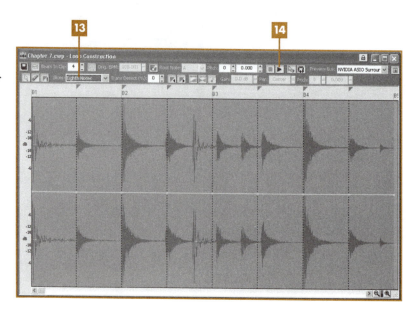

15 Click between the plus (+) and minus (–) buttons at the right of the Trans Detect (%) box and drag upward to increase the value. As it reaches 73%, slicing markers will appear at the sixteenth notes just before and just after B3.

16 Drag the B3 slicing marker and the next slicing marker prior to B4 slightly to the right so they line up with the peaks of the waveform. The markers will appear where you place them.

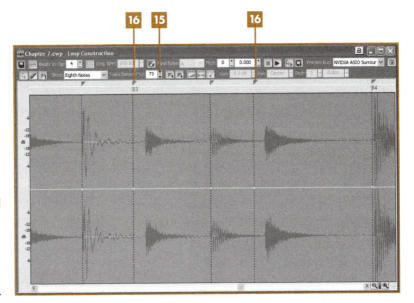

17 Preview the clip. It will sound almost perfect, but there will still be a glitch in the final hi-hat note.

18 Zoom in on the end of the loop and double-click in the top half of the Loop Construction view's timeline, right above the last sixteenth note. A slicing marker will be created where you double-clicked.

19 Drag the new slicing marker so it aligns exactly with the sixteenth note's peak. The marker will be relocated.

20 Preview the clip. It will finally sound correct and, as promised, it will sound even better than it did with SONAR's default slicing way back in Step 7!

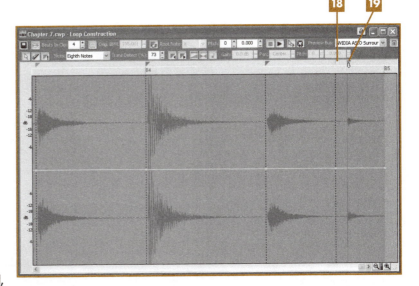

Slice, Detect, Tweak

For best results, start by setting the Slice size to a note value that covers most of a loop. Then get the subtler details by bumping up the Trans Detect (%) value. Make your final tweaks manually.

PART III

Creating Your Own Audio

Chapter 8: Recording Your Own Audio

Chapter 9: Editing Audio

Chapter 10: Managing Audio

87

8 Recording Your Own Audio

So far, you've seen that loops and groove clips are powerful tools for creating music, and that they can speed up the process of developing a song considerably. If you're a saxophonist like me, however—or a singer or a guitarist or any other kind of skilled performer—loops only get you part of the way there. Sooner or later you're going to want to put your own "voice" into your song, and that means audio recording. Never mind later, let's do it sooner—as in now! In this chapter, you'll learn how to:

* Choose audio inputs and outputs
* Prepare an audio track for recording
* Record audio
* Use punch record and loop record

Choosing Audio Inputs and Outputs

One of the most important concepts in SONAR 5—or, for that matter, any music-production situation—is *signal flow*. Although this is a pretty straightforward term—it really does refer to audio and MIDI signals flowing into, through, and out of your system—it is one of those "minutes to learn, lifetime to master" concepts. Throughout the rest of this book your understanding of signal flow will grow step by step. You've already managed the "out of" part by playing back songs, clips, loops, and groove clips. Now you'll handle the "into" part by getting new audio and eventually new MIDI information into SONAR. When you get to mixing, you'll see the internal signal flow, the "through" part.

For this chapter, I will assume that you have a microphone, guitar, keyboard, or other instrument properly connected to your audio card's physical input jack or jacks. Naturally, what you see onscreen will reflect your particular audio card and will therefore be slightly different from what you see on these pages. If you have technical difficulties, start by consulting your audio card's documentation. Appendix A, "Setup and Troubleshooting," also has some tips for troubleshooting audio problems, and the SONAR 5 manual and help system are full of useful information.

❄ Protect Your Ears!

Whenever you are dealing with audio devices, you are pointing amplified sound at your ears. Ordinarily, this is a good and benign thing. However, any system capable of giving you satisfyingly high-quality playback is also capable of blasting your ears with accidental loud sounds, such as *feedback*. Feedback happens when a sound runs through the same signal path repeatedly, getting amplified more and more each time until it produces an ear-splitting squawk or squeal. The most common cause of feedback is when a sound going into a microphone comes out the speakers and is picked up again by the microphone. This is one reason performers wear headphones when recording. Although this isn't a common occurrence and can be avoided by skillful and careful engineering practices, if it does happen you will want to stop it immediately. Turn off the microphone, turn off the track's record-arm button, turn down the volume of your speakers, or stop SONAR's audio engine, as explained later. Protect your ears!

1 Click on the I/O tab in the Track pane. The I/O tab will come to the front.

2 Click on the down arrow at the right of the track input drop-down list.

3 Click on the name of the input from which you want to record. The list will close, and the input will be displayed in the track's input field.

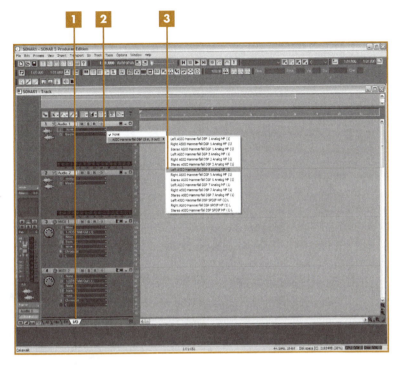

❊ **Input Names**

SONAR lists inputs in pairs, so if, for example, you have a stereo (two-input) soundcard called the "Feldspar 9000J," you will see something like Left Feldspar, Right Feldspar, and Stereo Feldspar listed as your available input options. If you have a mono (one-channel) source plugged into your soundcard, you will need to choose one of your mono track inputs, most likely Left Feldspar. If you're recording from a stereo source, you would simply choose Stereo Feldspar.

❊ ❊ ❊

4 Click on the down arrow at the right of the track output drop-down list.

5 Click on the name of the output to which you ordinarily listen.

6 Click on the All tab in the Track pane. The All tab will come to the front.

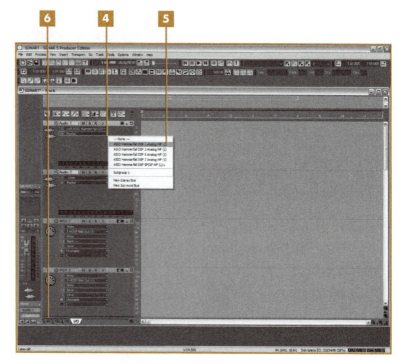

❋ No Master

If you're working from SONAR's Normal template, you will see that the track output is already set to Master. Although this seems like a perfectly reasonable output, go ahead and choose your audio card's primary stereo output as the track's output. I'll discuss exactly what that Master is when I discuss mixing.

❋ I/O versus All

Notice that the input and output you just chose in the I/O tab are both displayed in the All tab as well. This is because the Mix, FX, and I/O tabs are all *subsets* of the information displayed in the All tab. The subset tabs are useful for helping you find the specific parameters you need quickly. They are also an efficient way to squeeze a limited amount of information about a whole bunch of tracks into the window all at once.

Preparing an Audio Track for Recording

Once you've chosen your track's input and output, there are just a couple more things you need to do before you can successfully record audio into SONAR 5. You need to be sure you or the artist you're recording can hear what's being recorded, and you need to "arm" the track for recording so SONAR will actually commit it to disk.

Arming a Track for Recording

Every recording device, whether it's based on hardware or software, requires you to specify what tracks are going to be recorded at any given time. This is known as *record-arming* a track. Essentially, it tells SONAR to direct what's coming in on that track to the hard disk for storage and eventual playback. It doesn't get any simpler than this, as you'll see in the next steps.

1 Click on the Record (R) button on the track to which you want to record. The Record button will turn red, and the track itself will turn a different color to indicate it is armed.

2 Play your instrument or sing into the microphone. The track's input meter will show the level of the input signal. If you don't see any signal, consult your soundcard's documentation.

3 If necessary, adjust the track input level by increasing or decreasing the output volume of your instrument or microphone pre-amp. The input meter will reflect any changes.

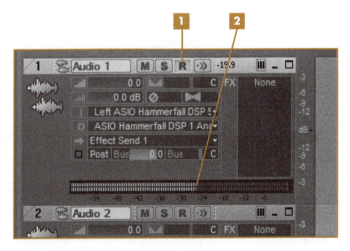

✳ Setting Levels

Finding the answer to the question, "How loud should I make my input?" would require almost an entire book by itself in order to sort out the technical hows and whys and the different schools of thought, and to filter through all the misinformation. The simplest solution is that, because SONAR's meters are *peak* meters by default, you should set your input so that when you sing or play your loudest, the input meter approaches *but never hits* the top of the scale. Notice that the scale in the Track Inspector is larger and therefore gives you more precise information than the meter in the Track pane. SONAR has no way of adjusting the volume of an input, so to make the input louder, you need to sing louder, play harder, or turn up the volume of your instrument or microphone pre-amp.

Starting and Stopping SONAR's Audio Engine

When feedback or digital distortion occurs, it can be uncomfortable and even dangerous, so you need to be able to fix it quickly. For this purpose SONAR has a button that can turn off its audio engine, stopping all audio activity and interrupting the feedback so you can remedy it. Here's how to turn SONAR's audio engine off and back on.

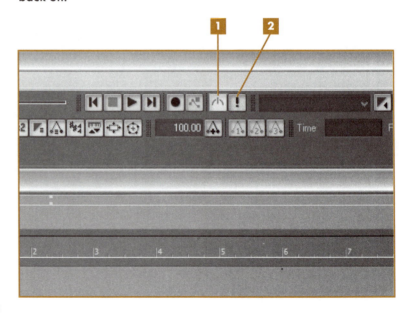

1 With at least one audio track record-armed, click on the Audio Engine button. The button will be grayed out, indicating that the audio engine is off, and no sound will be recorded or played.

2 Click on the Reset button. Playback or recording will stop, and the audio engine will be turned off.

3 Click on the Audio Engine button again. The button will be illuminated, and the words "Audio Running" will appear in the status bar at the bottom of the screen.

❋ **Reset**

When you are in the middle of recording or playing, the Audio Engine button will already be grayed out, and you will need to use the Reset button instead.

Enabling Input Echo

If you can hear yourself in your headphones, you can probably skip this section. Appendix A will give you a more detailed explanation of when and why you need Input Echo, but for now it's sufficient to say that if you have record-armed a track and you can't hear yourself, you will need to turn Input Echo on. Here's how to do exactly that.

1 Click on the Input Echo button. The button will illuminate, and you will be able to hear the input.

2 Click again on the Input Echo button. The button will be grayed out, and you will no longer hear the input.

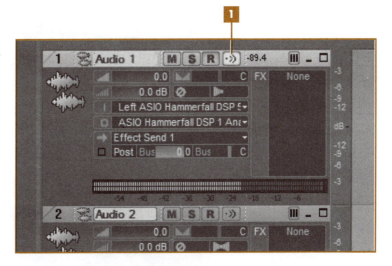

Making Your First Audio Recording

If you haven't read this chapter from the beginning, please do so now. It will save you frustration and reduce the risk of ugly and potentially dangerous distortion and feedback. If you have read the preceding steps already, then you are *finally* ready to record audio! It's really pretty simple if you've prepared properly.

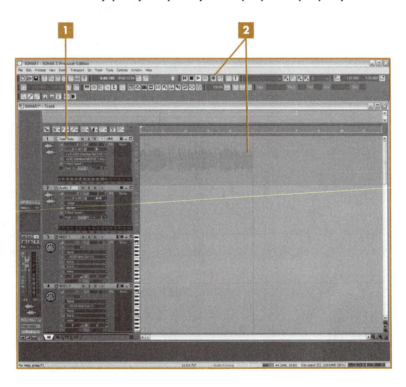

1 Double-click on the track name field and type in an informative name.

2 Click on the Record button. Recording will begin, the Now time will advance, and a waveform representing your input will be drawn in the recording track.

❄ Name That Track

It's essential that you name your tracks before you start recording. SONAR automatically names all audio files after the tracks to which they are recorded, making it much easier to find important files later on.

3 Click on the Stop button. Recording will stop, the Now time will reset to its previous position, and an audio clip will appear, showing the waveform of what was just recorded.

4 Click on the Play button. The clip you just recorded will play back.

5 Click on Edit.

6 Click on Undo Recording. The clip you recorded will disappear. Nobody gets it perfect on the first take!

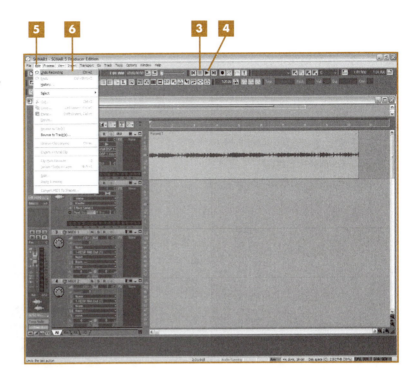

Using Punch Record

One of the great innovations in recording technology is the ability to *punch in* and replace only a portion of a recording. This allows engineers to retain the good parts of a "take" and replace only the parts that have mistakes or imperfections. SONAR's Auto-Punch record mode brings this same innovation to your desktop.

1 Drag in the Time Ruler to select the area you want to replace.

2 Right-click in the Time Ruler. The context menu will appear.

3 Click on Set Punch Points. Red punch markers will appear at the ends of the selection.

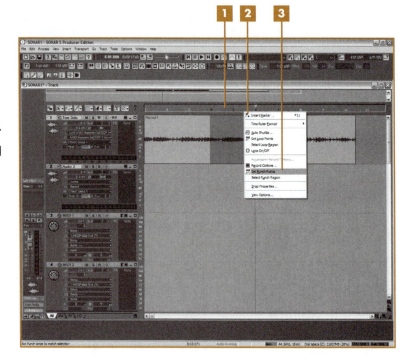

4 Right-click in the Time Ruler to open the context menu.

5 Click on Record Options. The Record Options dialog box will open.

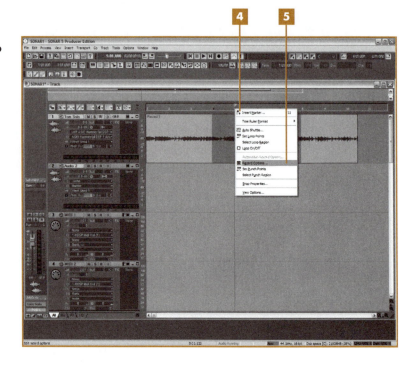

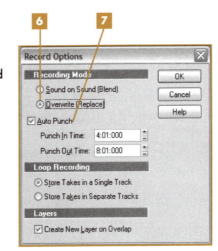

6 Click on Overwrite (Replace). This will cause newly recorded audio to replace the previous take.

7 If Auto Punch is not already enabled, click to enable it. This will cause SONAR to record between the punch-in and punch-out times.

8 Click on OK.

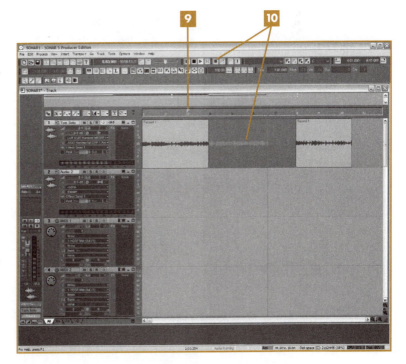

9 Click in the Time Ruler to set the Now time to some convenient point prior to the punch region.

10 Click on the Record button. Playback will begin at the Now time, and recording will begin at the punch-in marker and end at the punch-out marker.

11 Click on the Stop button. Playback will stop, and a new clip will appear between the punch markers.

Loop Recording

Sometimes in the search for that elusive perfect take, you'll want to try recording a passage several times in a row. Loop record mode allows you to do this without interruption. Simply set up the time you want to loop, hit Record, and repeat the passage until you get a keeper. These steps show you how.

1 Drag in the Time Ruler from the start of the loop to the end of the loop.

2 Right-click in the Time Ruler and choose Set Loop Points from the context menu. The selection will be bracketed by yellow loop markers, and the Loop On/Off button will be turned on.

3 Right-click in the Time Ruler and choose Record Options from the context menu. The Record Options dialog box will open.

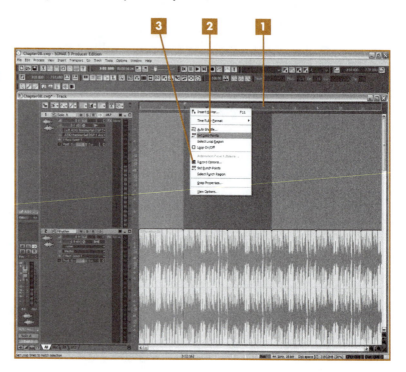

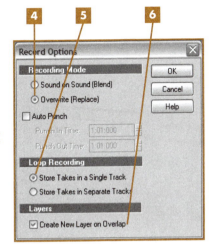

4 Click on Overwrite (Replace).

5 Click on Store Takes in a Single Track.

6 Click on Create New Layer on Overlap, and then click on OK to close the dialog box.

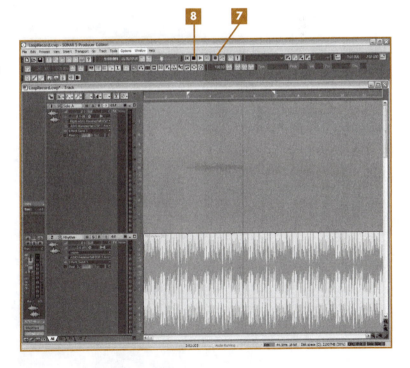

7 Click on the Record button. Recording will begin, looping from the end back to the beginning until you stop it.

8 Click on the Stop button. Recording will stop, and the last take will appear in the track.

❄ **Can't Choose Just One?**

If you find that you like part of one take and part of another, you can combine the best of both by editing them together. That's what the next chapter is all about!

9 Click on the Mute Tool button. The button will be highlighted, and the cursor will appear as an arrow with a mute symbol next to it.

10 Click on the drop-down arrow at the right of the Mute Tool button. The Click+Drag Behavior menu will appear.

11 Choose Mute Entire Clips (Alt+Drag Mutes Time Ranges) from the menu.

12 Click on the track's Track Layers button. The button will be highlighted, and the various takes will appear in parallel layers within the Track view.

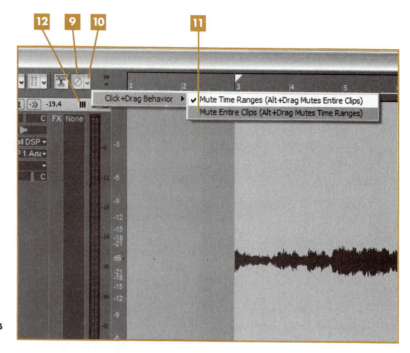

13 Click on the Play button. The selection will play, looping from the end back to the beginning.

14 Click on the clips to mute and un-mute them one by one so you can choose the best take.

15 Once you have chosen the best take and muted the rest, click on the Track Layers button to hide the unused takes. You will hear and see only the good take.

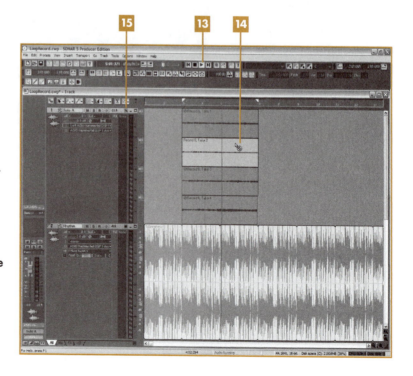

9 Editing Audio

One of the real breakthroughs of the computer-music revolution is the ability to dissect and manipulate audio recordings down to the level of a single sample. Some folks blame this editing magic for the proliferation of talentless-but-cute pop stars who are fixed and tuned and polished by skilled engineers in order to sell records, and there may be some truth to that! At the same time, giving creative musicians more efficient tools with which to make music is never a bad thing. In this chapter, you'll learn how to:

* Use SONAR's grid for precise editing
* Split audio clips
* Select partial clips
* Slip-edit audio clips
* Create fades and crossfades
* Use destructive processes on clips

Using Snap to Grid

SONAR 5 allows you the option of conforming certain edit functions to a timing grid. The grid can be based on musical bars and beats, on minutes and seconds, or on other SONAR events such as markers. This means that depending on how you set the Snap to Grid options, you could move a clip exactly to a marker, move a clip exactly one beat earlier, select exactly one second of a clip, or split a clip precisely one minute into a song. Of course, sometimes you don't want to be constrained by a grid, so you can easily turn Snap to Grid off. These steps walk you through the most common scenarios.

1 Click on the Snap to Grid button. The button will be highlighted, indicating that Snap to Grid is enabled.

2 Click on the Snap to Grid down arrow. The Snap to Grid dialog box will open.

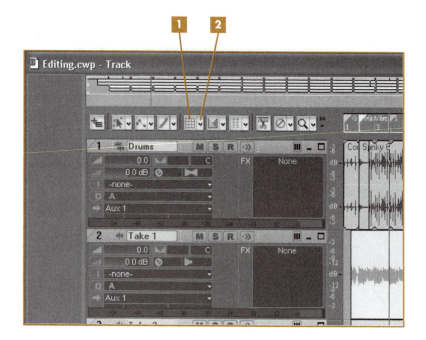

3 Click on an option. The most common options include:

❋ **Musical Time.** Sets the grid to musical values such as a measure, a quarter note, or an eighth note, allowing you to make rhythmic edits.

❋ **Clip Boundaries.** Makes the beginning and end of any clip into a grid point, allowing you to drag one clip against another with no space and no overlap.

❋ **Absolute Time.** Sets the grid to clock values, such as minutes or seconds, allowing you to make precise time-based edits.

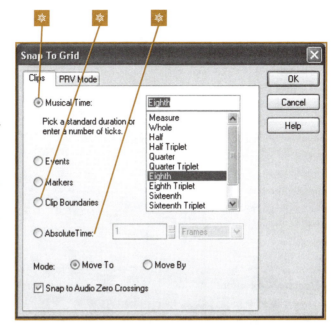

❋ **Mode.** Applies only to moving and copying clips within a Musical Time or Absolute Time grid.

• **Move To.** Snaps the moved clip to the nearest grid point, so, for example, the clip will start exactly at a particular quarter note or a specific second.

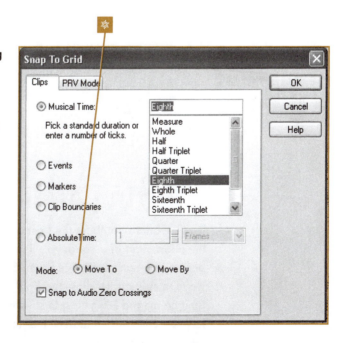

- **Move By.** Constrains the *distance* a clip moves to a multiple of a grid value, so, for example, a clip will end up exactly one measure earlier or 10 seconds later. If the clip started just before or after a grid point, it will end up exactly the same distance away from the nearest grid point when it has been moved.

※ **Snap to Audio Zero Crossings.** Forces the Now time, selection boundaries, and slip-edits to snap to the nearest point at which the waveform crosses the zero volt line, helping to avoid clicks and pops at clip boundaries. This preference is independent of all other options in the Snap to Grid dialog box, and it takes precedence over the chosen grid value.

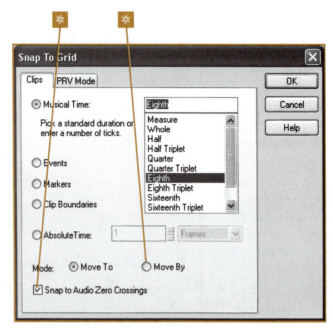

※ **Snap to Audio Zero Crossings**

As a rule, you should leave Snap to Audio Zero Crossings on all the time. It will save you a lot of time and trouble fixing the sort of nasty little clicks and pops that you would otherwise hear at the beginning and end of audio clips.

Splitting Audio Clips

If you want to combine the best parts of several vocal takes or cut the chorus out of a song, you'll need to chop up the audio clips before you can rearrange them. SONAR gives you two different ways to split audio clips—the Split command and the Split tool. The Split command lets you split several clips at once, and the Split tool lets you cut a segment from the middle of a clip just by dragging. Here's how they work.

1 Select one or more clips.

2 Click in the Time Ruler at the point where you want to split the clips. The Now time will be set to that position.

3 Press the S key on your keyboard. The clips will all be split at the Now time.

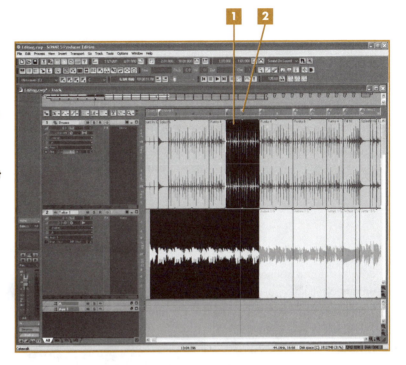

4 Click on the Split tool. A scissors icon will appear with the mouse pointer.

5 Click on an audio clip. The clip will split into two clips at the position at which you clicked.

6 Drag the mouse pointer within an audio clip. When you release the mouse button, the clip will be split at the beginning and end of where you dragged.

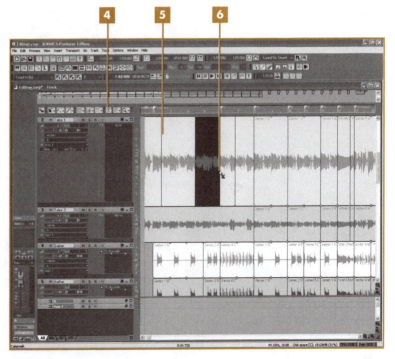

❀❀❀

Selecting Partial Clips

In Chapter 3 you worked with whole clips—selecting them, copying them, pasting them, and even deleting them. Sometimes, however, careful editing requires working with smaller sections of audio; fortunately, SONAR allows you to select partial clips. You can then copy, paste, and delete the partial clips. Selection of partial clips conforms to the grid if it's enabled, so you can select only the fourth bar of a clip or exactly 10 seconds of an ambience loop.

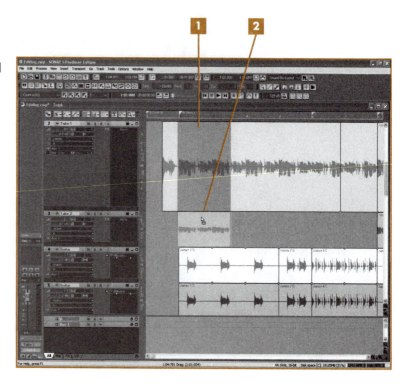

1 Press and hold the Alt key and drag the mouse pointer within an audio clip. The portion of the clip over which you Alt+dragged will be selected.

2 Drag the selection to a new location. The selection be cut and pasted.

3 Hold the Shift key while you drag to prevent the selection from moving earlier or later as you drag it.

❄ The Same, Only Different

Choosing Cut, Copy, Paste, or Delete from the Edit menu or context menu will achieve the same results as discussed in Chapter 3, except that the selected partial clip will be the object of the action rather than the entire clip.

Slip-Editing a Clip

The term *slip-editing* refers to the process of trimming a clip non-destructively. In SONAR, this is accomplished simply by grabbing one end of a clip and dragging it to make the clip shorter. The technique is the same one you used to roll out loops and groove clips, but slip-editing is usually used to reduce the length of a clip. You can lengthen a clip, but if the clip is not looped, you might only add silence to the end of the clip. Note that when slip-editing, you will see the clip jump to grid values—this is intended to help you make grid-based edits if you wish, but it does not restrict you from placing the clip boundary off the grid if you want. The only Snap to Grid option that applies strictly to slip-editing is Snap to Audio Zero Crossings.

1 Position the mouse pointer at one end of an audio clip. The pointer will change to a slip-editing icon.

2 Drag the end of the clip to make the clip shorter or longer.

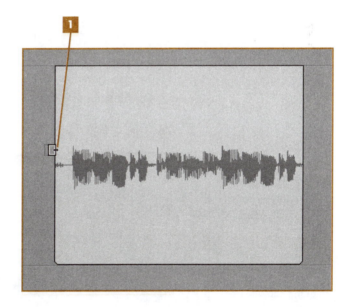

❀ **Slip-Editing**

You can change your mind all day long about the length of a clip, because slip-editing is entirely non-destructive. If you lengthen a clip beyond its original length, however, you will see a straight line instead of a waveform, indicating silence where there is no real sound.

Using Fades and Crossfades

The best way to think of what fades and crossfades can do for you is to listen to a good DJ, either the radio kind or the club kind. DJs are always fading a song in after they talk over the intro, fading a song out because they need to read the weather, and fading one song out while they fade another one in—that's a *crossfade*—so nobody gets the notion to leave the dance floor. On a smaller scale, fades and crossfades are also essential tools for creative *splicing* of different takes and other sonic surgery. If you have chosen not to enable Snap to Audio Zero Crossings, fading the ends of and crossfading the seams between clips is highly recommended.

Fading In and Out

Fading a clip in or out in SONAR couldn't be simpler, as you'll see in these steps. It's always a good idea when a clip is fairly exposed to fade it in and out to remove any abrupt changes to and from silence. You might also want to fade out applause early at the end of a live track—three minutes of applause is gratifying on stage, but annoying on a CD!

1 Position the mouse pointer at the upper-left corner of an audio clip. The pointer will turn into a triangle (the Fade tool).

2 Click and drag the mouse pointer from the corner inward. The left end of the clip will be shaded, and a line will appear indicating the changing volume of the clip as it fades in.

3 Play the clip. The clip will start from silence and gradually get louder until it reaches full volume at the end of the shaded area.

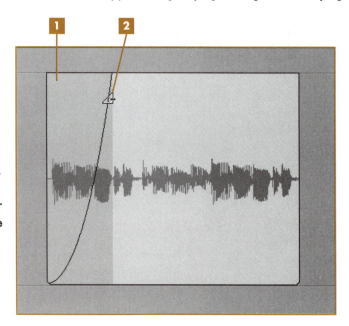

4 Drag the upper-right corner of the clip inward. This will create a fade-out.

5 Right-click at the top of the fade curve. The Fade Curve menu will appear. Its options include:

❋ Linear. The fade takes place at a steady pace over the clip's entire length.

❋ Slow Curve. The fade-in or fade-out starts slowly and then accelerates, with most of the volume change occurring toward the end of the fade.

❋ Fast Curve. The fade-in or fade-out starts quickly and then slows down, with most of the volume change occurring toward the beginning of the fade.

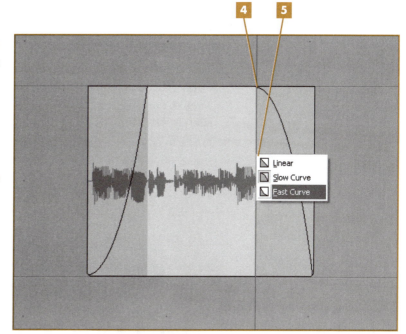

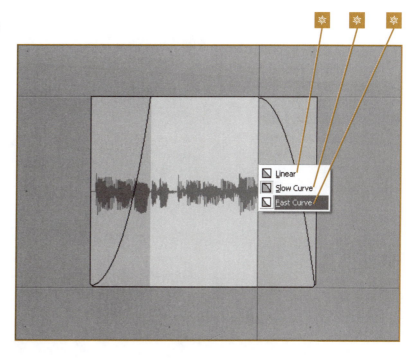

Creating Crossfades

Crossfading clips is as easy as fading them in or out. It's an important function for any kind of meticulous editing because it lets you make the transition from one clip to another smooth and gradual. It's a great way to cover up any glitches or changes in volume from one take to another. This technique can also be used to blend the end of one song seamlessly into the start of another.

1 Click on the Enable/Disable Automatic Crossfades button.

2 Drag a clip so that it overlaps another. The Drag and Drop Options dialog box will open.

3 Click on Blend Old and New, and then click on OK. Fade-in and fade-out curves will appear where the clips overlap.

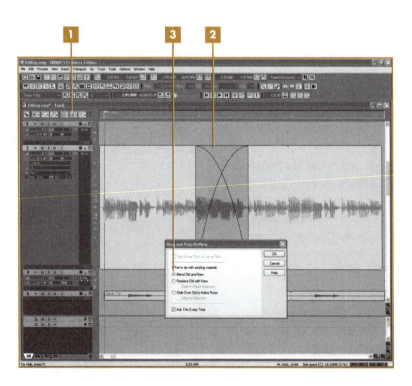

Saving Time

If you are doing this sort of thing often, you can save yourself time by setting the default Drag and Drop Options (in Global Options, Editing) to Blend Old and New and deselecting Ask This Every Time.

Setting Default Fade Curves

SONAR lets you choose default curves for fades and crossfades. You can always edit the curve via the Fade Curve menu, as discussed previously, but if you find yourself using one curve more than the others, you can save yourself time by setting it as the default curve.

1 Click on the Enable/Disable Automatic Crossfades down arrow.

2 Point to the fade type for which you want to set a default.

3 Click on the desired fade curve.

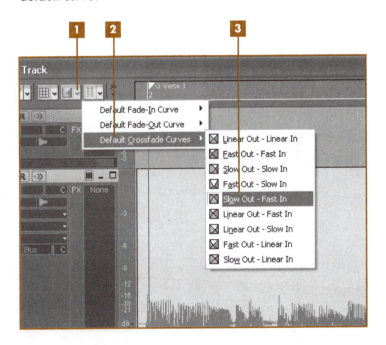

❋ **Suggested Default Fades**

Although circumstances and your ears will dictate the best curve for any given situation, you might want to start with the following defaults: Slow fade-in; Fast fade-out; and Slow Out-Fast In crossfade.

Processing Audio

SONAR features a number of powerful audio-processing functions. Some of these take the form of non-destructive real-time audio effects, such as reverb and delay, which I'll cover in Chapter 16, "Using Audio Effects." First, though, turn your attention to a special category of processes that must be performed *offline*, meaning that they must take place before playback. You could also call these *file-based* processes, because they operate directly on the audio data contained in audio clips.

Normalizing Audio

To *normalize* an audio clip is to raise its volume to the highest possible level without distortion. SONAR looks through the clip to find its highest peak, measures the distance from that peak to just below the onset of distortion, and then raises the volume of the entire clip by that amount. It is not necessary to normalize all of your clips, but if a clip is too soft, normalizing is a quick fix.

> ❄ **Danger, Danger!**
>
> These processes are *destructive*, changing the actual data in audio clips. You can use Undo if you change your mind during editing, but after you close a project, the changes are permanent. A cautious approach is to *clone* a track (as discussed in Chapter 10, "Managing Audio") before applying destructive processes.

1 Select a whole or partial clip.

2 Click on Process.

3 Point to Audio.

4 Click on Normalize. The Normalize dialog box will open.

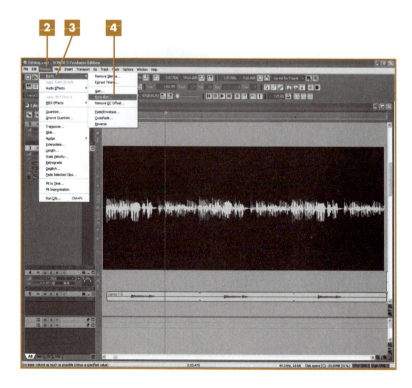

5a Choose a preset from the drop-down menu at the top of the dialog box.

OR

5b Drag the slider or type in a number box to set the Normalize Level.

6 Click on OK to process the selected audio.

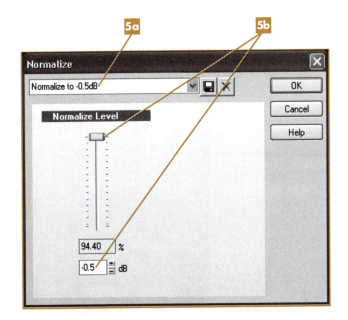

✲ **Abnormalization**

Normalization is no panacea. When you make the clip louder, you also make any background noise in the clip louder. The best solution is always to record your audio at proper levels to begin with.

Reversing Audio

Back in the '60s and '70s, there was a popular and controversial recording technique called *backward masking*. Rock stars were accused of putting subliminal messages in their records by mixing in phrases that had been played in reverse. Of course, whether anybody could understand the messages well enough to be influenced by them was another matter, but musicians, engineers, and fans were fascinated by the unnatural sound of backward voices and instruments. SONAR makes child's play out of reversing audio.

1 Select all or part of an audio clip.

2 Click on Process.

3 Point to Audio.

4 Click on Reverse. The selected audio will be reversed.

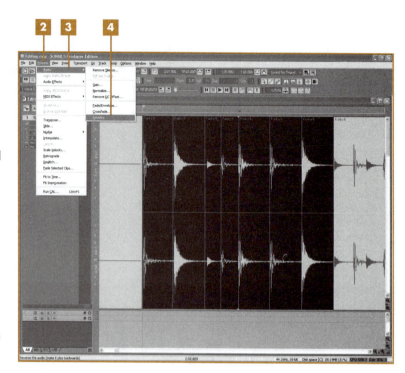

Removing Silence

SONAR can automatically find and remove the silent parts of a clip. One reason for doing this is that silence is rarely really silent! The background noise when musicians aren't playing might seem insignificant in a single part, but when there's background noise on each of several tracks it can add up and be noticeable. Removing the "silent" parts of those tracks keeps the noise from accumulating. Anyone familiar with the engineering term *gate* will recognize this function. Another reason for removing silence is to split a clip into multiple clips between phrases for easier handling. This is especially useful in dialogue or narration editing, but it has its uses in music production as well.

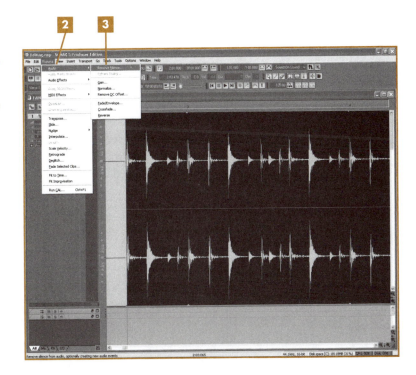

1 Select all or part of an audio clip.

2 Click on Process and point to Audio.

3 Click on Remove Silence. The Remove Silence dialog box will open.

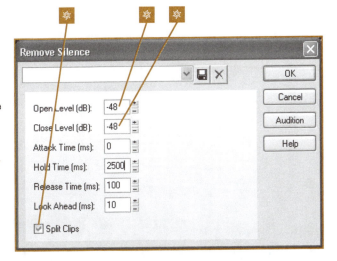

4 Enter values for the various parameters. Key options include:

❋ **Open Level (dB).** Sound above this volume will not be considered silence and will be kept.

❋ **Close Level (dB).** Sound below this volume will be considered silence and will be removed.

❋ **Split Clips.** The clip will be divided up into smaller clips wherever silence is removed.

5 Click on OK. The silence will be removed.

❋ **Hold It**

Hold Time sets a minimum length for a clip so you don't end up with too many tiny clips. Look Ahead extends the resulting clip earlier in time to catch the subtlety of a sound's attack. Your ears will tell you when this is necessary.

❋❋❋

10 Managing Audio

When working with audio in SONAR, you can find yourself accumulating a lot of tracks and eating up a lot of space on your hard disk. Keeping your project file and your hard disk well organized is the key to managing your virtual studio. You already know that naming your tracks and projects wisely is a step in the right direction. In this chapter, you'll learn how to:

* Archive, clone, and wipe audio tracks
* Retrieve hard disk space by applying trimming and consolidating audio
* Clean up your audio folders

Archiving Audio Tracks

In Chapter 2, you learned how to mute and solo tracks to control what parts of a project you could hear. Archiving a track can be considered a special case of muting. When you mute a track it is silenced, but it is still active. You can un-mute a track during playback. It's as though it were running alongside the rest of the tracks, ready to jump in at any moment. When you archive a track it is essentially made inactive. You can't reactivate it without stopping playback, and it doesn't use any system resources at all. An archived track is a great place to store tracks that you aren't using but that contain alternate takes or other elements you might need later.

1 Select one or more tracks.

2 Right-click on the track number of a selected track. The context menu will appear.

3 Click on Archive. The menu will close, and the letter A will appear on the Mute button of the track(s). The track(s) will also turn a darker color to indicate archive status. Repeat the process to return selected tracks to normal status.

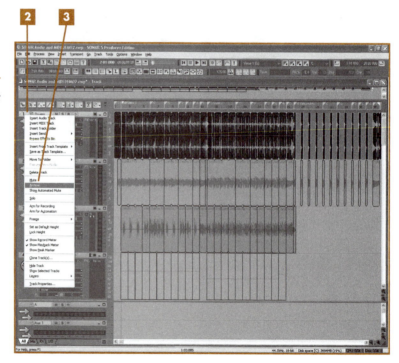

✳ Archiving Tracks

If a track was muted when it was archived, it will still be muted when you un-archive it.

Cloning a Track

Cloning a track is exactly what it sounds like—making an identical copy, including all clips, effects, and settings. By itself, all it does is reinforce the original track, making it slightly louder without changing the sound at all. Delay the clone slightly and pan it to one side, though, and the interaction becomes more complex. You can vary the effects and edits on the clone and do all sorts of things to add variety to the sound. Another great use for a clone is as a safety copy before you start doing complex or destructive edits to the original. Simply clone a track, archive the original or the clone (because they're identical, it doesn't matter which), and go wild!

1 Select one or more tracks.

2 Right-click on the track number of a selected track. The context menu will appear.

3 Click on Clone Track(s). The Clone Track(s) dialog box will open.

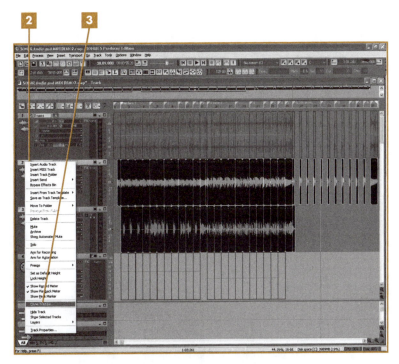

4 Click to choose desired options, which include:

❋ **Clone Events.** All clips will be cloned.

❋ **Link to Original Clip(s).** All cloned clips will be linked to the source track's clips.

❋ **Clone Properties.** Cloned tracks will have the same name and I/O settings as source tracks.

❋ **Clone Effects/Sends.** Cloned tracks will have the same effects and/or sends as source tracks.

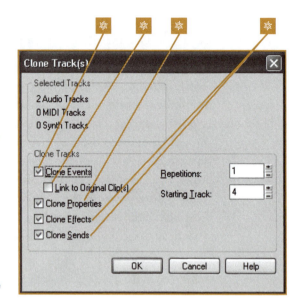

5 Type the desired number of repetitions in the Repetitions field. This is how many clones will be created.

6 Type a number for the desired target track in the Starting Track box. Existing tracks from that number down will move downward to make room.

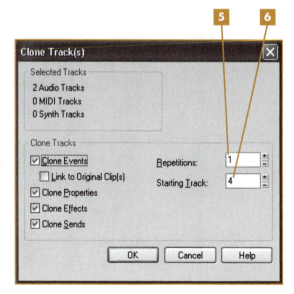

❋ **A Quick Way to Set Up for Recording**

A quick way to set up a track for recording additional takes is to clone only the track properties. The cloned track will be blank, but its input and output will be set the same as the track in which you recorded the previous take.

Wiping a Track

Even you have an idea or performance that turns out to be less than you had hoped for now and then, right? There's no shame in it—it happens to us all. Using SONAR's Wipe Track command, you can destroy any evidence of that fact! Wiping a track removes all clips from a track while leaving the track itself and all of its I/O settings intact.

1 Select one or more tracks.

2 Click on Track. The Track menu will appear.

3 Click on Wipe. The track will be cleared of all clips.

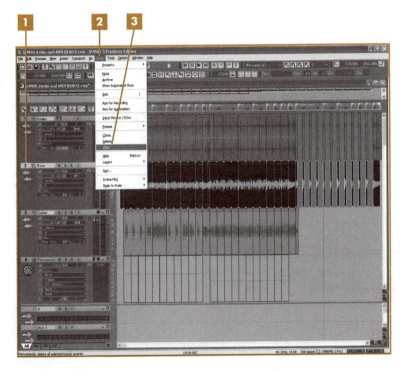

Consolidating Project Audio

If you haven't been using per-project audio folders, or if you've imported audio into your project, the audio from any given project may be both intermingled with audio from other projects and scattered among several folders on your hard disk. To organize your data better, you can use the Consolidate Project Audio command. It collects all audio files from an open project in a single subfolder of the Audio Data folder.

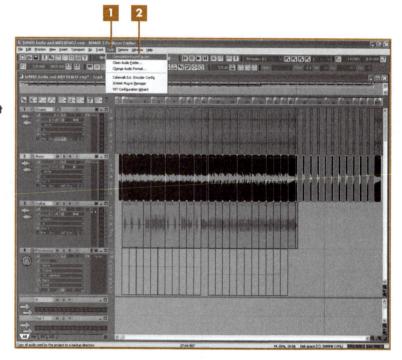

1 Click on Tools. The Tools menu will appear.

2 Click on Consolidate Project Audio. The Consolidate Project Audio dialog box will open.

❋ Don't Forget the Project File!

Be aware that the folder that now contains all of the project's audio files does not include the project file itself. If you back up the consolidated folder *and* the project file you will have a complete backup of your project.

3 Click on OK. The dialog box will close, and SONAR will place copies of the project's audio files into a single folder.

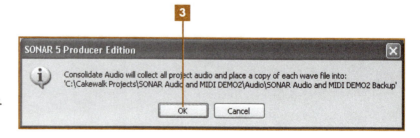

Applying Clip Trimming

Because SONAR's slip-editing is nondestructive, it leaves a lot of unused audio data on your hard disk. This is great if you change your mind about an edit, but it's a big waste of space once you get to a point in a project where you're committed to the arrangement. You can reclaim this wasted space by permanently deleting the audio that has been trimmed away. That's what the Apply Trimming command does, and here's how to use it.

1 Select the clips from which you want to delete slip-edited data.

2 Click on Edit. The Edit menu will appear.

3 Click on Apply Trimming. The trimmed audio will be deleted.

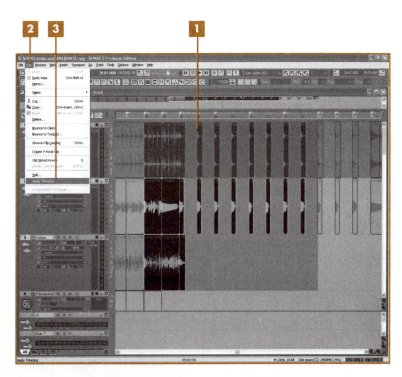

❋ **Saving Space**

When it's time to archive a project, you might want to select all of your clips (Edit, Select All) and then apply trimming to them all. That will ensure that you're not wasting storage space on a lot of data you don't want.

Cleaning Audio Folders

Sooner or later—actually, there's no later about it when you're dealing with audio files—you're going to find your hard disk overflowing with audio files, and you'll want to clean off any unused data to make room for more creativity. It's best to let SONAR handle this for you, because each project file knows exactly what files it owns. The Clean Audio Folder command will search your system for project files and then build a list of audio files that don't belong to any project. You can then delete these files and reclaim the wasted drive space.

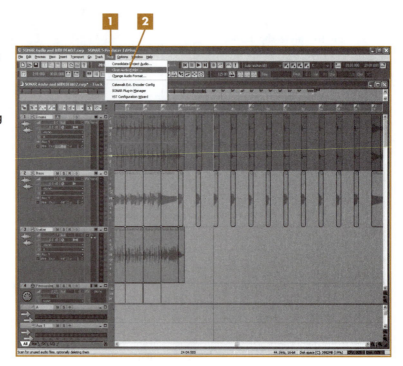

1 Click on Tools. The Tools menu will appear.

2 Click on Clean Audio Folder. The Clean Audio Folder dialog box will open.

3a Type the name of the folder you want to search in the Audio Path box.

OR

3b Click on the Browse button and navigate to the folder you want to search.

4 Optionally, click on Recurse (All Wave files below this point belong to SONAR Projects) to tell SONAR to look for audio files in subfolders of the chosen folder.

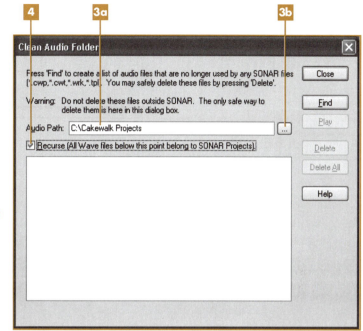

5 Click on Find. SONAR will search the specified folder and display a list of orphaned files.

6 Optionally, click on Play to audition files.

7 Click on Delete or Delete All. The selected file or all files, respectively, will be deleted from your hard disk.

❋ **Searching High and Low**

SONAR will search your entire hard drive for project files, but it will only search the folder you choose for audio files to delete.

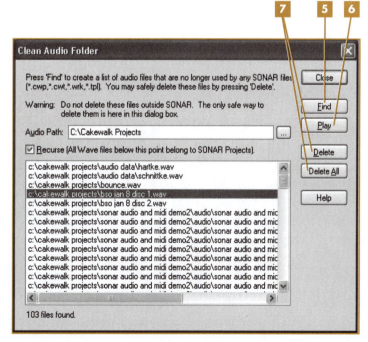

PART IV

Working with MIDI

Chapter 11: Using the Cakewalk TTS-1

Chapter 12: Editing MIDI

Chapter 13: Recording MIDI Tracks

Chapter 14: Cleaning Up Your MIDI Act

Chapter 15: Mastering MIDI's Ins and Outs

11 } Using the Cakewalk TTS-1

MIDI is a powerful language for controlling synthesizers, and SONAR 5 gives you every bit of control the MIDI language allows. One of the great things about MIDI is that it uses a common set of instructions that can be applied to any MIDI-capable synthesizer, regardless of its brand, model, or vintage. That means that all of the tools and functions in the next few chapters will work on whatever synthesizers you already own. To keep things consistent, though, I'll use the Cakewalk TTS-1 that is included with SONAR 5. It's a software synthesizer—sometimes called a *virtual instrument*—that runs directly within SONAR. Depending on your level of experience with MIDI synthesizers, you will probably find it useful to follow along using the TTS-1 and then later apply the lessons to other instruments. In this chapter, you'll learn how to:

* Use the Synth Rack to start the TTS-1
* Assign MIDI track outputs
* Change patches on the TTS-1
* Control the tempo of a project

Opening the Tutorial Project

Cakewalk has included several tutorials with SONAR, and you should go through them to help solidify all of the concepts you're learning. I'm going to use the first tutorial project as an example in this chapter, but of course everything here applies to any project. You'll start by opening the tutorial project and making the most of the available screen space.

1 Open the first tutorial project, TUTORIAL1.cwp. You'll find it in the folder C:\Program Files\Cakewalk\SONAR 5 Producer Edition\Tutorials.

Studio Edition

If you have SONAR 5 Studio Edition, the path will be C:\Program Files\Cakewalk\SONAR 5 Studio Edition\Tutorials.

2 Drag the lower-right corner of the Track view to fill the window.

3 If necessary, click on the Show/Hide Bus Pane button to close the Bus Pane.

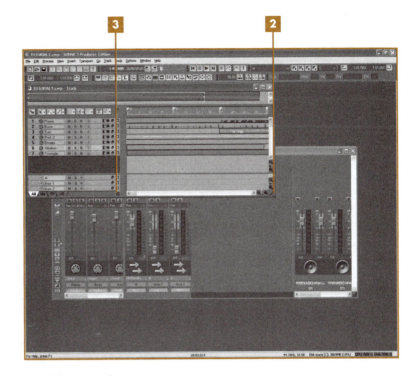

4 Click on the down arrow to the right of the Zoom tool. The View Options menu will appear.

5 Click on Fit Project to Window. The tracks will be resized to fill the window.

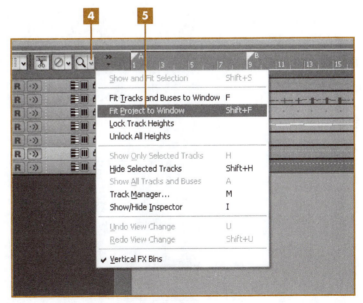

133
❈❈❈

Using the Synth Rack

The Synth Rack is SONAR's tool for starting and managing virtual instruments. It gives you a unified set of tools for starting or deleting any of the available DXi synthesizers, and it lets you open their editing interfaces for mad tweaking. Although it's possible to insert software synthesizers directly on tracks, it's usually more useful to create them from the Synth Rack. All of the software synthesizers you are currently running will appear in the Synth Rack regardless of how you created them initially.

Starting the TTS-1

The TTS-1 is a General MIDI 2 synthesizer that uses Roland's acclaimed Sound Canvas sound set. The following steps apply equally well to any of the numerous third-party software synthesizers available.

1 Click on the Synth Rack button. The Synth Rack will appear.

2 Click on the Insert button. The Insert menu will appear.

3 Click on Cakewalk TTS-1. The Insert Soft Synth Options dialog box will open.

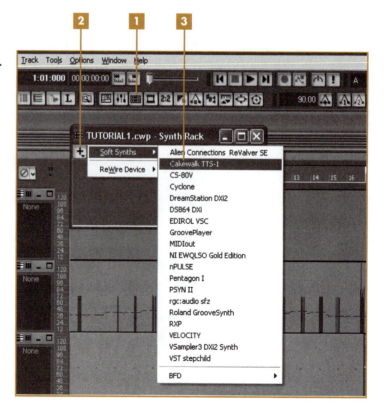

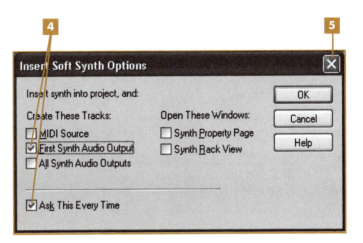

4 Click on the First Synth Audio Output and Ask This Every Time options to select them, and deselect all others. A ☑ will appear next to only those two options.

5 Click on OK. The dialog box will close, and the TTS-1 will appear in the Synth Rack.

❆ **Closing the Synth Rack**

It's okay to close the Synth Rack or the editing page of any soft synth—simply click on its Close button. Although an application's Close button ends the program completely, it doesn't work the same way for windows within SONAR, except for the Track view. You can always reopen the Synth Rack from the toolbar or the View menu, and you can reopen any synth from the Synth Rack.

Assigning MIDI Track Outputs

To hear the results of MIDI notes in a track, you must assign the output of the track to that instrument. This causes MIDI data to be sent from the track to a synthesizer, where the synthesizer responds by playing those notes.

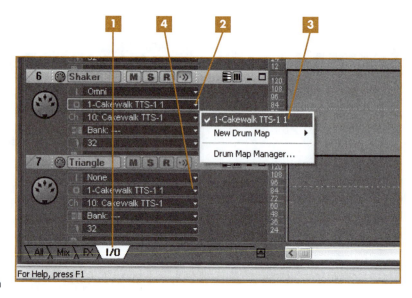

1 Click on the I/O tab in the Track pane. The I/O tab will come to the front.

2 Click on the down arrow to the right of a track output field. The track output menu will appear.

3 Click on Cakewalk TTS-1 1. The menu will close, and the track output field will display "Cakewalk TTS-1 1."

4 Repeat Steps 2 and 3 for each track. All outputs will show "Cakewalk TTS-1 1."

Playing the Tutorial Project

Now that you've got all of your MIDI tracks assigned to the TTS-1, you're ready to hear the results. Each track will now feed its information to the synthesizer, and the synthesizer will respond by playing its sounds according to the MIDI instructions.

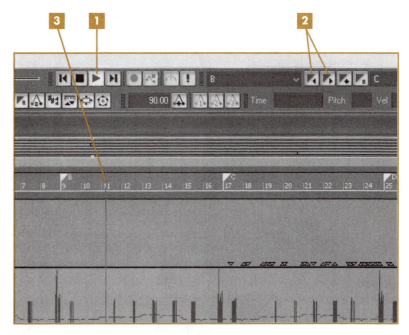

1. Click on the Play button. The tutorial project will play through the TTS-1.

2. Click on the Next/Previous Marker buttons. The Now time will skip immediately to the next or previous marker, and playback will continue from that point.

3. Click anywhere in the Time Ruler. The Now time will skip immediately to that point, and playback will continue.

Changing Patches

The various instrument sounds that a synthesizer can make are organized into *banks* and *patches*. A patch is an individual timbre, and a bank is a collection of 128 patches.

Setting the Default Bank and Patch

Each MIDI track is assigned to play back on a specific patch of a specific bank. These settings are located near the track output assignment.

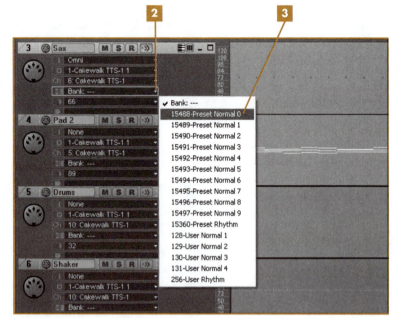

1. Press Ctrl+down arrow a few times to increase the track height until the Bank and Patch fields are visible.

2. Click on the down arrow to the right of the Bank field. The Bank assignment menu will appear.

3. Click on a bank.

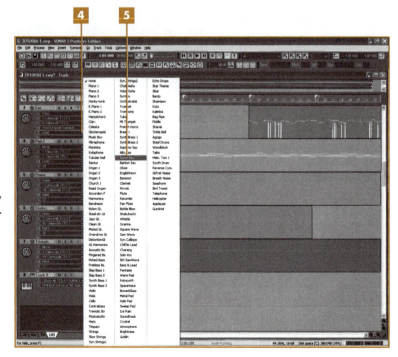

4. Click on the down arrow to the right of the Patch field. The Patch assignment menu will appear.

5. Click on a patch.

❋ Auditioning Patches

Changing banks and patches on the fly during playback is a great way to hear the difference immediately. You might find it useful to use Loop playback (see Chapter 2) so you can hear a section played in different sounds.

Inserting a Patch Change

SONAR even lets you change a track's assigned patch in the middle of a song. This is a convenient way to generate some sonic variety in an arrangement.

1 **Click** on the **Next Marker button**. The Now time will move to the next marker.

2 **Click** on the **track number** of the track into which you want to insert a patch change. The track will be highlighted.

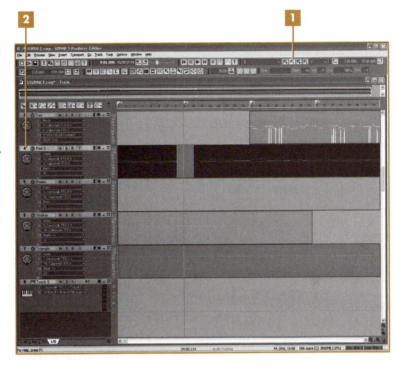

3 **Click** on **Insert**. The Insert menu will appear.

4 **Click** on **Bank/Patch Change**. The Bank/Patch Change dialog box will open.

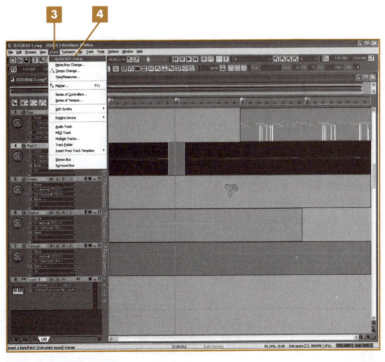

5 Click on the Bank down arrow and choose a bank from the drop-down list.

6 Click on the Patch down arrow and choose a patch from the drop-down list.

7 Click on OK. The dialog box will close, and on playback the new bank and patch will take effect at the current Now time.

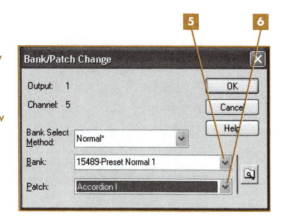

Changing Tempo Gradually

In Chapter 6, I covered setting and changing the project tempo, but what do you do if you want to accelerate or decelerate during a song? It's no problem—SONAR can do it.

1 Click on the Tempo button. The Tempo view will appear.

2 Click on the Draw Line button. The mouse pointer will appear as a plus sign (+).

3 Drag in the tempo grid. A line will appear connecting the point at which you clicked the mouse to the point at which you released the mouse.

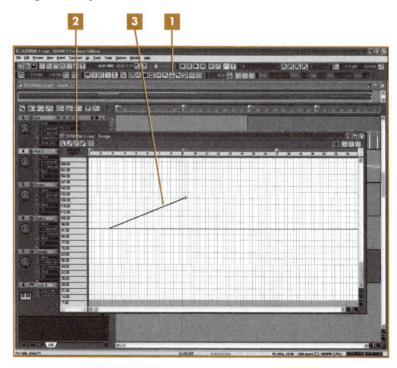

❋ **Timing Is Everything**

To make very precise tempo changes, use the zoom controls in the lower-right corner of the Tempo view to zoom in closely.

4 Play the project. The tempo will change gradually according to the line you drew.

5 Click on the Eraser button. The mouse pointer will have a circle with a slash through it (denoting the Eraser tool).

6 Drag in the tempo grid. Any existing tempo changes in the area in which you drag will be deleted.

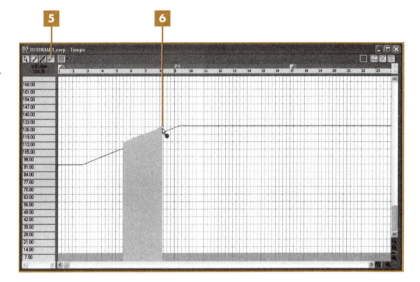

12 } Editing MIDI

You can think of MIDI information in SONAR as a blueprint that your synthesizers will follow. You are the architect of your project, and you can change your mind whenever you want. Each time your synthesizers "build the house," they will check the most recent blueprint and follow your instructions to the letter. In this chapter, you'll learn how to:

* ❉ Slip-edit and transpose MIDI clips
* ❉ Reverse and change the length of MIDI clips
* ❉ Edit notes in the Piano Roll view
* ❉ Add and delete notes
* ❉ Use the Controller pane to edit control data

Using MIDI Clips

SONAR 5 makes editing simple by using the same set of tools for both audio and MIDI data. That means that most of what you already know about editing audio clips applies equally well to editing MIDI clips. Because MIDI is a different sort of information from audio, though, there are a couple of differences, including the ability to transpose MIDI freely.

Slip-Editing MIDI Clips

Audio clips are made up of a series of samples, each of which is a miniscule fraction of a second long. It takes thousands of samples to make up an audio clip. MIDI clips, on the other hand, are primarily series of messages telling a synthesizer to turn notes on and off. The highly technical terms for these two messages are *Note On* and *Note Off*. This means when you slip-edit a MIDI clip so that you cut off a Note On message, the note will never be heard, even if the Note Off message is still present in the clip. If you slip-edit a MIDI clip so that you cut off a Note Off message, SONAR will simply slide the Note Off message along with the end of the clip, making the note shorter.

1 Drag the mouse pointer up or down on the MIDI Scale (the piano keyboard at the left edge of the Clips pane) to make the notes larger or smaller.

2 Right-click on the MIDI Scale and drag the mouse pointer up and down to scroll the notes.

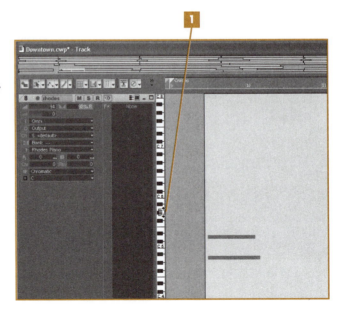

3 Point to the left edge of a MIDI clip. The mouse pointer will turn into the Slip-Editing tool.

4 Drag the mouse pointer to the right to make the clip shorter.

5 Drag the mouse pointer past the beginning of a MIDI note. The note will disappear.

6 Drag the mouse pointer back to the left to make the note reappear.

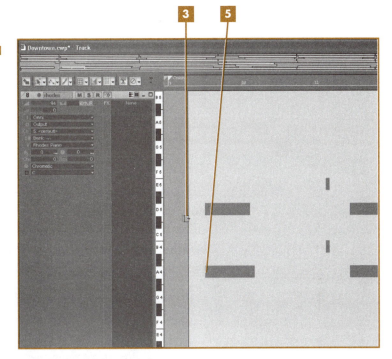

7 Point to the right edge of a MIDI clip.

8 Drag the mouse pointer to the left to make the clip shorter.

9 Drag the mouse pointer past the end of a MIDI note. The note will become shorter along with the clip.

10 Drag the mouse pointer past the beginning of a MIDI note. The note will disappear.

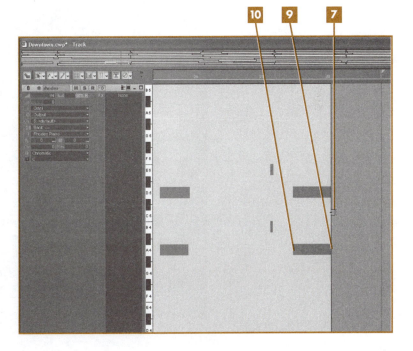

❄ **Gone and Back Again**

When you drag the end of the clip back to the right, the note will reappear, eventually reaching its original length. The note will never end up being longer than it was originally, though.

Transposing Clips

Because MIDI clips are just instructions, changing their pitches is as easy as telling SONAR to add or subtract a few numbers from the original notes. You can transpose *chromatically*, meaning that a series of notes will retain their absolute pitch relationships, or *diatonically*, meaning that the intervals between notes will adapt to the scale tones of the project's key.

1 Click to select one or more MIDI clips.

2 Click on Process.

3 Click on Transpose. The Transpose dialog box will open.

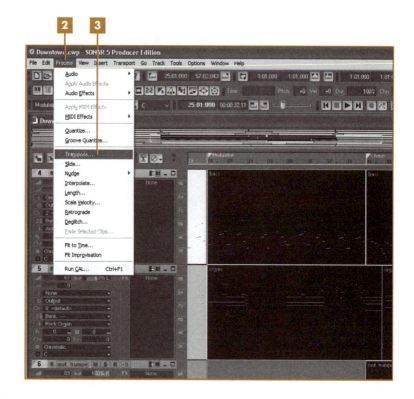

4 Type a positive or negative number in the Amount field. This is the number of semitones SONAR will transpose the clip(s).

5 Optionally, click in the Diatonic Math check box.

6 Click on OK. The clip(s) will be transposed accordingly.

✸ **Transposition Tip**

If you want something to sound as though it's in a completely different key, use chromatic transposition. Diatonic transposition is great for generating parallel harmony parts within the original key. Try cloning a melodic MIDI track and transposing the clone diatonically up or down by three (a diatonic third).

Reversing MIDI Clips

Reversing MIDI clips achieves a different effect than reversing audio clips. Instead of the unnatural backward-masking sound you get with reversed audio, reversed MIDI data simply plays the notes in reverse order. The notes sound like normal notes because SONAR just turns the whole clip around and then turns all Note Ons into Note Offs and vice versa. This can be a great tool for generating new ideas and jarring a creative block loose.

1 Select a MIDI clip.

2 Click on Process.

3 Click on Retrograde. The notes within the clip will be reversed.

❄ **One by One**

It's usually best to reverse MIDI clips one at a time. When you reverse multiple clips, the clip outlines don't move with the data, so you end up having to re-trim the clips.

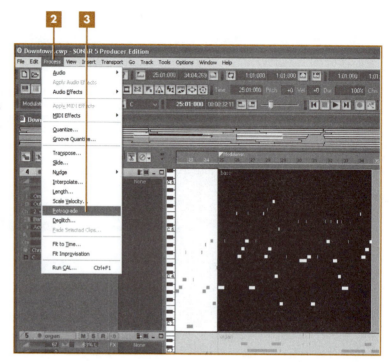

Changing the Length of MIDI Notes

The duration of a MIDI note is simply the time elapsed between its Note On and its Note Off messages. That simple fact makes it easy to change the length of a note, a series of notes, or an entire clip.

1 Select one or more MIDI clips.

2 Click on Process.

3 Click on Length. The Length dialog box will open.

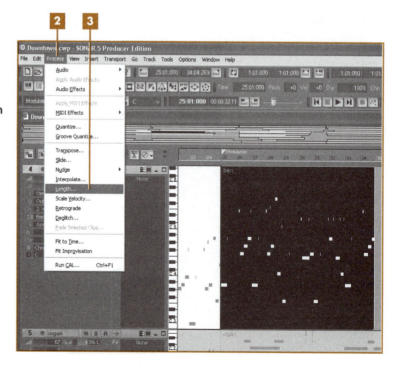

4 Click on the desired options. Available options include:

❋ Start Times. Causes the spacing of Note On messages to be increased or decreased.

❋ Durations. Causes the distance between Note On and Note Off messages to be increased or decreased.

5 Type a value in the By Percent field. This will determine the amount of change.

6 Click on OK. The length of the selected MIDI data (and the clip, if necessary) will be changed by the specified percentage.

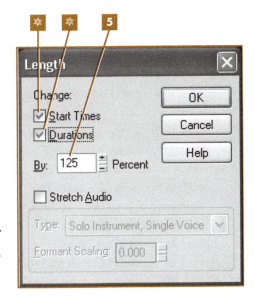

❋ The Finer Points of Articulation

To change the length of notes—in musical terms, to make the notes more *staccato* or *legato*—without changing the overall timing of the clip, choose only the Durations option. To speed up or slow down the clip without changing note length, choose only the Start Times option. To make the whole clip faster or slower without changing its internal feel, choose both.

Editing MIDI in the Piano Roll View

Clips are a convenient way of organizing blocks of MIDI events, but if you need to edit MIDI right down to the note level, the Piano Roll view (PRV) is your tool of choice. One look and you'll know why it's called Piano Roll—it looks and acts just like the big paper rolls that made old-fashioned player pianos work. Each note had a rectangle cut into the paper, and when the piano's mechanism encountered the beginning of a cutout it would press a key, releasing the key at the end of the cutout. SONAR's Piano Roll shows Note On messages as the beginning of rectangular "cutouts" and Note Off messages as the ends of the rectangles. A grid shows you where notes are vertically and where beats are horizontally. What could be easier?

Moving and Copying Notes

In PRV mode, you can move or copy individual notes or groups of notes earlier or later, and you can also change their pitches by dragging them up or down.

Inline or Out of Line?

In previous versions of SONAR the Piano Roll view was a floating window, but SONAR 5 introduces the "inline" PRV. This allows you to switch MIDI tracks between Clips mode and PRV mode without leaving the Track view. The floating PRV window is still available from the View menu, and you'll use it in Chapter 21, "Using Drum Maps and the Drum Grid."

1 Click on a track's PRV button.

2 Right-click in the track.

3 Point to PRV Tool.

4 Click on Select. The cursor will be the default pointer.

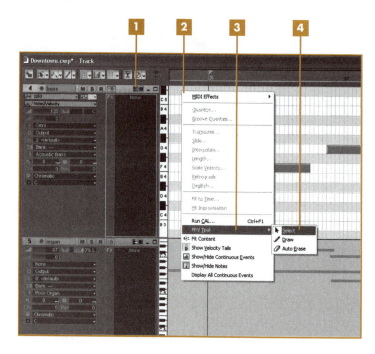

5 Drag around one or more notes to "lasso" them.

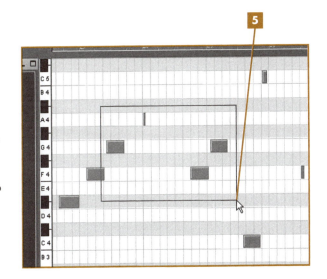

❋ Lasso That Note

When you lasso notes in this way, be sure to completely enclose all notes you want to include in the selection. Only notes that fall entirely within the lasso's outline will be selected.

6 Drag the note(s) to their new time and/or pitch.

7 Ctrl+drag the note(s) to copy them.

❋ The Same, Only Different

Selecting only some of the notes in a phrase and copying them is a great way to build variety in your compositions. This is because our ears like the familiarity of repetition, but too precise a repetition causes us to lose interest.

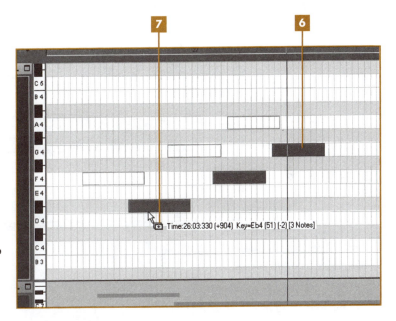

Changing a Note's Length

Sometimes you've got a performance that's almost perfect—if only you'd held that note just a tiny bit longer! SONAR lets you tweak the length of individual notes in the Piano Roll view, naturally.

1 Right-click in a MIDI track.

2 Choose Draw from the PRV Tool menu.

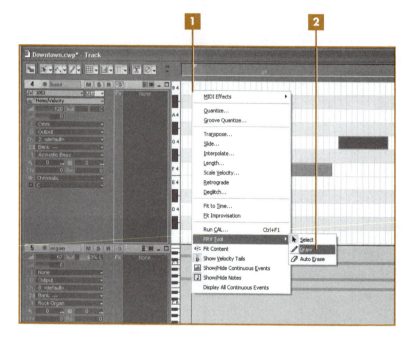

3 Point to the beginning or end of a note. The mouse pointer will appear as a two-headed horizontal arrow.

4 Drag the beginning or end of the note earlier or later. The note's start or end time will change accordingly.

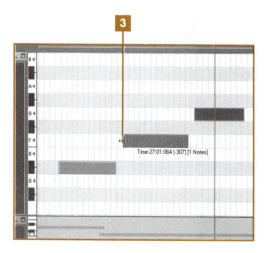

Adding and Deleting Notes

It will come as no surprise that within SONAR's graphical Piano Roll view, the tools to add and delete notes are drawing tools: a pencil and an eraser.

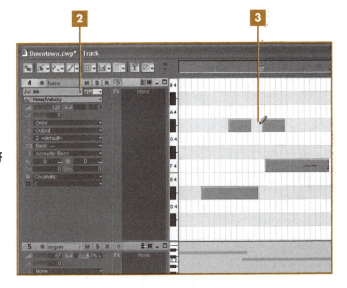

1 Choose **Draw** from the PRV Tool menu. The mouse pointer will appear as a pencil.

2 Choose a **note duration** from the drop-down list.

3 **Click** within the **grid**. A note of the specified duration will be created at that point.

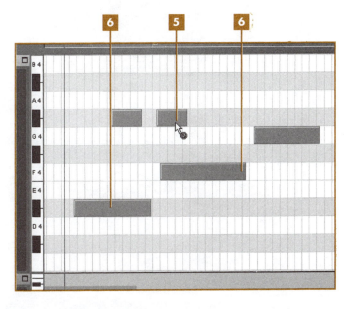

4 Choose **Auto Erase** from the PRV tool menu. The mouse pointer will appear as an arrow with a slashed circle attached.

5 **Click** on a **note**. The note will be deleted.

6 **Drag** across **multiple notes**. Each note will be deleted as the mouse pointer touches it.

Editing Note Velocities

The strength of individual notes is defined by a parameter called *velocity*, a measure of how hard your finger strikes a key. In addition to note volume, velocity often affects note timbre to some degree as well. Here's how to edit note velocity in the PRV.

1 Choose the Draw tool from the PRV toolbar.

2 Choose Show Velocity Tails from the PRV toolbar.

3 Point to the upper-middle third of a note. The pencil-shaped cursor will grow a small ladder—the velocity tail.

4 Drag the mouse up or down to change the note's velocity. A vertical line will indicate the velocity value.

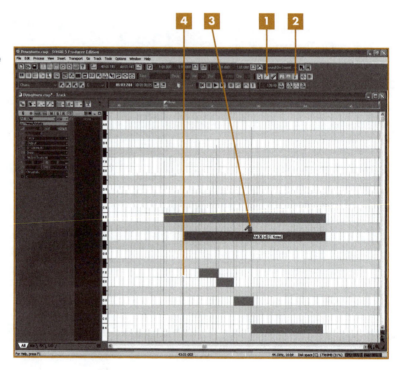

✳ Group Velocities

If you use the Select tool to select multiple notes, you can edit their velocities as a group.

Drawing Controllers and Other Events

MIDI needs more than Note On and Note Off messages to achieve expressive results, so the language includes a number of other parameters that let you control pitch bend, volume, and various other real-time performance controls. Most of these parameters are called *controllers*, and SONAR lets you edit them right alongside the notes they affect.

1 Click on the MIDI Event Type drop-down list.

2 Click on New Value Type. The MIDI Event Type dialog box will open.

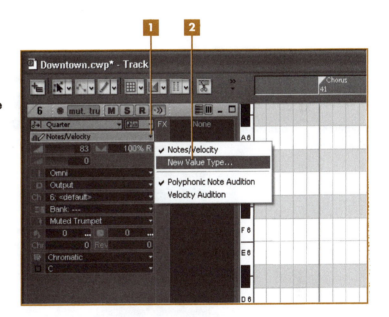

3 Choose **the desired** controller **or other** event type **from the drop-down lists.**

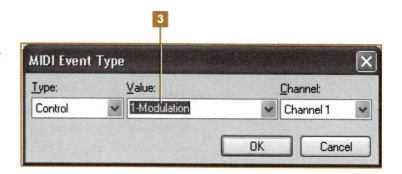

4 Choose **the** Draw tool **from the PRV toolbar.**

5 Drag **in the** track **to draw the desired controller.**

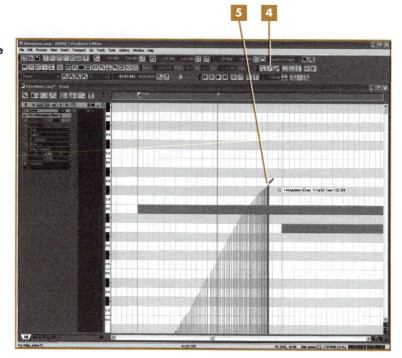

6 Choose the Select tool from the PRV toolbar.

7 Drag to lasso controller data.

8 Drag the selected data up or down to change its values or left or right to change its timing.

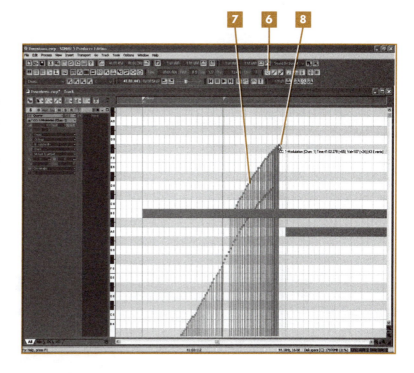

❋ **Speed Counts**

As you draw controller data, the more slowly you drag the mouse, the denser the data. Although there are times when extremely precise controller data is necessary, most of the time it's a good idea to keep the data relatively sparse.

13 Recording MIDI Tracks

Now that you've got a solid grasp of how SONAR displays and manages MIDI data, it's time to generate some of your own Note Ons and Note Offs. The process is quite similar to the process of recording audio, so most of what you learned in Chapter 8 will apply here as well. As you've seen, though, MIDI is more flexible than audio, so you have some additional options that can help you achieve great performances. Of course, you've still got the Undo option for those occasional less-than-great performances. In this chapter, you'll learn how to:

* Choose your MIDI inputs and outputs
* Configure the metronome
* Set up a MIDI track for recording
* Record, punch-record, and loop-record MIDI

Choosing MIDI Inputs and Outputs

So far, you've dealt only with internal MIDI connections by using the Cakewalk TTS-1. To record MIDI you'll need at least one MIDI Input port enabled, and if you're going to trigger hardware synthesizers you'll need at least one MIDI Output port enabled.

1 Click on Options. The Options menu will appear.

2 Click on MIDI Devices. The MIDI Devices dialog box will open.

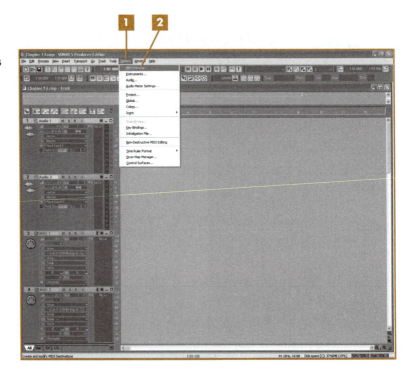

3 Click to enable one or more MIDI inputs. The inputs will be highlighted.

4 Click to enable one or more MIDI outputs. The outputs will be highlighted.

5 Click on OK to close the dialog box.

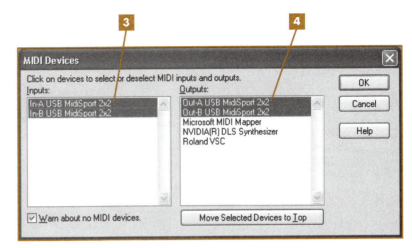

 Highlighting MIDI I/O

It's not necessary to Ctrl+click or Shift+click to select multiple MIDI inputs or outputs in this window. They stay highlighted until you click on them again to deselect them.

Configuring the Metronome

If you want to use SONAR's Time Ruler and grid to edit your performance, you need to know where SONAR's beats are. That's what the metronome does for you. Some musicians refer to the metronome as a *click track*, a series of audible clicks that helps them keep track of the tempo. The metronome will follow any tempo changes you have in your session, too.

1 Click on Options. The Options menu will appear.

2 Click on Project. The Project Options dialog box will open.

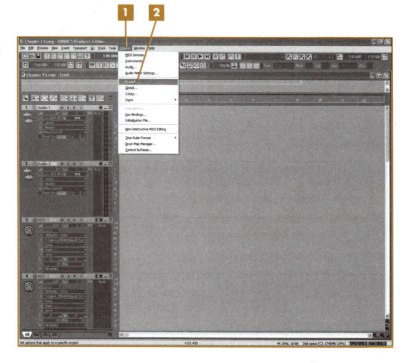

3 Click on the Metronome tab. The Metronome tab will come to the front.

4 Click on an option. A ✓ will be placed by the option. Typical options include:

❀ Recording. This option will cause the metronome to play during recording.

❀ Record Count-in. This option will tell the metronome to click a specified number of measures or beats prior to the Now time.

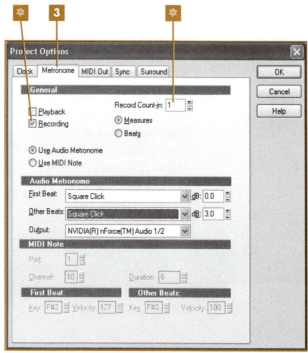

❄ **Use Audio Metronome.** This option utilizes a dedicated software metronome whose parameters are specified in the Audio Metronome section below.

❄ **First Beat/Other Beats.** You can choose a different sound for the first beat of each bar, or you can set the volume (dB) of the first beat to be louder than the rest.

❄ **Use MIDI Note.** This option causes the metronome to play the click through a hardware synthesizer connected to the port and channel specified in the MIDI Note section below.

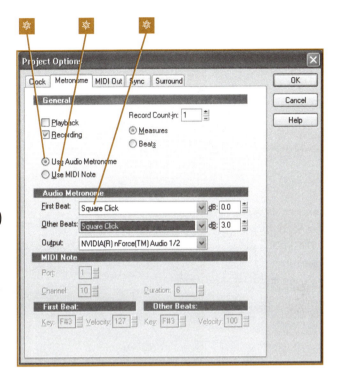

❄ **Precious Polyphony**

Using the audio metronome saves you from wasting polyphony on a hardware synthesizer.

Setting Up for Recording

There are just a few things you need to do to be sure you're ready to make your first MIDI recording. After you do this a couple of times, it will become second nature.

Assigning the MIDI Track Input and Output

By default, MIDI tracks are set up with no input so you don't get any surprises. Just as when you assigned audio inputs and MIDI and audio outputs, you simply have to choose your source from a menu.

❄ **Your Choice**

You can use either the TTS-1 or a hardware synthesizer for the following steps. If you want to use the TTS-1, open the Synth Rack and start the TTS-1 as you did in Chapter 11 before continuing.

1 Click on the down arrow to the right of a MIDI track's Input field. The MIDI Input menu will appear.

2 Point to All Inputs or to a specific MIDI input. The Channels submenu will appear.

3 Click on MIDI Omni or on a specific MIDI channel. The menu will close, and the track's Input field will display your choice.

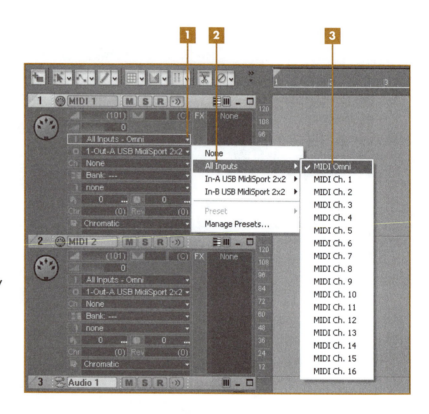

❄ **All Inputs or Not?**

Most of the time, you can choose All Inputs, MIDI Omni for all of your MIDI tracks. This setting lets any incoming MIDI data from any connected MIDI device be recognized by the track. If you want to take advantage of SONAR 5's multi-channel MIDI input recording (we'll get to that in Chapter 15, "Mastering MIDI's Ins and Outs"), you'll want to set each track's input to a specific MIDI input and channel.

4 Click on the down arrow to the right of the MIDI Output field. The MIDI Output menu will appear.

5 Click on Cakewalk TTS-1 or the physical MIDI output to which your hardware synthesizer is connected. The menu will close, and the MIDI Output field will reflect your choice.

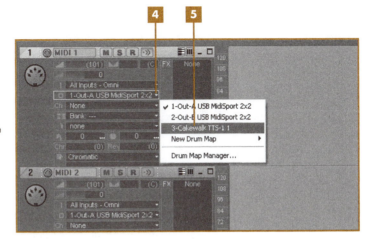

6 Click on the down arrow to the right of the MIDI Channel field. The MIDI Channel menu will appear.

7 Click on the MIDI channel you want this track to trigger. The menu will close, and the MIDI Channel field will reflect your choice.

8 Choose the bank and patch you want this track to use, following the procedure used in Chapter 11. The Bank and Patch fields will reflect your choices.

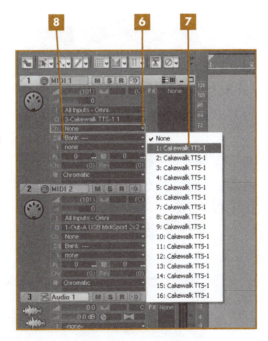

If you are using a hardware synthesizer, your Bank and Patch menus will show only numbers, not names. Chapter 15 will cover using SONAR's instrument definitions to fix this. For now, check your synthesizer's documentation for the bank and patch numbers to use. You could also set them from your synthesizer's front panel, in which case you should set the track's Bank and Patch to None.

Getting Ready to Record

Your track is now wired correctly to accept MIDI coming in from your keyboard and pass it on to a hardware or software synthesizer. Now all you need to do is tell the track to capture that data and spit it back out, and you're ready to record.

1 Click on Options. The Options menu will appear.

2 Click on Global. The Global Options dialog box will open.

❋ **Local Control**

If your controller keyboard has its own synthesizer sounds, you should turn its Local setting to Off. If Local is set to On, you will hear every note you play being doubled.

3 Click on the General tab.

4 Deselect the Allow MIDI Recording without an Armed Track option.

5 Deselect the Always Echo Current MIDI Track option.

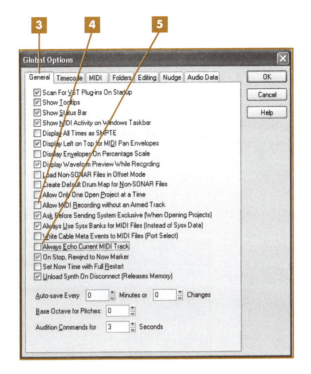

6 Click on the Input Echo button of a MIDI track. The button will be highlighted, and any MIDI notes you play on your keyboard will be played through the track's MIDI output.

7 Click on the Record Arm button of the MIDI track. The button will turn red.

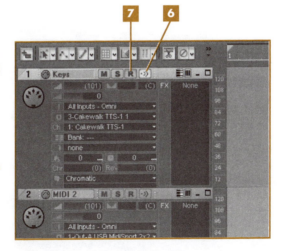

❈ Latency

If you hear a time lag between pressing a key and hearing the TTS-1, refer to Appendix A, "Setup and Troubleshooting," for suggestions on reducing latency.

Recording Your First MIDI Part

You've got your MIDI inputs and outputs enabled and assigned, you've got the metronome set to give you a steady click, and you've got your MIDI track set up both to record and to echo your performance. Now pick a tempo and go for it!

1 Click on the Tempo display. The current tempo will be highlighted.

2 Type in a tempo and press Enter.

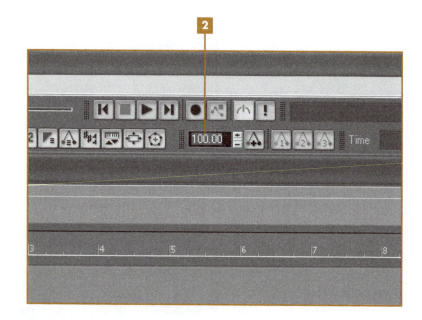

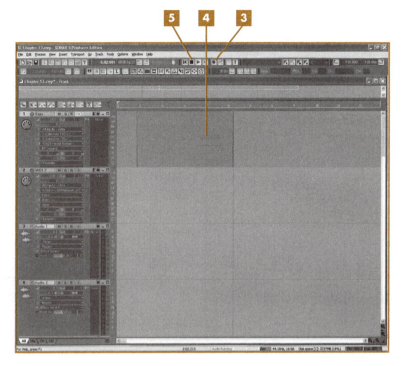

3 Click on Record. The metronome will click the count-off you specified, and then recording will begin.

4 Play on your MIDI instrument. SONAR will draw a new MIDI clip starting wherever you played your first note, and each new note will be displayed within that clip.

5 Click on Stop. Recording will cease, and the new MIDI clip will appear in the track, beginning at the first note you played and ending at the release of the last note you played.

6 In the unlikely event that your performance was less than perfect, press Ctrl+Z to undo the recording. The MIDI clip will be deleted.

Punch-Recording MIDI

You can punch in and replace portions of MIDI recordings using the Auto Punch technique you learned in Chapter 8. MIDI recording offers the additional option of punching in and out manually, allowing you to punch in multiple times in a single pass. This is not quite as precise as Auto Punch, but it's the only way to do multiple punches.

1 With a MIDI track prepared for recording as described earlier, in the section "Setting Up for Recording," right-click in the Time Ruler. The context menu will appear.

2 Click on Record Options. The Record Options dialog box will open.

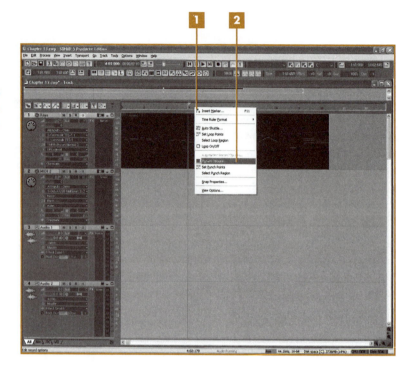

3 Click to enable Overwrite (Replace).

4 If necessary, click to disable Auto Punch.

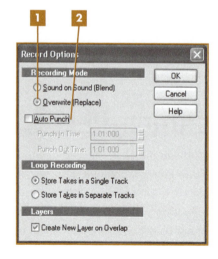

❄ **Replace or Blend?**

Choosing Sound on Sound (Blend) would cause SONAR to combine your new performance with the old. You could use that technique to add a harmony part.

5 Set the Now time to a few bars before the first phrase you want to replace.

6 Click on Play. Playback will begin, and you will hear the existing MIDI part.

7 At the point in the phrase you want to replace, click on Record and play the new part. The track will record your MIDI input, replacing the existing MIDI data.

8 At the end of the replacement part, click on Record again. Playback will continue, and you will once again hear the existing MIDI part.

9 Continue to punch in and out by clicking Record. Each time you punch in and out, a new MIDI clip will appear at that point, replacing the previous MIDI performance.

❄ **Play and Record Shortcuts**

You might find it much easier to press the R key on your keyboard than to click on Record each time you punch in and punch out. For that matter, you will probably find it easier to use the spacebar than to click on Play and Stop(it does both).

Loop Recording

Loop-recording MIDI is a time-honored tradition—at least, as close as you can come to time-honored in such a new field. In particular, virtually every R&B beat you've heard in the last decade has started with a producer laying down a kick drum and then layering first a snare and then a hi-hat as the kick track looped. This is slightly different from the way you loop-recorded audio in Chapter 8. Note that this is only a convention, and you can use either type of loop record with MIDI or audio.

1 Drag in the Time Ruler from the start of the loop to the end of the loop. The selection will be highlighted.

2 Right-click in the Time Ruler. The context menu will appear.

3 Click on Set Loop Points. The selection will be bracketed by yellow loop markers, and the Loop On/Off button will be turned on.

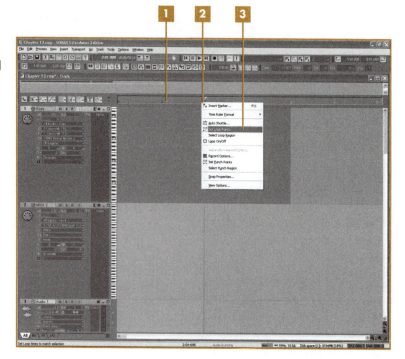

4 Right-click in the Time Ruler. The context menu will appear.

5 Click on Record Options. The Record Options dialog box will open.

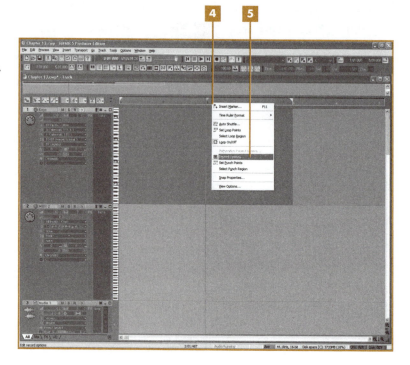

6 Click on Sound on Sound (Blend). The option will be selected.

7 Click on Store Takes in a Single Track. The option will be selected.

8 Click on OK. The dialog box will close.

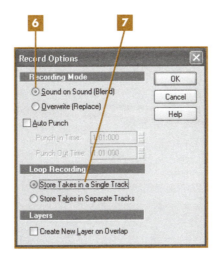

9 Click on the Record button and play the first part. Recording will begin, looping from the end back to the beginning until you stop it.

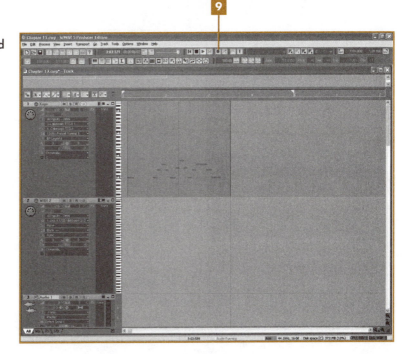

※ **Take Your Time**

When the loop starts over, you will hear whatever you played on the first pass. You can either start the second part immediately, or you can listen to the first part until inspiration strikes. SONAR will continue to loop, waiting for your next note, until you're ready.

10 Click on the Stop button. Recording will stop, and the most recent take will appear in the track, with the other takes hidden beneath.

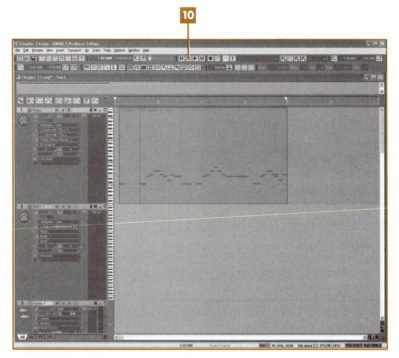

※ **Merging Takes**

If you're happy with the way the part turned out, you can merge the different layers into a single clip by dragging around them to select them all and choosing Bounce to Clip(s) from the Edit menu. This will make it easier to copy, paste, trim, and otherwise edit and manipulate the part.

14 } Cleaning Up Your MIDI Act

One of the things that makes MIDI and computers such a good match is that they're both mathematical in nature. MIDI expresses every aspect of a performance as a number—note numbers, channel numbers, and patch numbers—and a computer is fundamentally an overgrown calculator. This makes manipulating, fixing, and modifying MIDI an absolute cakewalk for a computer (pun intended). In this chapter, you'll learn how to:

* Fix timings using Quantize
* Improve timings using Groove Quantize
* Use logical processes to modify MIDI data
* Use track parameters to alter a performance

Fixing Timing with Quantize

Because SONAR knows the tempo, generates the metronome, and records the timing of every note you record, it can easily compare what you played with its own timing grid and, at your request, fix the timing. This is called *quantization*, and it's not only a convenient tool for correcting a performance, it's also a major stylistic component of modern dance music. Strictly quantized drum beats are fundamental for generating that driving dance-floor groove. Here's how to make it happen.

1 Right-click on a MIDI clip. The context menu will appear.

2 Move the mouse pointer to View and then click on Piano Roll. The Piano Roll view will appear.

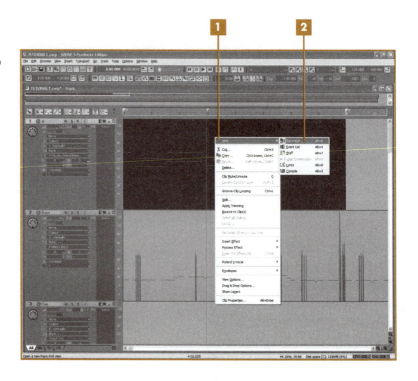

✳ Just for Appearances

You don't have to be in Piano Roll view to quantize, but it will help you see the notes snap to the grid as you quantize them.

3 Click on Process. The Process menu will appear.

4 Click on Quantize. The Quantize dialog box will open.

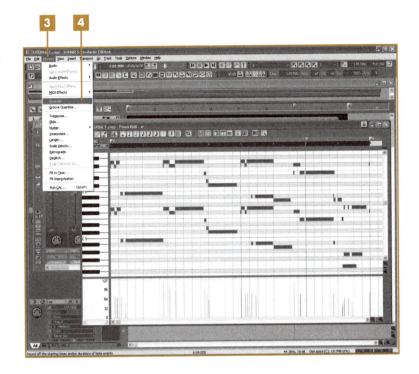

5 Click on the down arrow at the right of the Duration drop-down list box. The list will open.

6 Click on the desired duration.

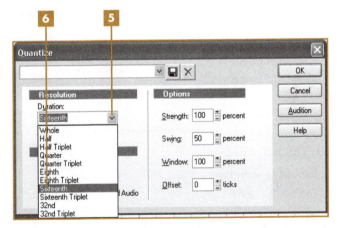

✳ Lowest Common Denominator

For best results, always choose the smallest rhythmic subdivision of the passage you're quantizing.

7 Click to choose the desired Change parameters, which include:

❋ Start Times. The beginnings of notes (the Note On messages) will be quantized.

❋ Note Durations. The ends of notes (the Note Off messages) will be quantized.

❋ Only Notes, Lyrics, and Audio. All other MIDI data will be exempt from being quantized.

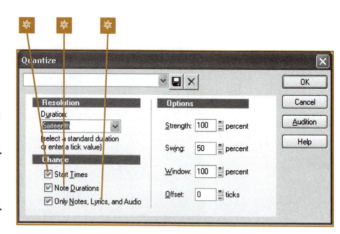

8 Enter values for the desired Options, which include:

❋ Strength. Values below 100 leave some human imperfections in the timing.

❋ Swing. A value of 66 is "textbook swing," and a value of 50 is "even eighths."

❋ Window. Values below 100 allow notes that are way off the grid to go unchanged.

❋ Offset. This option shifts the quantization grid slightly earlier (negative values) or later (positive values).

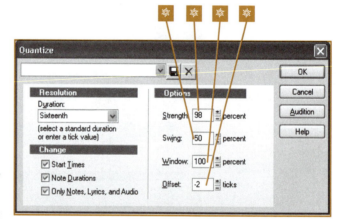

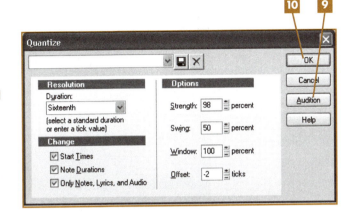

9 Optionally, click on Audition to preview the results. A few seconds of the selected clip will be quantized and played for your approval.

10 Click on OK. The dialog box will close, and the selected MIDI data will be quantized.

❈ **Critical Quantization**

To tighten up the timing of a performance without making it sound too mechanical, quantize start times but not durations, and use a Strength value of less than 100. To eliminate gaps between notes—to make them more *legato*—quantize both start times and durations.

Better Timing with Groove Quantize

Being perfect isn't all it's cracked up to be—trust me on this! There are subtle rhythmic variations that skilled musicians do that transcend mechanical accuracy. Performers *push* a beat to unsettle you and *pull* a beat to relieve the tension, and Quantize doesn't understand that stuff. Fortunately, SONAR also provides Groove Quantize, a more intelligent and flexible way of defining a quantization grid that "breathes" like a human.

1 Click on a MIDI clip. The clip will be highlighted.

2 Click on Process. The Process menu will appear.

3 Click on Groove Quantize. The Groove Quantize dialog box will open.

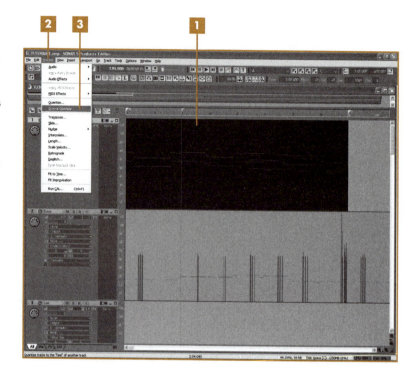

4 Choose a Groove File. This file contains the groove patterns.

5 Choose a Groove Pattern. Each pattern represents a different style or variation.

6 Choose a Resolution. As with regular Quantize, your choice should reflect the smallest rhythmic subdivision of the selected clip.

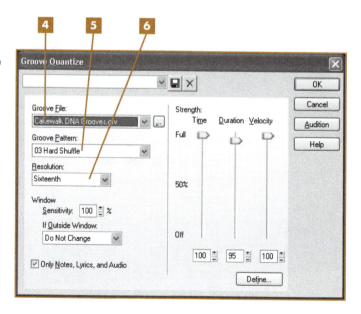

7 Drag **the Strength sliders** to the appropriate values:

❀ Time. This affects how close to the Groove Quantize grid Note On messages will be moved. A value of 100% moves all Note On messages precisely to the grid.

❀ Duration. This affects how close to the Groove Quantize grid Note Off messages will be moved.

❀ Velocity. This affects how close to the Groove Quantize template note velocities will be changed.

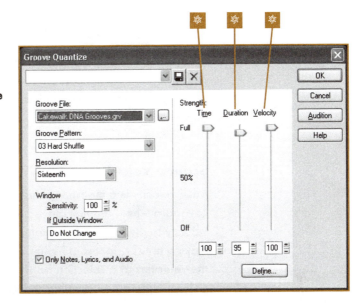

❀ **Keeping the Groove**

Groove patterns have a separate grid for Note Off messages, so although it was more natural not to quantize durations with the standard Quantize feature, you should at least audition Groove Quantize with Duration Strength set at or near 100% and then adjust to taste. Note also that Groove Quantize takes velocity into consideration, comparing the clip to its own pattern of accents.

Using Logical MIDI Processes

A *logical process* is any function that performs some kind of numerical evaluation of MIDI data and then makes changes according to what it finds. Quantize and Groove Quantize are two examples of logical processes, but SONAR has several more. Let's explore a few of them.

Scaling Velocity

MIDI *velocity* is a measure of how hard you struck the controller keyboard when you first played the note. Most synthesizers map velocity to the intensity of a note, and some map it also to timbre, making notes brighter at higher velocities. SONAR lets you scale the velocities of a selection from low to high, creating a *crescendo*, or from high to low, creating a *decrescendo*.

1. Select a MIDI clip or a group of notes.

2. Right-click in the Piano Roll view. The context menu will appear.

3. Click on Scale Velocity. The Scale Velocity dialog box will open.

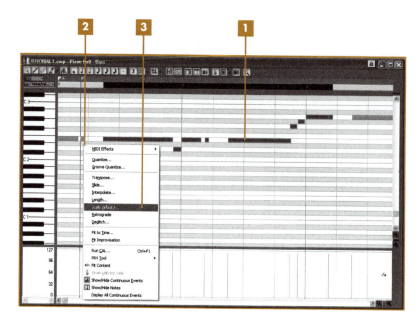

4 Enter a Begin value. This velocity will be assigned to the first note in the selection.

5 Enter an End value. This velocity will be assigned to the last note in the selection.

6 Optionally, click on the Percentages check box. A ☑ will appear in the box, and the velocities of the selected notes will be scaled by a percentage of their current values, rather than adjusted absolutely.

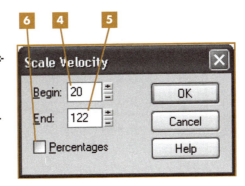

✸ **It's All Relative**

Scaling by percentage retains some of the "feel" of the original performance. In fact, if you like a performance but it's just too soft, try scaling by percentage with Begin and End values of 125 or so. This will increase every velocity in the selection by 25% while maintaining their relative values.

Sliding MIDI Data

SONAR gives you many different ways to move notes and clips around. You can drag them, quantize them, copy and paste them, and *slide* them. Sliding data is just another way of moving it earlier or later. Its advantage is that it's more precise than dragging and less mechanical than quantizing. Like the way you played a phrase, except that you dragged a bit? Slide it earlier. Want to write a new two-measure turnaround before the bridge? Slide the bridge two bars later.

1. Select a MIDI clip or a group of MIDI notes.

2. Right-click in the Piano Roll view. The context menu will appear.

3. Click on Slide. The Slide dialog box will open.

❋ Right-Clicking Power

The Piano Roll view's context menu is almost identical to the Process menu, so if you're in Piano Roll view already, it's easier to right-click if you want access to these functions.

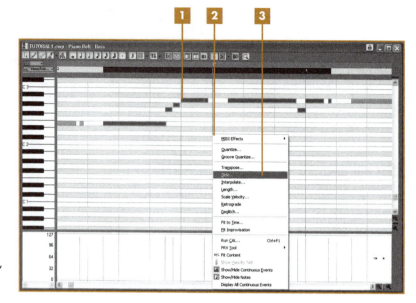

4. If necessary, click on Events in Tracks. A ☑ will appear next to the option.

5. Enter a By value. Positive numbers will move the selection later, and negative numbers will move the selection earlier.

6. Click on the desired unit of movement, and then click on OK.

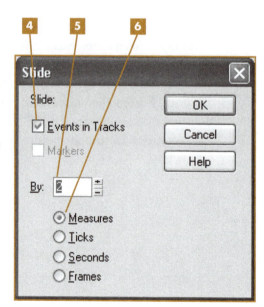

Using Track Parameters

Each MIDI track in SONAR has a set of MIDI parameters that are used to adjust playback of that track. These parameters don't change the MIDI notes themselves; they simply alter the way the MIDI notes are played. These parameters are found in the All tab of the Track view.

Using Velocity Trim (Vel+)

Velocity Trim adds or subtracts a specified value from the velocity of every note in the track. This preserves the relative velocities of a performance while boosting or cutting the overall intensity. Positive values will increase intensity, and negative values will decrease the track's intensity.

1a Drag the Velocity Trim slider. The Velocity Trim value will increase or decrease accordingly.

OR

1b Click on the Velocity Trim field and then press the plus (+) or minus (−) keys. The value will increase or decrease accordingly.

2 Double-click on the Velocity Trim field. The Velocity Trim value will be reset to zero.

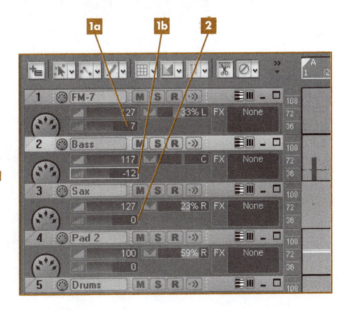

Using Time Offset (Time+)

Time Offset adds or subtracts a specified value from the time position of every note in a track. One time you might use this is if you had quantized a synth pad, but its slow attack made it sound late. By "cheating" the track a bit earlier using Time Offset, you could make the pad sound on time. Positive Time+ values will delay a track, and negative values will cause it to play earlier.

1 Click on the ellipsis (...) at the right of the Time+ field. The current value will be highlighted, and plus (+) and minus (–) buttons will appear.

2a Click on the plus (+) or minus (–) buttons. The Time+ value will be adjusted accordingly.

OR

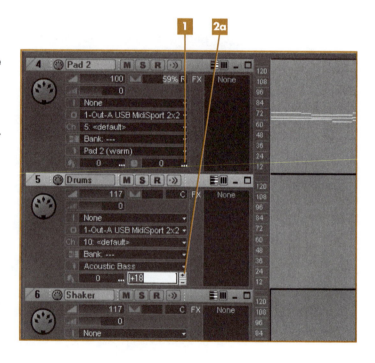

2b Point the mouse pointer at the small space between the buttons. The mouse pointer will appear as a double-headed vertical arrow.

2c Drag the mouse pointer up or down. The Time+ value will be adjusted up or down quickly.

3 Press Enter or Tab to confirm the new time offset.

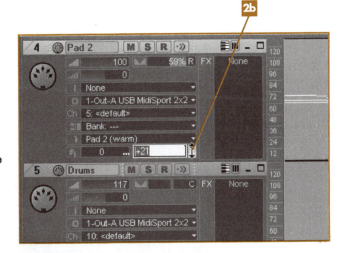

❋ Different Strokes

You can use either of these techniques for Key+, and you can use the technique described next for Key+ to adjust Time+. You can also use the plus and minus keys for either, as described previously in the section "Using Velocity Trim (Vel+)." Find the technique that makes you comfortable and stick with it!

Using Key Offset (Key+)

In a manner similar to Velocity Trim and Time Offset, Key Offset applies a non-destructive adjustment to the pitches of all *notes* in a track. The most common use for this is to drop a bass line down an octave. In fact, if you have a MIDI keyboard with limited range, you can use this adjustment during recording. Every note that you play from your keyboard will be echoed back to the assigned synth an octave lower (or whatever you set it to) than you play it. You never have to play in a difficult key again! Positive values will transpose a track up by semitones, and negative values will transpose it down by semitones. A value of 12, for example, will cause the track to play back one octave higher.

1 Double-click on the Key Offset field's icon or value. The value will be highlighted.

2 Type a new value and press Enter or Tab. The Key+ field will return to normal and display the value you entered.

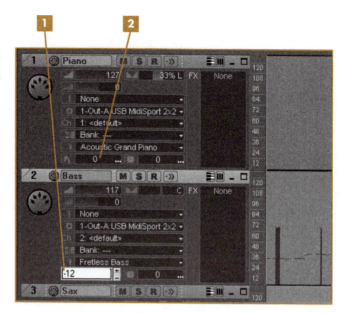

Menu Items

There's another way to adjust these three parameters. Under Track, Properties, you can open a dialog box for each of them. If you select multiple tracks and then open the parameter dialog box, your adjustment will be applied to all of the selected tracks.

Using MIDI Effects

For information about using SONAR's MIDI effects, including real-time Quantize, real-time Transpose, Cakewalk FX Velocity, and Arpeggiator, as well as information about how to create echoes and delays, see this book's companion Web site at http://www.courseptr.com/downloads.

15 } Mastering MIDI's Ins and Outs

MIDI was designed to be a universal language, allowing you to control synthesizers and other devices with a standard set of instructions regardless of brand or model. This universality makes a comprehensive sequencing environment, such as SONAR, powerful enough to control many instruments at once, but it can also make managing your MIDI inputs and outputs seem quite complex. SONAR gives you tools to manage this complexity, and with a little advance work you can set things up so you won't have to stop in the middle of a creative thought to decipher your MIDI setup. In this chapter, you'll learn how to:

✽ Import and use SONAR's Instrument Definitions feature
✽ Record from multiple MIDI instruments simultaneously
✽ Filter out unwanted MIDI input messages

Using Instrument Definitions

MIDI labels everything with numbers—channel 10, bank 0, patch 117—so it can be adapted to any manufacturer's devices. Unfortunately, this sometimes makes dealing with MIDI a little too much like balancing your checkbook. SONAR's Instrument Definitions allow you to give meaningful names to the various channels and patches of the hardware synthesizers you have connected to your system.

Assigning Instruments

Instruments are defined at each channel of each MIDI output. Before you can define instruments on a MIDI output, the output must be enabled under Options, MIDI Devices, as discussed in Chapter 13. To assign an instrument definition, follow these steps.

1 Click on Options. The Options menu will appear.

2 Click on Instruments. The Assign Instruments dialog box will open.

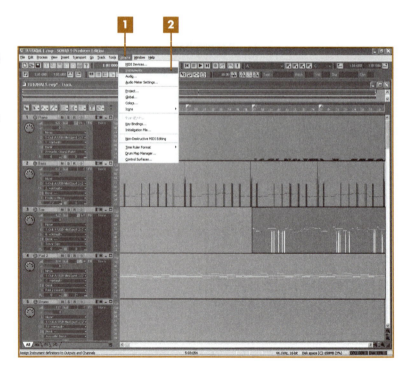

3 Click to select a specific channel or channels of a particular output in the Output/Channel pane.

4 Click on an instrument in the Uses Instrument pane. A black line will connect the selected channel(s) and the instrument.

5 Click on Save Changes for Next Session. The assignment of instruments will be recalled for subsequent sessions.

6 Click on OK. The dialog box will close, and your choices will be remembered.

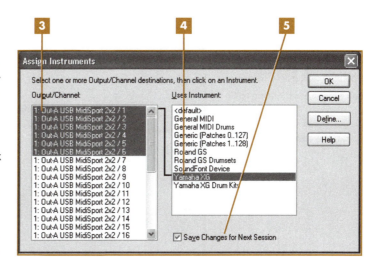

❈ GM Drums

It's customary to use channel 10 for all drum sounds on a General MIDI instrument. For GM instruments, assign channel 10 to General MIDI drums. Do the same for GS and XG instruments, choosing Roland GS drum sets and Yamaha XG drum kits, respectively.

7 Click on the MIDI Output field of a MIDI track. The MIDI Output menu will show all enabled MIDI outputs.

8 Click on the MIDI output to which you just assigned an instrument.

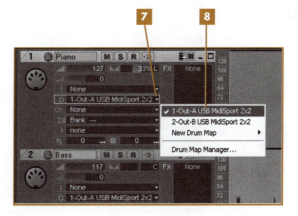

❈❈❈

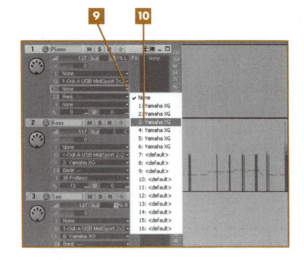

9 Click on the Channel field of the MIDI track. The Channel menu will show the name of the instrument you assigned.

10 Click on the desired channel.

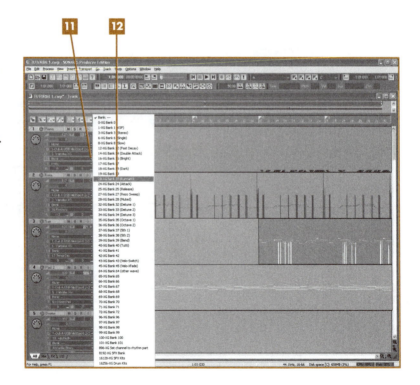

11 Click on the Bank field of the MIDI track. The Bank menu will show the specific bank names of the instrument you assigned to that MIDI output.

12 Click on the desired bank.

13 Click on the Patch field of the MIDI track. The Patch menu will show the names of all patches available in the chosen bank of the instrument you assigned.

14 Click on the desired patch.

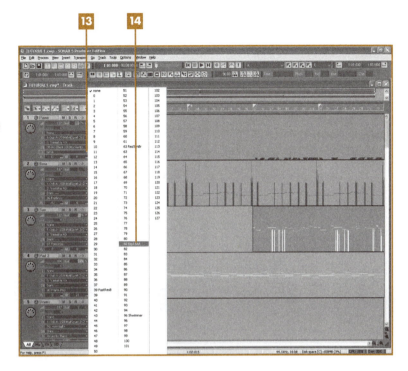

❋ **That's More Like It!**

You can see that assigning a specific instrument definition to that particular MIDI output made choosing banks, channels, and patches a lot friendlier. Once you've got your whole studio set up this way, you'll be more efficient than ever!

Importing Instrument Definitions

By default, SONAR gets its list of available instrument definitions from a master file that contains a few common instrument definitions. For many instruments, especially newer or less-common instruments, you will have to add information about your instrument by importing an instrument-definition (INS) file (characterized by the .ins file extension). Such files are available on the SONAR installation discs and online at www.cakewalk.com. Here's how to import the required information about your instrument.

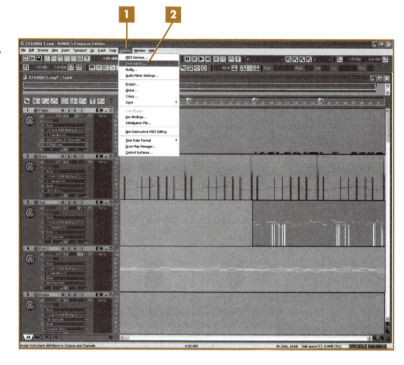

1 Click on Options. The Options menu will appear.

2 Click on Instruments. The Assign Instruments dialog box will open.

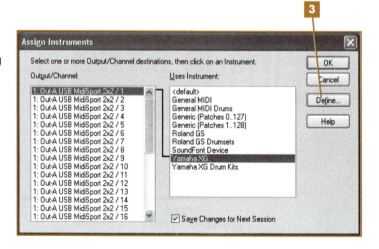

3 Click on Define. The Define Instruments and Names dialog box will open.

4 Click on Import. The Import Instrument Definitions dialog box will open.

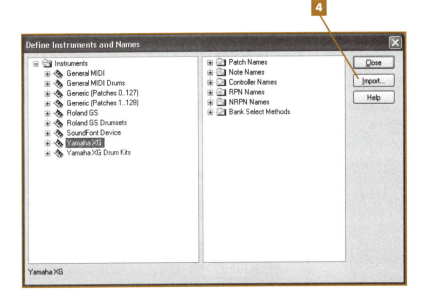

5 If necessary, navigate to the location of the desired instrument-definition file.

6 Click to select an instrument-definition file.

7 Click on Open. The dialog box will show a list of available instruments.

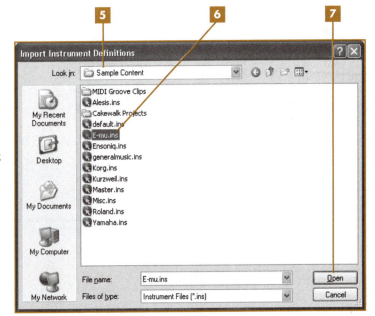

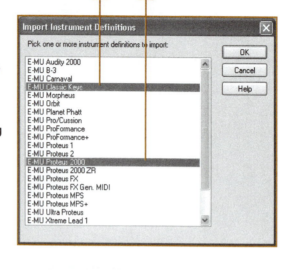

8 Click to select the desired instrument.

9 Optionally, Ctrl+click to select additional instruments.

10 Click on OK. The Define Instruments and Names dialog box will be updated to list the imported instruments.

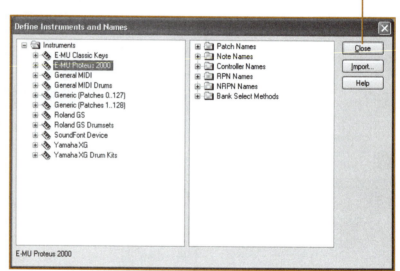

11 Click on Close. The imported instruments will now be listed in the Uses Instrument pane of the Assign Instruments dialog box.

12 Assign the imported instruments to the desired channels as described previously in the "Assigning Instruments" section.

❄ INS Files

As you've seen, SONAR's instrument definitions reside in files with the extension .ins, many of which are quite small. These files can reside anywhere on your hard drive, or even on a CD or other removable drive. The files that ship with SONAR 5 are grouped by manufacturer, and each file contains definitions for a number of different models. In the event your model is not listed, you might find it at Cakewalk's Web site.

Recording Multiple Inputs

By default, SONAR accepts MIDI input from any enabled input port. In fact, if it receives input from more than one input at a time, it combines all the input into one stream of data and echoes and records it as though it were from a single input. There are times when you don't want this to happen, such as when you are playing a bass line with your left hand on one synthesizer and a lead line with your right hand on another. In this case, you would want SONAR to distinguish between the two inputs and allow you to direct what your right hand plays to one track and what your left hand plays to another. SONAR makes this easy to set up.

1 Click on the down arrow at the right of the MIDI Input field of a track.

2 Point to the desired MIDI input for that track.

3 Click on the desired channel.

4 Repeat steps 1–3 for any additional tracks. SONAR will direct MIDI input from each input/channel combination to the specified track.

5 Record your music as usual. MIDI input from the various inputs/channels will be recorded into separate tracks.

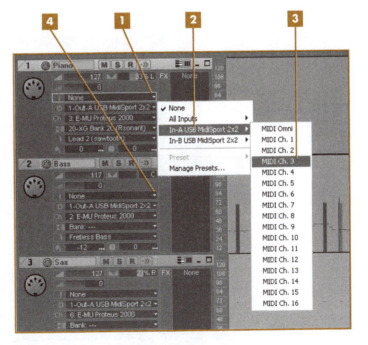

❋ **All Inputs**

To return to SONAR's default behavior of merging all MIDI inputs, simply choose All Inputs, Omni as a track's MIDI input.

Filtering MIDI Input

MIDI instruments are capable of sending a wide variety of messages. Sometimes these messages aren't entirely necessary, but even so they take up space in the MIDI pipeline. In extreme cases, these extraneous messages can clog things up and disrupt playback. Although you can always select and delete the data after it has been recorded, it's often more efficient to prevent it from being recorded in the first place. This is the purpose of SONAR's MIDI Input filter.

1. Click on Options. The Options menu will appear.

2. Click on Global. The Global Options dialog box will open.

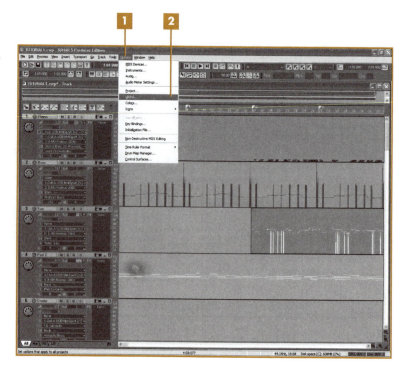

3 Click on the MIDI tab. The tab will come to the front.

4 Click on the messages you want to record. A ✓ will appear next to messages you choose to record, and everything else will be filtered.

5 Click on OK. Only the chosen messages will be recorded and echoed.

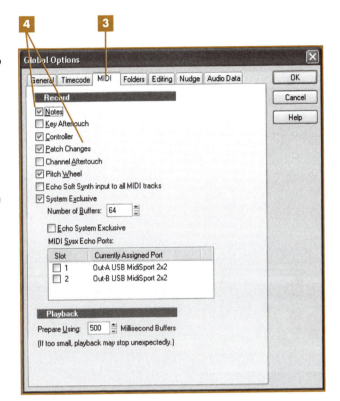

❄ **Filter What?**

SONAR's default setting is to record everything but Key (mono) Aftertouch and Channel (poly) Aftertouch messages, because few synthesizers use them. Filtering Controller messages can be useful as a troubleshooting technique, and on some instruments it's helpful to filter Pitch Wheel messages.

PART V

Effects and Mixing

Chapter 16: Using Audio Effects

Chapter 17: Mastering Audio's Ins and Outs

Chapter 18: Using the Console View

Chapter 19: Capturing Your Mix for CD and the Internet

16 } Using Audio Effects

Except for the most purist classical projects, much of the sound of modern recordings is shaped by the judicious use of audio effects. Reverberation, delay, equalization, and compression—these are primary tools for the mix engineer. A traditional studio has racks full of hardware boxes that provide these effects, but SONAR includes numerous software effects that let you process the sound without ever leaving the computer. In this chapter, you'll learn how to:

❋ Use real-time audio effects

❋ Use and create plug-in presets

❋ Bypass and change the order of effects

❋ Apply audio effects offline

Using Real-Time Audio Effects

If you've ever used a stomp-box with your guitar, run your vocals through a reverb—heck, if you've even used the tone controls on your stereo—you've used real-time audio effects. These effects modify the sound of the audio during playback without permanently changing the source files.

SONAR's real-time audio effects operate as *plug-ins*, separate programs that only run within a host program, such as SONAR. This plug-in architecture allows you to buy third-party effects to expand your sonic palette, although SONAR includes plenty of high-quality effects to begin with. There are, in fact, far more plug-ins in SONAR than I can cover, so let's take a look at some representative real-time effects. The following examples cover the techniques you need to know to explore and experiment with the whole collection. Some of the windows may look slightly different depending on whether you use them on a mono or stereo track.

Using Cakewalk FxChorus

A *chorus* effect makes a sound seem thicker or denser by layering it with slightly altered copies of itself. This is similar to the sound of someone singing the same thing several times and then blending the various takes together (think Enya). Cakewalk's FxChorus is one of several effects in the DSP-FX series, designed for high quality and efficient use of CPU resources.

1 Right-click in the FX Bin of an audio track. The FX menu will appear.

2 Point to Audio Effects. The Audio Effects submenu will appear.

3 Point to Cakewalk. The Cakewalk effects submenu will appear.

4 Click on FxChorus. The FxChorus window will appear.

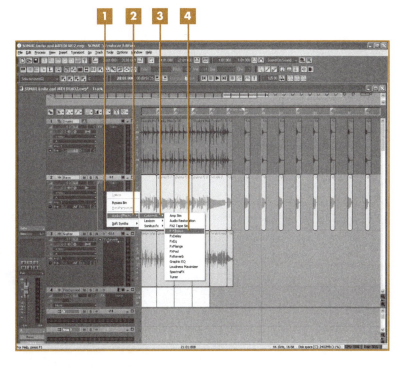

5 Click on a voice's on button to toggle it on and off.

6 Drag a voice's gain slider to increase or decrease the voice's volume.

7 Click on a voice's Select (sel.) button to show the voice's parameters in the Voice Settings displays at the top of the window.

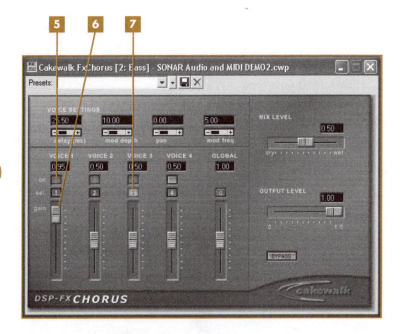

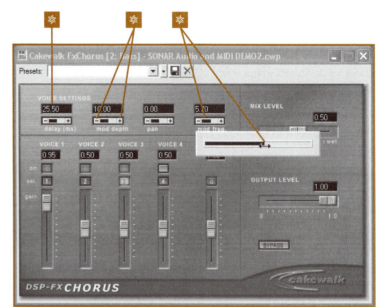

8 Adjust the various Voice Settings using the following techniques:

* Double-click in a field and type a value.

* Click on a field's plus (+) or minus (–) buttons.

* Click and drag on a value slider. An expanded value slider will appear, and the value will be updated as you drag the expanded slider.

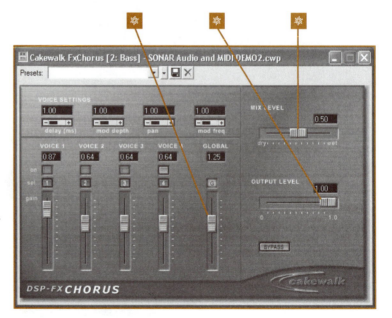

9 Drag the various global parameter sliders. The global parameters include:

* Mix Level. This slider controls the relative level of the original (dry) signal and the processed (wet) signal.

* Output Level. This slider allows you to lower the final volume of the effect's output in case the addition of the four voices adds too much volume or causes clipping.

* Global. This slider adjusts the gain of the four voices while maintaining their relative values.

Close the Window

Once you've adjusted the parameters of a plug-in, you can either minimize or close the plug-in window. Neither will stop the plug-in from processing the audio. To re-open a plug-in window, simply double-click on the plug-in's name in the FX Bin.

Using Sonitus:fx Equalizer

EQ stands for *equalization*, which is a way of shaping the frequency content of a signal. The bass and treble controls on your stereo are elementary forms of EQ. The Sonitus:fx Equalizer is part of the exceptional Sonitus:fx Suite included with SONAR 5. This plug-in not only shows you a graphical display of the effect, it lets you edit parameters directly from the display.

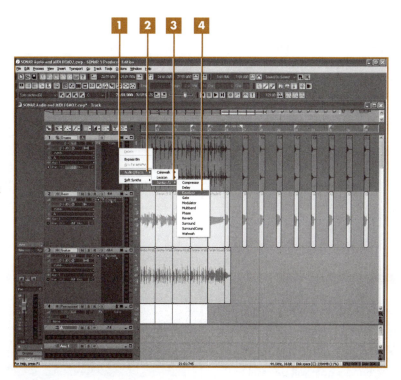

1 Right-click in the FX Bin of an audio track. The FX menu will appear.

2 Point to Audio Effects. The Audio Effects submenu will appear.

3 Point to Sonitus:fx. The Sonitus:fx submenu will appear.

4 Click on Equalizer. The Sonitus:fx Equalizer window will appear.

❋ **More Than One Way**

You can use the same techniques to adjust the Sonitus:fx equalizer's settings that you used in FxChorus—dragging sliders, toggling buttons, and typing values. The following steps explore additional techniques.

5a Click on a band's Filter Type button to cycle through the five filter types.

OR

5b Choose a filter type from the Filter Type drop-down list.

6 Click and drag in a value field. Dragging up or to the right will increase the value, and dragging down or to the left will decrease the value.

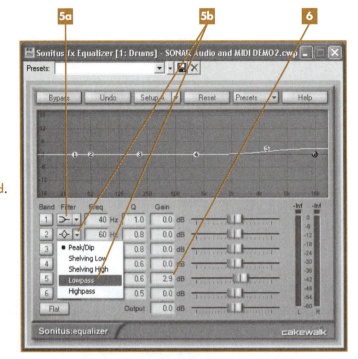

7 Drag a yellow filter marker. The gain and frequency of the band will be adjusted accordingly.

8 Double-click on a slider. The band's gain will be reset to 0.

9 Click on the Flat button. All bands' gains will be reset to 0.

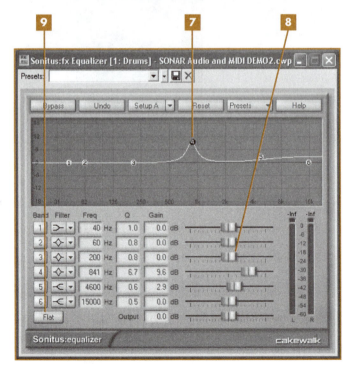

10 Click on the Presets down arrow. The Presets drop-down list will appear.

11 Click to choose the desired preset from the list.

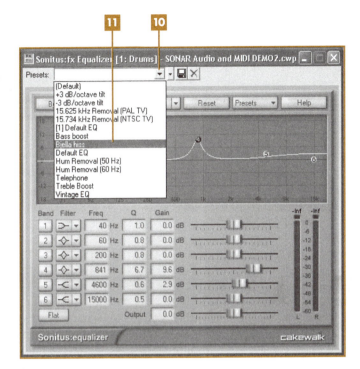

All plug-ins in SONAR have the Presets list at the top of the window. The Sonitus:fx plug-ins have a separate Presets drop-down list that gives you the same list of presets.

❋ Use Your Ears

You can (and should) adjust effects parameters while you are playing the audio. This allows you to hear exactly what the changes are doing to the sound. Remember: The parameter values are useful for reference, but the only thing that really matters is what it sounds like!

Using Sonitus:fx Compressor

A *compressor* is used to control the dynamics of audio. In essence, it narrows the gap between loud sounds and soft sounds by turning down any sounds that exceed a certain volume. You could theoretically accomplish the same thing by keeping your hand on the volume control and turning the volume down whenever it gets loud and back up whenever it gets soft, but you wouldn't be able to react as quickly or as precisely as a compressor. Sonitus:fx Compressor's controls operate in much the same way as those of Sonitus:fx Equalizer. Here are the pertinent functions for controlling dynamics with this plug-in.

* **Threshold.** This is the volume above which the signal will be attenuated (turned down).

* **Ratio.** This is how aggressively the signal will be attenuated. Higher ratios attenuate the signal more severely.

* **Attack.** This is how quickly the compressor will kick in once a signal exceeds the threshold.

* **Release.** This is how quickly the compressor will let go once a signal drops below the threshold.

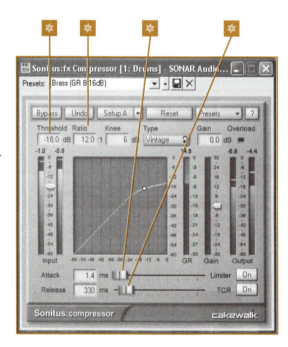

Creating Effects Presets

As you've seen, it's very helpful to be able to recall all parameters of a plug-in by choosing a preset. A *preset* is simply a snapshot of all the settings, and you can save presets of your own to use along with all of the included presets.

1 Adjust the parameters of a plug-in as desired.

2 Click in the Presets field and type a name for your preset.

3 Click on the Save button next to the Presets field. The parameters will be saved under the preset name you typed.

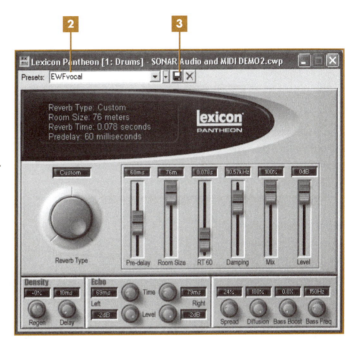

❋ **Save Carefully**

If you click on the Save button while the name of an existing preset is displayed, you will write the current parameters to that preset, replacing whatever values were originally stored under that name.

❋❋❋

Bypassing an Effect

It's often useful to be able to hear the original, unprocessed sound of a track or a mix. When you *bypass* an effect, you effectively re-route audio past the effect so it does nothing to the sound. Most plug-ins have a bypass button, but some (including the Pantheon reverb) don't, so SONAR gives you a bypass button for each plug-in in the FX Bin.

1a Click on the green button to the left of a plug-in's name in the FX Bin. The button will turn grey, indicating that the effect is bypassed.

OR

1b Click on the Bypass button in the plug-in's edit window. The button will turn yellow, indicating that the effect is bypassed.

2 Click on either button again. The button will return to its normal color, indicating that the effect is active.

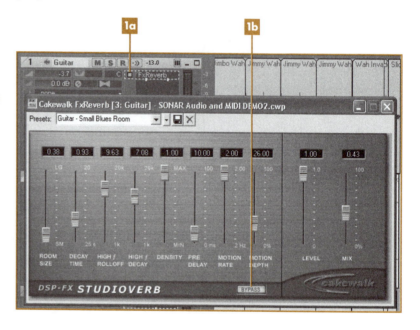

❋ **Double Bypass**

These two bypass buttons work independently of each other, so if either one is in bypass mode, the effect will not be heard. Both must be in normal mode for the effect to be heard.

Changing the Order of Effects

Ask any guitarist: The order in which effects processing is applied can change the results completely. Do you want to compress the EQ or EQ the compressor? The answer is different depending on the situation, and experimentation is the key to finding the right order. SONAR makes it easy to change the order of effects without changing anything else about them, so you can switch, listen, and switch back as often as you like.

1 Click and hold on a plug-in's name in the FX Bin. The plug-in name will be outlined, and a red line will appear just above it.

2 Drag the plug-in up or down in the FX Bin. The red line will indicate the plug-in's new position.

3 Release the mouse button. The plug-in will appear in its new position, and the order of processing will reflect the new sequence of plug-ins.

4 Drag or Ctrl+drag a plug-in to the FX Bin of a different track. The plug-in will be moved or copied to the new track.

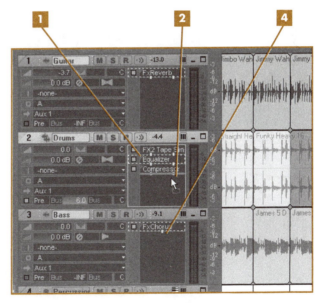

Using Clip-Based Audio Effects

In addition to processing entire tracks, SONAR allows you to apply real-time effects to individual audio clips. Say you've edited together a lead vocal track from multiple takes, and one phrase is a bit bright compared to the rest. SONAR's clip-based effects allow you to apply an EQ plug-in to match that phrase's timbre to the clips surrounding it.

1 Right-click on a clip.

2 Point to Insert Effect.

3 Point to Audio.

4 Click on an effect or choose an effect from a submenu.

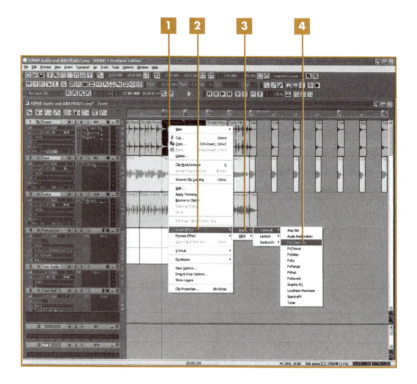

5 Choose a preset as discussed previously or adjust individual parameters.

6 Click on the clip's FX icon to open the Clip FX Bin.

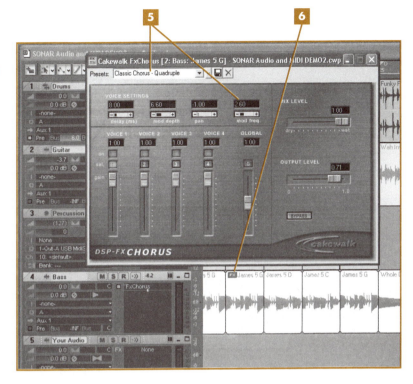

7 Use the Clip FX Bin in the same way you did the Track FX Bin to bypass and reorder effects and to open a plug-in window.

❄ **Order, Order!**

As you know, it's important to have your effects in the right order. Clip-based effects always come before track-based effects.

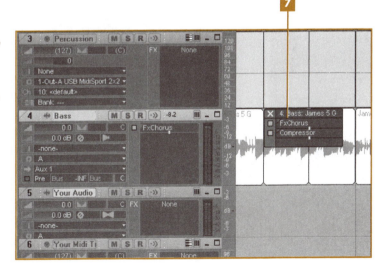

Freezing Audio Tracks

In a host-based system such as SONAR, where all audio processing is handled by the computer's CPU, it's almost inevitable that you will want to add more effects than your system can handle in real time. When this happens, you can use SONAR's Freeze function to apply a track's real-time effects to the clips as though they were file-based processes. After SONAR has applied the effects, it bypasses the FX Bin, thereby freeing up some of your CPU's attention for those additional effects you wanted to add.

1 Right-click on an audio track to open the context menu.

2 Point to Freeze.

3 Click on Freeze Track. All clips on the track will be processed with effects to new clips, and the track's FX Bin will be bypassed, freeing up CPU resources.

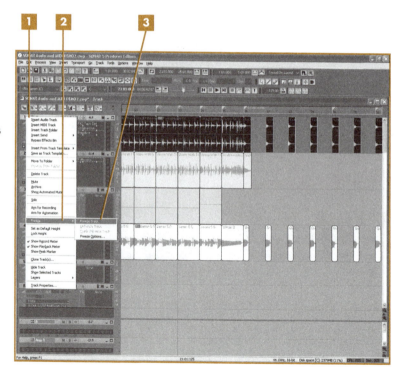

❄ **Unfreezing**

If you want to change something in a frozen track, simply select the track and choose Unfreeze Track from the Track, Freeze menu. The original clips will be restored, and the FX Bin will be enabled. You can edit the audio or tweak the plug-ins and then re-freeze the track.

17 } Mastering Audio's Ins and Outs

You've already seen how SONAR lets you communicate with the outside world—recording from inputs on your audio interface and playing back through outputs on your audio interface. Now it's time to explore the inner world of SONAR audio. In this chapter, you'll learn how to:

❋ Work with buses

❋ Create a headphone mix and add effects to it

❋ Use sends to control reverb effects

❋ Create subgroups, submixes, and stems

❋ Use SONAR Producer Edition's surround features

Using the Bus Pane

A *bus* can be thought of as an internal audio pathway, kind of like a virtual audio cable that you can use to connect from some internal source to some internal destination. It's a powerful way to be able to group signals together for efficient processing or to recombine them in a way that is different from the main output. In this first section you'll create a few buses that you'll then use throughout the rest of the chapter. First, make a clean start by creating a blank project.

> ❊ **Multi-Channel or Stereo**
>
> Some of the procedures in this chapter assume that you have a multi-channel audio interface. If you have a stereo (two-channel) interface, your capabilities will be somewhat reduced—obviously surround mixing is out of the question—but the same principles apply.

1 Click on File. The File menu will appear.

2 Click on New. The New Project File dialog box will open.

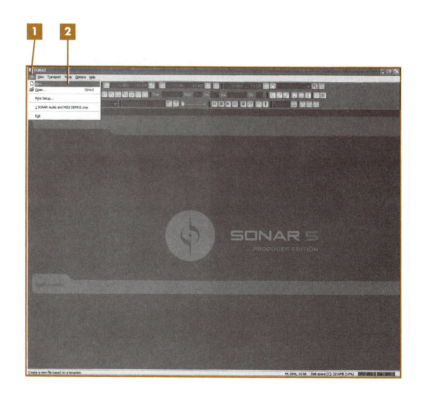

3 Click in the Name field and type a name for the project.

4 Click on the Blank (no tracks or buses) template.

5 Click on OK. A project with no tracks of any kind will open.

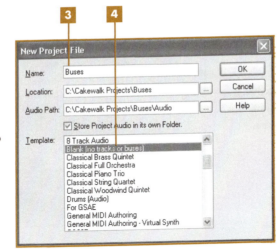

6 If necessary, click on the Show/Hide Bus Pane button.

7 Drag the splitter bar upward to enlarge the Bus pane.

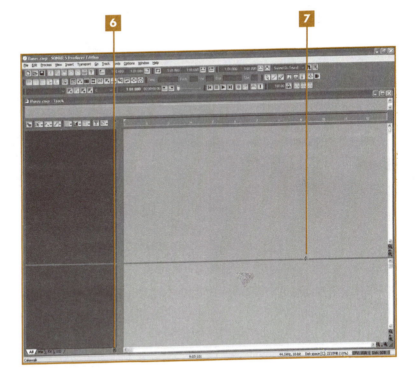

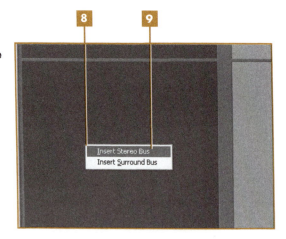

8 Right-click in the left side of the Bus pane.

9 Click on Insert Stereo Bus. A new stereo bus will be created in the Bus pane.

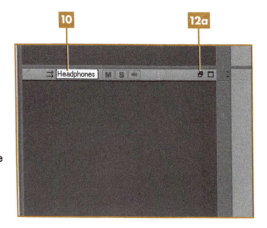

10 Double-click on the bus name and type Headphones.

11 Press Enter to confirm the new name.

12a If necessary, click on the Restore Strip Size button. The track will expand vertically.

OR

12b If necessary, drag the bottom border of the track down.

13 Create four new stereo buses using the preceding steps, and name them Reverb Return, Drums, Music, and Dialog.

14 If the Bus Output field does not already list the name of your primary stereo output, click on the down arrow at the right of the Bus Output field for each bus and click on the name of your main stereo output. The output of the bus will be assigned to the main stereo output.

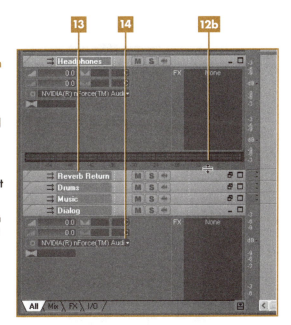

❄ **Buses for the Future**

You will be using these buses throughout the rest of this chapter to explore some common procedures that take advantage of SONAR 5's sophisticated bus architecture.

Creating a Headphone Mix

Unless you are doing live classical recording, you will almost always need to set up a *cue mix*, which is routed to the headphones so the performers can hear themselves along with any existing tracks. Although it's sometimes sufficient to have them listen to exactly what is coming through your monitors, it's a good idea to have a separate headphone mix. Two of the many reasons why you might choose to do this are that it allows you to change the balance of parts the performers are hearing without affecting your mix, and it allows you to change the volume of their mix independently of yours. You ordinarily accomplish this by using a send.

❀ ❀ ❀

Creating an Interface Send

A *send* creates an exact copy of the audio running through a track. By sending this copy to the headphones, you create the cue mix. Once you have sent the copy, you can use a bus to modify it as needed. You can start by creating a simple headphone mix that sends the signal straight out your interface—where you presumably have a headphone amplifier connected—without passing through a bus.

1 Create a new audio track and name it Dialog 1.

2 Right-click on the track number.

3 Point to Insert Send.

4 Click on an interface output. A new send will be created on the track.

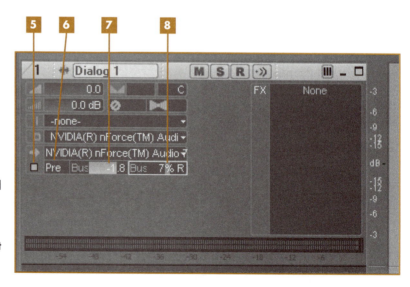

5 Click on the enable button. The button will turn green, and the send will be active.

6 Click on the Post/Pre button to enable pre-fader operation. When "Pre" is displayed, the send's level is independent of the track's volume fader.

7 Drag the Send Level slider to control the volume of the signal being sent to the headphone output.

8 Drag the Send Pan slider to set the pan position of the signal being sent to the headphone output.

Creating a Bus Send

Now it's time to put one of those buses to good use. By running the headphone mix through a bus first, you can control the level of the headphone mix and add effects to it if you want.

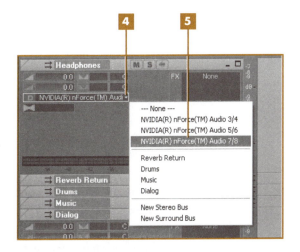

1 Click on the down arrow at the right of the Send Output drop-down list on the Dialog 1 track.

2 Point to Reassign Send.

3 Click on Headphones. The send output will be reassigned to the Headphones bus.

4 Click on the down arrow at the right of the Bus Output drop-down list on the Headphones bus.

5 Click on the name of the interface output to which the send has been assigned. The bus output will be reassigned to that interface output.

❀ A Different Route

The signal from the send is still going to the output where your headphone system is connected, but it passes through the Headphones bus first. With one source track this doesn't seem like a big deal, but if you've got 20 or 30 tracks being mixed to the headphones, you'll be glad to have the bus to control them. Imagine having to adjust 20–30 send faders every time the singer says, "Make it a little louder," and then "Make it a little softer!"

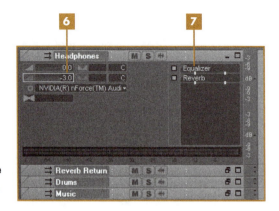

6 As desired, adjust the mute, volume, and pan status of the Headphone bus. These changes will be heard only in the headphones and will not affect your main mix.

7 As desired, add plug-ins to the Headphone bus. These effects will affect only the cue mix, not your main mix.

❊ Volume versus Balance

Control the overall volume of the headphone mix from the bus, and control the balance of the headphone mix from the send levels of the various tracks.

❊ One-Click Control

As you can see, routing the headphone mix through a bus gives you one-click control over muting and volume, and it allows you to sweeten the mix to make the performers more comfortable. Keep in mind that you have done all this without affecting your control-room mix in the least.

Using a Send to Apply Reverb

The technique you learned in Chapter 16—inserting an effect directly on the audio track—is generally considered standard procedure for effects such as compression and equalization, where you want to change the signal completely. However, when engineers use time-based effects, such as reverb, it's common to mix the original (dry) signal with the processed (wet) signal. There are historical, practical, and aesthetic reasons behind this practice, and although in music no rule is absolute, it's always a good idea to learn the standard way before breaking the rules.

This technique, then, can be considered the standard routing for adding reverb effects to your tracks. It involves using a send from each track to split off a copy of its audio; all of these copies are then sent to a single bus. A reverb is inserted on the bus and set to 100% wet. This gives you complete, independent control over the balance of dry (the audio tracks) and wet (the bus), so you can make the simulated reverb chamber as big or as small as you want without having to edit a setting on every single audio track. If you're familiar with mixing consoles, you'll recognize this as a typical aux send/aux return scenario.

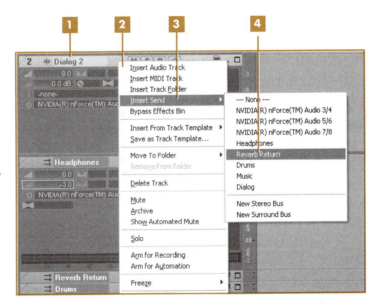

1 Create a new audio track and name it Dialog 2.

2 Right-click on the track's title bar.

3 Point to Insert Send.

4 Click on Reverb Return. A new send will be created on the track.

5 Repeat the process to create a new send for Dialog 1.

6 Click on the Send enable button of each audio track. Leave them post-fader.

7 Right-click in the FX Bin of the Reverb Return bus.

8 Assign the Lexicon Pantheon reverb plug-in. The Pantheon edit window will appear.

❋ **Studio Edition**

If you have SONAR 5 Studio Edition, you have Lexicon Pantheon LE, which lacks some of the bells and whistles of the full version. It might look slightly different, but it will work the same way for the purposes of this exercise.

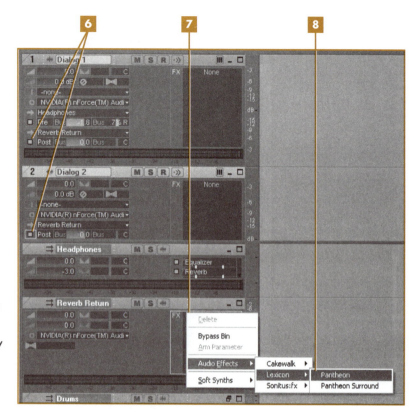

9 Adjust parameters or choose a preset as desired.

10 If necessary, drag the Mix slider up to 100%. Pantheon will now pass nothing but wet signal. This is standard practice for mixing reverb on a bus.

11 Click on the Close button. The Pantheon edit window will close.

12 Click and drag **the** Output Volume slider **on the Reverb Return bus. The volume of the wet mix will increase or decrease, while the volume of the dry mix will stay constant.**

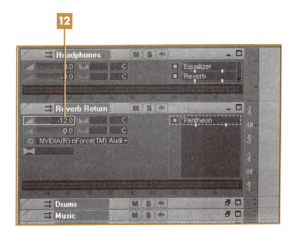

❄ Wet versus Dry

Change the dry mix—the balance of the audio tracks—by adjusting the volume faders on the audio tracks. Change the wet mix—the balance of the audio tracks passing through the reverb—by adjusting the sends on the audio tracks. Change the wet/dry balance by adjusting the volume fader of the Reverb Return bus. This arrangement gives you complete and independent control over all aspects of your reverb processing.

Creating Subgroups, Submixes, and Stems

Subgroups, submixes, and stems are three different mix scenarios that use essentially the same technique. The real difference is how each is used. All three involve using a bus or buses to create a partial mix prior to the final output. Unlike the send/return scenarios discussed previously, this technique routes the *outputs* of audio tracks to buses.

Creating a Subgroup

A subgroup allows you to treat several audio tracks as a single unit. In this example, you will use a subgroup to combine all of your drum tracks to a single bus so you can apply a compressor plug-in to the entire kit at once.

❄ ❄ ❄

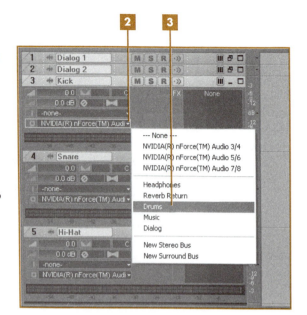

1. Create three audio tracks and name them Kick, Snare, and Hi-Hat.

2. Click on the down arrow at the right of the Track Output field of the Kick track.

3. Click on Drums. The output of the track will be reassigned to the Drums bus.

4. Repeat this process for the other two drum tracks. All of the drum kits will now be heard only through the Drums bus.

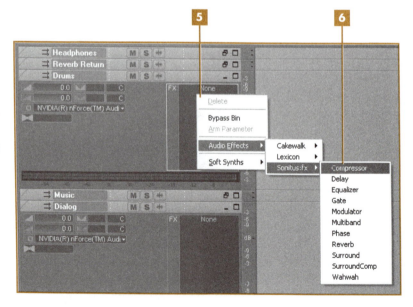

5. Right-click in the FX Bin of the Drums bus.

6. Assign the Sonitus:fx Compressor and adjust its settings to taste. The entire drum kit will be compressed through this plug-in.

One Way or Another

Although you could certainly apply a separate compressor to each audio track of the drum kit, that would eat up system resources and would produce a different sound than this technique, which compresses the entire kit as though it were a single instrument.

Creating a Submix or Stem

A *submix* is just what it sounds like: a small part of a larger mix. In the following example, you will use submixes to combine all of your instrumental parts to one bus and all of your dialogue parts to another bus, giving you the ability to change the relative volume of music and dialogue with only two faders. The term *stems* comes from the field of audio for film, and it refers to the many submixes that make balancing complex film mixes manageable.

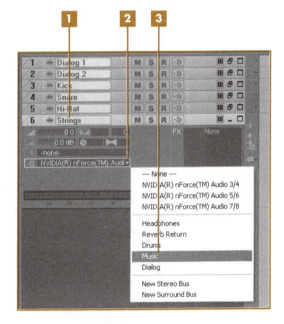

1 Create an audio track and name it Strings.

2 Click on the down arrow at the right of the Track Output field of the Strings track.

3 Click on Music. The output of the track will be reassigned to the Music bus.

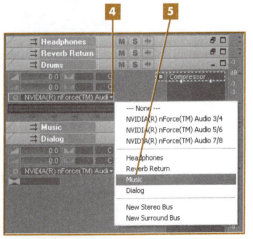

4 Click on the down arrow at the right of the Track Output field of the Drums bus.

5 Click on Music. The output of the bus will be reassigned to the Music bus.

Bus to Bus

That's right, the output of a bus can be routed to another bus! Because it all happens in the digital domain, there's no additional noise or sonic compromise to doing this. Why do it? The Drums bus is used for compressing the drum kit, and then you're combining the compressed drum kit with the strings to create a submix of all of the instrumental parts at the Music bus.

6 Using the same technique, assign the track outputs of the Dialog tracks to the Dialog bus. All of the dialogue audio will be heard only through the Dialog bus.

7 Adjust the volume, pan, and other parameters of the Music and Dialog buses to balance and blend the two submixes.

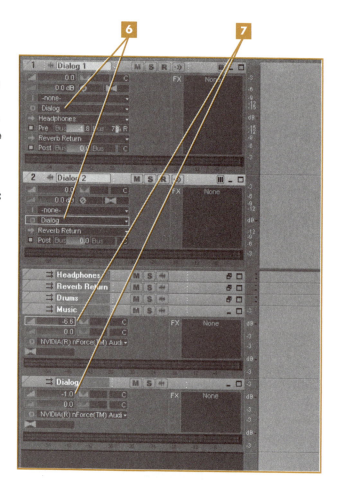

Keeping It Simple

Use this technique any time you have a complex mix to simplify the process of balancing different sections of the mix. In a typical rock/pop mix, you might have separate submixes for the keyboards, guitars, drums, and vocals. If the drums are too loud, you move one fader and fix it! You always have the ability to change the internal balance of the members of a submix by adjusting their track volume faders.

Surround Mixing

SONAR 5 Producer Edition brings the world of surround sound to your desktop. Almost any imaginable surround format up to 8.1—meaning eight surround channels plus a Low Frequency Effects (LFE) channel—can be used. Of course, you need to have enough output channels on your soundcard to be able to take advantage of this, and you also need corresponding speakers to experience the effect. Many home-theater systems have multi-channel analog inputs you can connect to your soundcard's outputs.

Surround sound raises the level of your project's complexity substantially, and the topic of surround could fill an entire book by itself. The discussion here will give you the tools you need to get SONAR ready for surround and to get started creating your own surround mixes.

Setting SONAR's Surround Format

Stereo mixing is a snap compared to surround mixing—you've got two channels, so you have a 50/50 chance of getting left and right routed to the correct outputs. For that matter, if you get them backwards, you may never notice! With more channels comes more possibility for error, so there are two things you must establish before you start. First, you need to decide how many channels you're going to use and how they are to be arranged. Second, you need to ensure that each channel is mapped to the correct physical output so you hear it coming from the correct speaker.

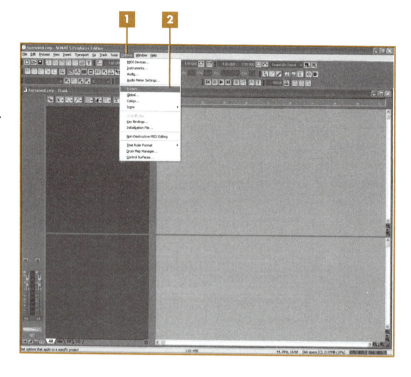

1 Starting with a new blank project, click on Options.

2 Click on Project. The Project Options dialog box will open.

3 Click on the Surround tab.

4 Click on the Surround Format drop-down list and choose a surround format.

5 Use the Output window's drop-down lists to change the output channel assignments so they match your speaker connections.

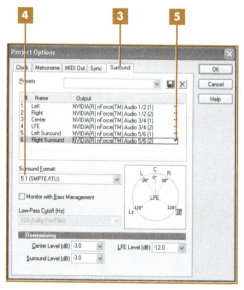

Surround Formats

The most common surround format is called 5.1, meaning five channels surrounding the listener and one Low-Frequency Effects (LFE) channel. Most DVDs feature 5.1 sound-tracks, and most home-theater systems use this format. I highly recommend that you start your surround experience by choosing 5.1 (SMPTE/ITU) from the Surround Format drop-down list.

The surround channels—Left, Right, Center, Left Surround, and Right Surround—should be arranged in a circle around the listening position, as shown in the dialog box. The subwoofer, which carries the LFE channel (as well as the bass content of the surround channels in most home-theater systems), can be placed almost anywhere.

Using Surround Tracks and Buses

Surround tracks and buses use the same basic concepts and controls as stereo tracks and buses. The biggest difference is, of course, in panning, which now covers a lot more ground. To deal with the increased possibilities, SONAR provides a dedicated Surround Panner window. That's where the real fun begins.

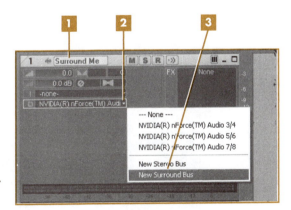

1 Create a new audio track and name it appropriately.

2 Click on the track's Output field.

3 Click on New Surround Bus. A new surround bus will be created, and the track's output will be assigned to that bus.

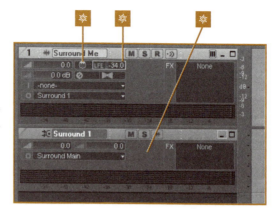

4 Note the following differences from what you've seen previously:

❋ The Pan control on the audio track is a small circle, representing the surrounding speakers. Although this control is functional, *it's tiny!* That's why there's a dedicated Surround Panner window.

❋ The audio track has a slider for LFE level so you can determine how much of its bass content should be included in the LFE channel.

❋ The surround bus has no panner at all. All surround panning happens at the track level.

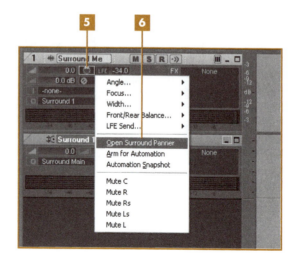

5 Right-click on the track's Pan control.

6 Click on Open Surround Panner.

7 Click on the plus sign (+) and drag the sound wherever you want it to go. This is the angle and focus marker, and it represents the position of the track's sound in the surround field.

8 Drag either of the width markers to change the apparent size of the track's signal.

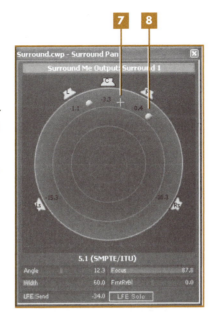

Other Surround Panner controls include:

❋ **Angle.** This controls whether the sound is in front of you, behind you, or to your side. Zero degrees is directly in front, –90 is to your left, and so on.

❋ **Width.** This is the same as the width markers. A setting of 0 makes the sound seem to come from a single speaker. Larger settings spread the sound across more speakers, making it seem wider.

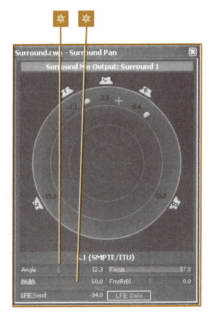

* **Focus.** This controls the distance from the listener. A setting of 100 is far away, and a setting of 0 is in your lap. You can also think of this as the size of the surround circle.

* **Front/Rear Balance (FrntRrBl).** This controls whether the sound comes from the front speakers or the rear speakers. Zero is equally balanced, positive numbers move the sound forward, and negative numbers move the sound backward.

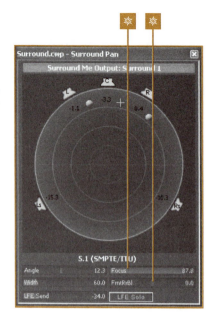

> ❊ **Going in Circles**
>
> Hold down the Alt key while panning to lock the Focus value. This lets you pan in a perfect circle. Just don't do it too much, or you'll get motion sickness!

Using Surround Effects

Using plug-ins for audio effects in a surround mix isn't that different from using stereo effects. There are two ways you can accomplish this. The first is by using dedicated multi-channel plug-ins, such as the Sonitus:fx Surround Compressor. This is ideal, because such plug-ins are smart enough to consider all six (or more) channels as a unit. The second way is to utilize your existing effects through SONAR's SurroundBridge, but you can only use the SurroundBridge on buses.

1 Right-click in the FX Bin of a surround track or surround bus.

2 Assign the Sonitus:fx Surround Compressor (SurroundComp).

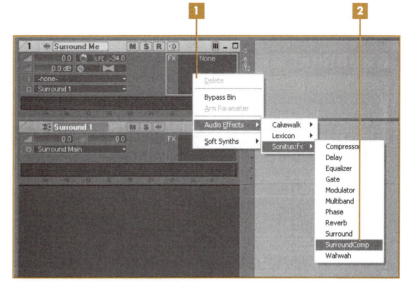

3a Choose a preset from the Presets drop-down list.

OR

3b Adjust individual parameters as needed.

❋ **Sonitus Presets**

Most of the Sonitus:fx plug-ins allow you to choose from the same set of presets whether you use the SONAR Presets drop-down list or the plug-in's Presets drop-down list. The Surround Compressor, however, keeps its own list separate from SONAR presets.

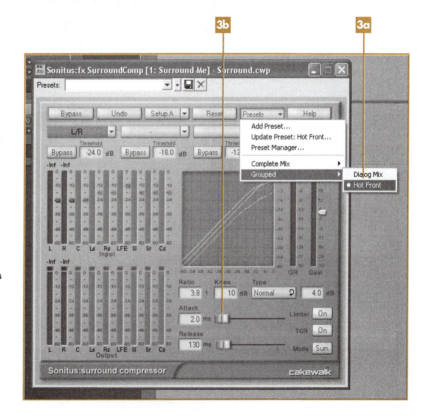

4 Right-click in the FX Bin of a surround bus.

5 Point to Audio Effects.

6 Point to a plug-in category.

7 Click on a non-surround plug-in. The plug-in's edit window will open.

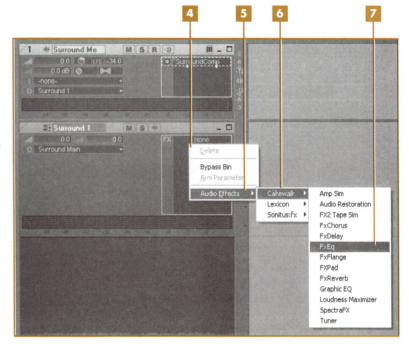

8a Choose a preset from the Presets drop-down list.

OR

8b Adjust individual parameters as needed.

※ Linking Plug-Ins with SurroundBridge

SONAR's SurroundBridge automatically creates multiple linked copies of stereo or mono plug-ins. Adjust a parameter or choose a preset within any of the linked copies, and the others will follow along. You can choose to unlink controls globally by clicking on the Unlink Controls button or selectively from the SurroundBridge Linker tab.

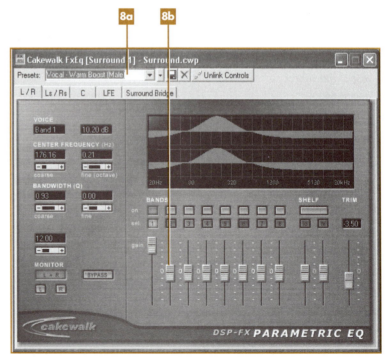

18 } Using the Console View

SONAR's Console view is modeled after a traditional mixer, with big faders and meters and individual vertical channel strips for each track. It really doesn't offer any functions that aren't available in the Track view, but it lays out the controls you need to mix your project in a very efficient, manageable, and—for anyone used to physical mixers—familiar way. To take advantage of this view, you simply need to understand its layout, control its display, and learn how to accomplish tasks you already know from the Track view. In this chapter, you'll learn how to:

❋ Show and hide Console view controls

❋ Assign inputs and outputs

❋ Adjust level and pan

❋ Create audio and MIDI tracks, buses, and sends

❋ Use the channel EQ (Producer Edition only)

❋ Configure the appearance of the Console view

Assigning Inputs and Outputs

The Console view is laid out in three sections: tracks, buses, and main outs. The main outs are the actual physical outputs of your audio interface, and the only control you have over them is for volume and mute. On the audio and MIDI tracks, however, you can also assign inputs and outputs just as you did in the Track view, and you can assign outputs to buses as well. Instead of being right next to each other, though, in the Console view the inputs are all the way at the top of the channel strip and the outputs are all the way at the bottom.

1 Click on the Console View button. The Console view will appear.

2 If necessary, Shift+click on the Show/Hide Input and Show/Hide Output buttons to show the Input and Output controls.

❄ **Show/Hide**

The Show/Hide buttons toggle on and off the display of various controls. Simply Shift+click on the button again to toggle the control's display status. You could just click, but holding Shift while you click prevents the Console view from resizing itself every time you show or hide a control.

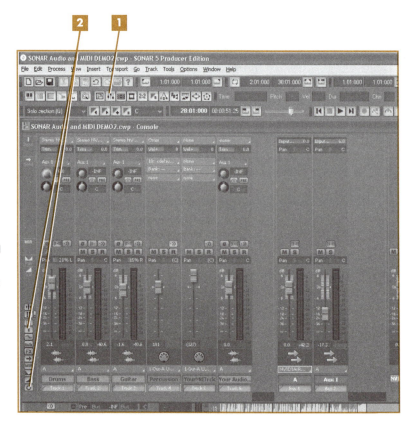

3 Click on the lower-right corner of the Input field of an audio track.

4 Point to the name of the desired audio interface.

5 Click on the name of the desired input.

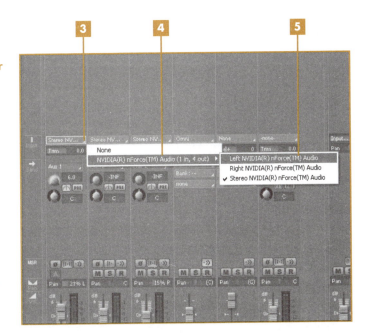

❈ **A Different View**

Your Input menu and any submenus might look quite different from the menu shown in this book, depending on your audio interface's options.

6 Click on the Output field of an audio track or bus. The Output menu will appear and display all available outputs and buses.

7 Click on the desired output or bus or on New Stereo Bus (or New Surround Bus). The menu will close, and the Output field will reflect your choice. If you choose New Stereo Bus or New Surround Bus, a new bus will be created and the output will be assigned to it.

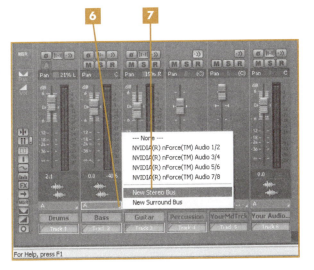

❈ **Only One at a Time**

Once you have chosen a particular bus or output in an audio track's Output field, it is no longer available in the Output field of a send on that track. The same rule applies to assigning outputs and sends on a bus.

Adjusting Level and Pan

The Console view is not simply a distillation of mixing controls from the Track view—its controls are truly optimized for their functions. For example, the volume fader on a track is several times larger in the Console view, allowing for more precise control.

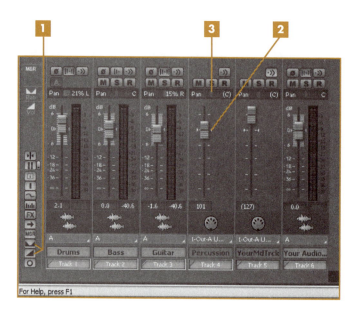

1 If necessary, Shift+click on the Show/Hide Volume or Show/Hide Pan button to display those controls.

2 Drag the volume fader of an audio or MIDI track, bus, or main out up or down.

3 Drag the Pan slider of an audio or MIDI track or bus left or right.

※ Snap-To

As in the Track view, if you double-click on a control it will snap to its default value. The default snap-to value for volume on an audio track is 0.0 dB. For MIDI volume, it's 101. Pan will snap to center.

Creating Tracks, Sends, and Buses

There's no need to return to the Track view to add audio or MIDI tracks, buses, or sends to your project. All of these functions are available from the context menu in the Console view.

1 Right-click in a blank area within a track or within the Track pane.

2 Click on Insert Audio Track or Insert MIDI Track to create the appropriate track.

3 Optionally, click and hold in any blank area within a track and drag the track left or right. The track order will change accordingly in both the Console and Track views.

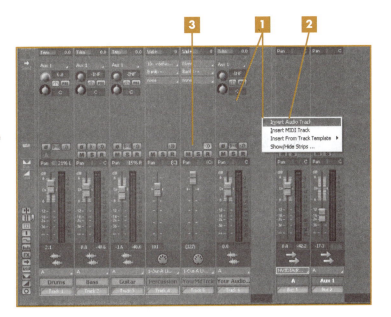

4 If necessary, Shift+click on the Show/Hide Sends button to display the Sends area.

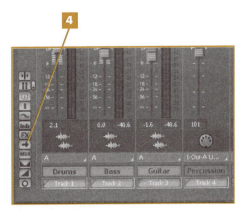

❈ Sends Views

The Sends area has three display modes: hidden, two sends, and four sends. If there are more sends on a track than the current mode can show, a scroll arrow will appear at the top or bottom of the Sends area.

243
❈❈❈

5 Right-click in the Sends area. The context menu will appear.

6 Point to Insert Send. The Insert Send submenu will appear, showing all available outputs and buses.

7 Click on the desired output or bus or on New Stereo Bus (or New Surround Bus). The menu will close, and the send will be assigned to the chosen bus or output. If you choose New Stereo Bus or New Surround Bus, a new bus will be created and the send will be assigned to it.

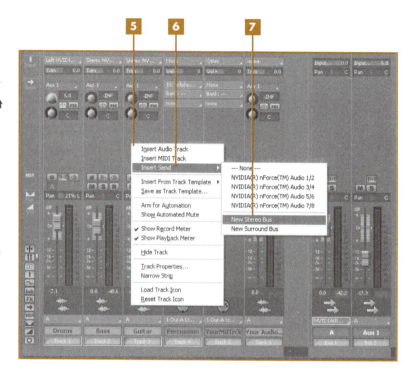

8 Right-click in any blank area within the Bus pane or within a bus.

9 Click on Insert Stereo Bus or Insert Surround Bus. A new bus will be created.

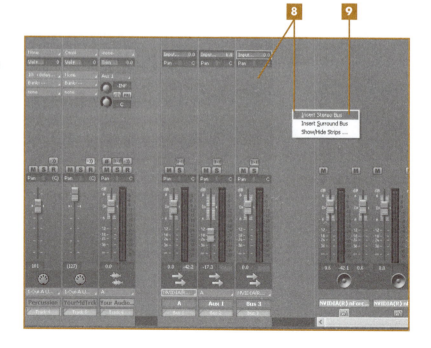

Using the Channel EQ (Producer Edition)

In a typical contemporary music mix, equalization is used to help parts fit together within a dense arrangement. As a result, most big-ticket consoles include EQ on every channel. SONAR 5 Producer Edition follows this tradition, but if you have the Studio Edition, never fear—you can still insert an EQ plug-in on as many channels as your CPU will allow. You haven't sacrificed sound, you only lack some conveniences.

1 If necessary, Shift+click on the Show/Hide EQ and Show/Hide Plot buttons to display those controls.

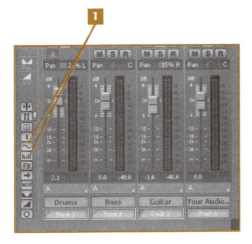

❋ EQ Views

Like the Sends area, the EQ display has three modes: hidden, one band, and four bands. Unlike the Sends area, though, you can't scroll to see the fifth and sixth bands. To see all six bands, you must open the EQ edit window by double-clicking on the *plot*—the graphic display of the frequency curve.

2 Click on the EQ Enable button. The button will turn green to indicate that the EQ is enabled.

3 Click on the Band Enable button. The button will be highlighted to indicate that the band is enabled.

4 Drag a parameter slider to adjust its value.

5 Click on a Band Type field and choose the desired band type.

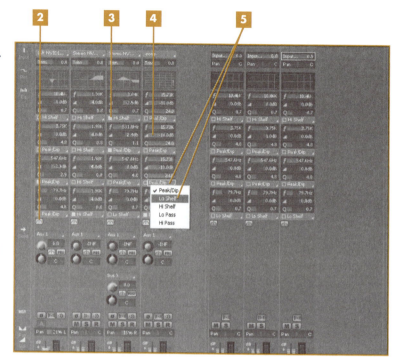

6 If only one band is visible, click on the Band # field.

7 Click on the desired band in the menu that appears.

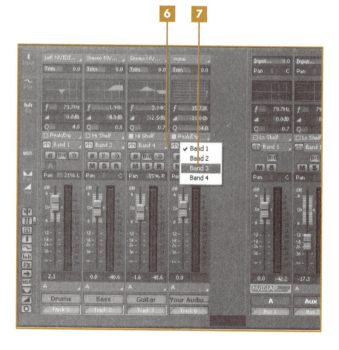

Configuring the Console View's Appearance

As you've seen, the Console view can expand to include quite a few different controls. When you display all of its controls across a large number of tracks, it can become cumbersome. SONAR lets you configure the Console's display so you can deal with a manageable number of tracks and controls. In addition to the Show/Hide buttons you've already used, you can make tracks narrow or wide, change the width of the three panes, and hide meters and even tracks.

1 Click on the Narrow/Widen All Strips button. All tracks, buses, and main outs will be made narrower.

2 Right-click on a track, bus, or main out.

3 Click on Narrow Strip in the menu that appears. The track will be widened.

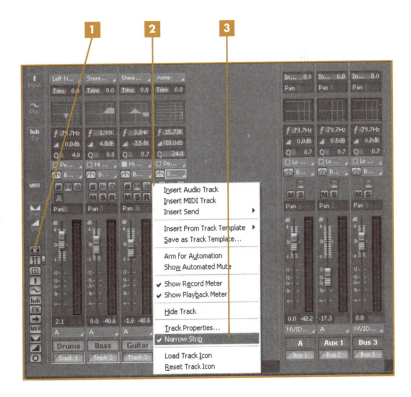

❋ **Toggling Track Width**

Clicking on the Narrow/Widen button or the Narrow Track command toggles the status of the track or tracks between narrow and wide display with each successive click.

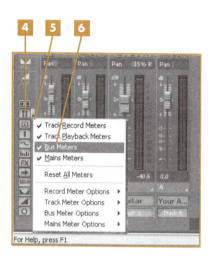

4 Click on the Show/Hide All Meters button. The display status of all meters in the Console view will be toggled on or off.

5 Click on the Meter Options button. The Meter Options menu will appear.

6 Click on a meter type. The menu will close, and the display status of that meter type will be toggled on or off.

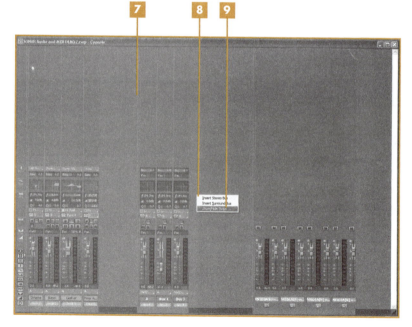

7 Drag the divider bar between two panes to resize the panes.

8 Right-click in the blank space of a pane.

9 Click on Show/Hide Strips. The Track Manager dialog box will open.

10 Click on a track's check box. The ☑ next to the track will toggle on or off, depending on its previous status.

11 Click on OK. The dialog box will close, and the track's display status will be updated as you specified.

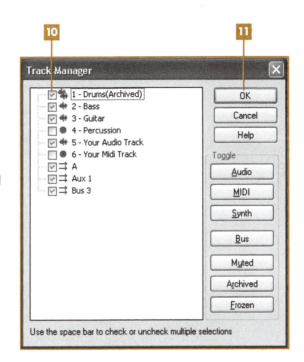

Track Manager

- ☑ 🎵 1 - Drums(Archived)
- ☑ 🔊 2 - Bass
- ☑ 🔊 3 - Guitar
- ☐ ⬤ 4 - Percussion
- ☑ 🔊 5 - Your Audio Track
- ☐ ⬤ 6 - Your Midi Track
- ☑ ⇉ A
- ☑ ⇉ Aux 1
- ☑ ⇉ Bus 3

OK
Cancel
Help

Toggle
Audio
MIDI
Synth
Bus
Muted
Archived
Frozen

Use the space bar to check or uncheck multiple selections

Capturing Your Mix for CD and the Internet

Sooner or later, your music will be ready to share with your adoring fans. When that time arrives, you will most likely produce a CD, streaming audio files such as MP3s, or both. It's increasingly common for musicians to post portions of their songs on their Web sites as MP3s to whet their fans' appetites for buying the CD, so SONAR gives you the tools to create several types of output files. SONAR can't burn the actual CD for you, but it will enable you to prepare files that are ready to be burned from your CD application. In this chapter, you'll learn how to:

* Record external synthesizer parts to audio tracks
* Export a mix ready for a CD
* Export a mix ready for the Internet

Recording External Synth Parts

If you don't have any MIDI tracks, you can go straight to the next section. If you do have MIDI parts, though, this is an extremely important step—and one that in many people's minds is shrouded in far more mystery than it deserves. It's quite simple, really: If you have any MIDI parts that are routed to hardware (external) synthesizers, you must record those synthesizers to audio tracks before you export your mix.

Like most host-based digital audio workstations, SONAR creates output files as quickly as your CPU can manage. A relatively simple mix can be turned into a stereo WAV file in a few seconds, and a complex mix with lots of effects can actually take longer than it would take to play the song through. This wreaks havoc on MIDI parts that are triggering external synthesizers, though, so SONAR doesn't even play them while it exports files. If you are using only DXi synthesizers, such as the Cakewalk TTS-1, SONAR will include those MIDI parts with no problem, but if you are using any external synthesizers, connect their outputs to inputs on your audio interface and follow these steps.

1 Click on the Solo button of a MIDI track that is triggering a hardware synthesizer. The track will be the only thing that plays.

2 Create a new audio track and name it after the MIDI track you're recording.

3 Assign the new track's input to the input to which your hardware synthesizer is connected.

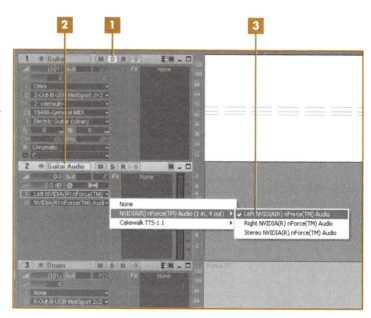

4 Click on the track's Record Arm button. The button will turn red and the track will be ready to record.

5 Click on the Rewind button to reset the Now time to the beginning of the project.

6 Click on the Record button. SONAR will record the synthesizer's output to the audio track.

7 When you reach the end of the MIDI track, click on the Stop button. Recording will stop and a new clip will appear in the audio track.

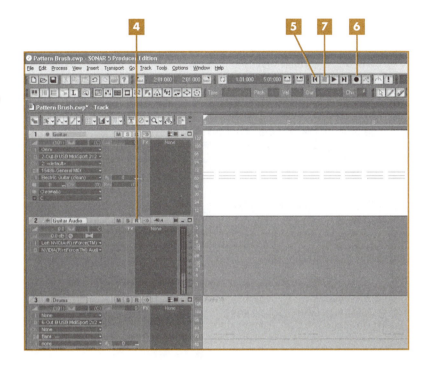

❊ Input Echo

If you want to hear the synthesizer track as it is being recorded, turn Input Echo on for the audio track. Don't forget the guidelines discussed in Chapter 8 in the "Preparing an Audio Track for Recording" section, about getting the right input volume for recording. (Hint: It depends on the volume of the synthesizer!)

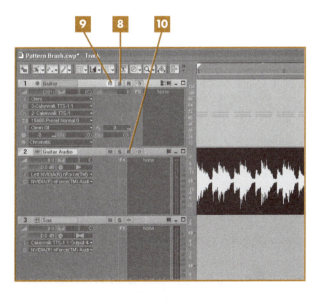

8 Click on the Solo button of the MIDI track. The button will turn grey.

9 Click on the Mute button of the MIDI track. The button will be highlighted, and the MIDI track will no longer play.

10 Click on the Record Arm button of the audio track. The button will turn grey.

11 Click on Play. The project will play back, with the new audio track substituting for the sound of the synthesizer being triggered by the MIDI track. If you are satisfied with the recorded track, repeat steps 1–10 for any other MIDI tracks that trigger hardware synthesizers.

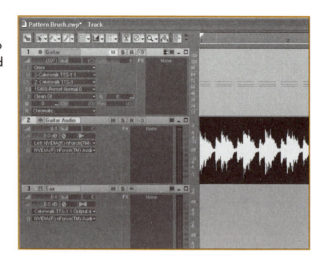

❄ Archive It

It's a good idea to archive each MIDI track as you commit it to an audio track. That way, you preserve its data for reference, but it will not play back.

❄ Don't Say That!

This process is often mistakenly called "converting MIDI to audio." Even SONAR's documentation uses this misnomer! You can't "convert" MIDI messages to audio, but you can (and just did) record the results of those MIDI messages as they trigger a synthesizer.

Exporting Audio

Now that you've got your MIDI tracks in shape, it's time to export your mix as a single file that can be burned to CD or posted to your Web site. The first part of this process is the same no matter what format you're exporting, so I'll cover it in detail for a WAV file and then discuss the differences for each of the other formats.

Exporting as a WAV File

All Windows computers and most Macintosh applications recognize a WAV file as a standard digital audio file. It has the advantage of being an uncompressed *linear* PCM file, so it doesn't suffer any degradation from the extreme data reduction used in streaming formats. The other side of the coin is that WAV files are quite large, requiring 10 MB for each minute of CD-quality audio.

This combination makes them ideal for creating audio CDs and impossible for Internet streaming.

1 Click on Edit.

2 Point to Select.

3 Click on All. All clips in all tracks will be selected.

If you have any effects, such as reverb, that have long decays, you will want to lengthen the selection so that you don't cut off the effect "tail." Shift+click in the Time Ruler about 2–3 seconds after the end of the project, and SONAR will continue exporting for long enough to catch the effect.

4 Click on File.

5 Point to Export.

6 Click on Audio. The Export Audio dialog box will open.

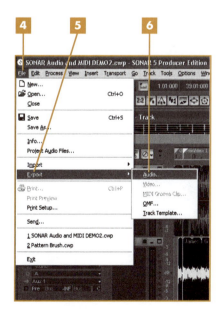

7 Navigate to the folder to which you want the file exported.

8 Type a name for the exported file in the File name field.

9 Choose RIFF Wave from the Files of type drop-down list.

10 Choose Entire Mix from the Source Category drop-down list.

❋ **Exporting Stems**

If you have split your mix out into stems, as discussed in Chapter 17, you can export each stem to a separate file by choosing Buses from the Source Category drop-down list.

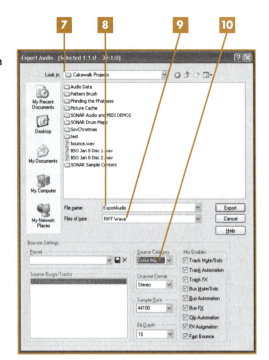

11 Choose Stereo from the Channel Format drop-down list.

12 Choose 44100 from the Sample Rate drop-down list.

13 Choose 16 from the Bit Depth drop-down list.

14 If necessary, click on the check box for any Mix Enables item that isn't already checked.

15 Click on Export. The file (or files) will be created.

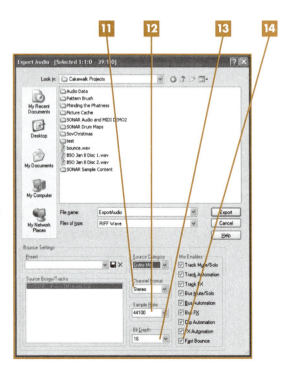

What Resolution?

If you are planning to burn this song to CD, 16 bits and 44,100 samples per second is the proper resolution. If, however, you are planning either to send the file to a mastering engineer or to work on it in a mastering program, you should instead export a 24-bit file at the sample rate of your session.

Bounce Presets

SONAR allows you to save your bounce settings as a preset. Before you click on Export, type a name for these settings in the Preset text box in the Bounce Settings area of the Export Audio dialog box, and click on the floppy disk icon. The next time you export audio, you can recall these settings from the Preset drop-down list.

Exporting an MP3 File

The term MP3 is one of those rare cases of a truly nerdy word becoming a household name. It refers to an industry-standard type of lossy data reduction for audio files. By applying psychoacoustic principles, scientists came up with a way of removing most of the data from an audio file while maintaining much of the original sound. The difference in sound quality between an MP3 file and the original audio file ranges from painfully obvious at very low bit rates to almost undetectable at higher bit rates. At higher bit rates, the file size can be reduced by 80–90% compared to the original WAV file, and at the lowest bit rates the file is only 1–2% of its original size!

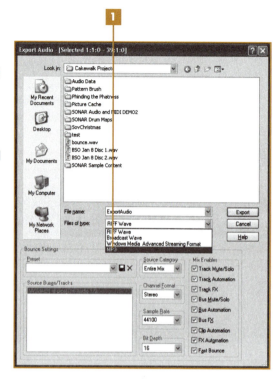

1 Follow the entire aforementioned procedure for exporting a WAV file, but at step 9, choose MP3 from the Files of type drop-down list. When you click on Export, the MP3 Export Options dialog box will open.

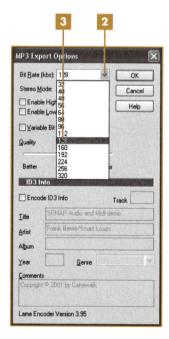

2 Click on the Bit Rate (kbs) drop-down list.

3 Click on the desired bit rate.

❋ What Rate?

If you intend to stream this file over the Internet, a bit rate of 32 kilobits per second (kbps) will allow users with dial-up connections to receive the stream in real time. If you plan only to play the file locally or if your intended audience members have broadband Internet connections, choosing a bit rate of 128 kbps or higher will yield a much better-sounding result.

4 Click on the Stereo Mode drop-down list and choose from the following options:

❊ **Stereo.** Stereo information is retained.

❊ **Joint Stereo.** Saves space by representing stereo information in a useful but less precise way. Use it as a compromise between mono and stereo.

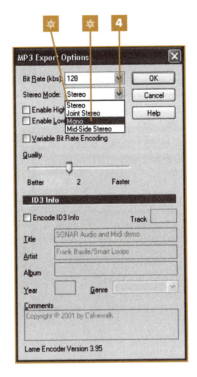

❊ **Mono.** Left and right channels will be combined, resulting in the loss of all panning and stereo effects. If the stereo image of your mix is not critical, this allows for better fidelity.

❊ **Mid-Side Stereo.** Similar to Joint Stereo, but especially useful when the mix has a lot of elements panned to the center.

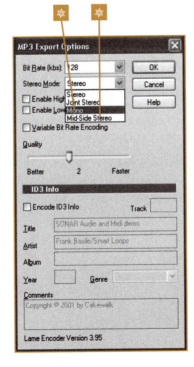

5 Drag the Quality slider to Better. This will cause the encoder to take longer and do a better job.

6 Optionally, click on Encode ID3 Info. A ☑ will appear next to the option.

7 Optionally, enter the desired information in the ID3 Info fields. This information will be displayed when the file is played in an ID3-compatible player.

8 Click on OK. A progress bar will appear, and when it completes the file will be ready.

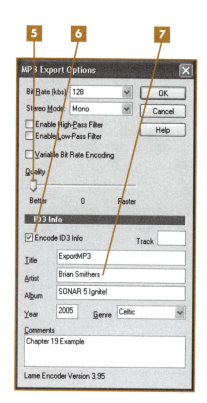

✳ MP3 Trial Period

SONAR allows you to export MP3s for 30 days, after which time you must pay a license fee for continued use.

PART VI

Hidden Magic

Chapter 20: Working with Notes and Lyrics

Chapter 21: Using Drum Maps and the Drum Grid

Chapter 22: Getting More Efficient

20 } Working with Notes and Lyrics

SONAR 5 includes two views that many musicians and songwriters will find essential—the Staff view and the Lyrics view. If you already read music, you may find the Staff view to be the most efficient way to get your ideas down, and if you don't read traditional music notation you'll find it helpful in communicating with musicians who do. Although SONAR won't actually sing your lyrics, it allows you to assign lyrics to notes in the Staff view and display them in a separate Lyrics view as well. To top it all off, you can print out scores, parts, and lead sheets, complete with chord symbols. In this chapter, you'll learn how to:

❋ Enter and edit notes in the Staff view

❋ Add expression marks

❋ Work with lyrics in the Staff and Lyrics views

❋ Print parts and scores

Using the Staff View

As a classically trained musician, I went straight for SONAR's Staff view when I first started sequencing. (To be completely honest, it was Cakewalk 3.0, 12 versions ago!) It just made sense to use the language I knew so well as a starting point when everything else about the program was so new to me. In the long run I have found that I use the Staff view less, because the Piano Roll is more efficient and represents MIDI data more precisely than the Staff view. This is because Piano Roll makes clear all the things that musicians take for granted when they see traditional notation, such as the different meanings of a staccato marking from one tempo to another. Still, SONAR's notation capabilities have many uses, as you'll see.

Configuring the Staff View

The Staff view can display a single track or multiple tracks, so you can print parts or a score. It offers several common clefs, including grand staff, and can even show you a fretboard layout so you can see your MIDI parts from a guitarist's perspective. Here's how to see just what you want to see in the Staff view.

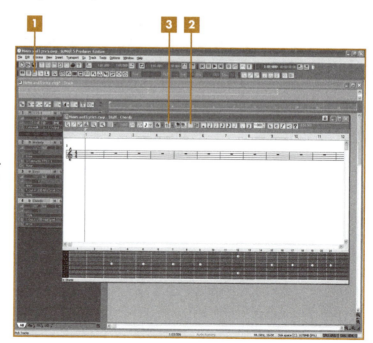

1 Click on the Staff View button. The Staff view will open.

2 Optionally, click on the Fret View button to toggle the Fret view open or closed.

3 Click on the Pick Tracks button. The Pick Tracks dialog box will open.

4 Click on the **name** of the track you want displayed.

5 Optionally, **Shift+click** or **Ctrl+click** to select **additional tracks**. The tracks will be added to the selection.

6 Click on **OK**. The dialog box will close, and the track(s) you chose will be displayed.

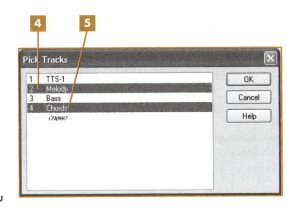

7 Click and hold on the **Zoom slider** and **drag up** or **down** to make the staves larger or smaller.

8 Click on the **Layout button**. The Staff View Layout dialog box will open.

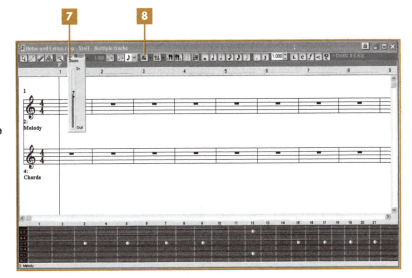

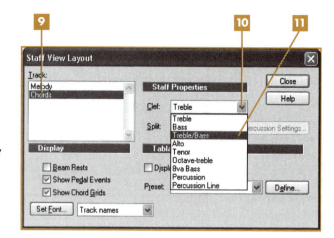

9 Click on a track name in the Track list.

10 Click in the Clef field.

11 Click on the desired clef.

12 Click on Close. The Staff view will be updated with your changes.

Working with Notes

Working with notes in SONAR's Staff view uses the same basic principles as adding and editing notes in the Piano Roll view. You enter notes with a pencil, remove them with an eraser, and drag them around with the mouse until you've got the right sound.

1 Click on the Draw Tool button. The mouse pointer will appear as a pencil.

2 Click on the desired note-duration button.

3 Click on the staff to place a note of the chosen duration.

4 Click elsewhere on the staff to place new notes. Appropriate rests will fill the spaces between notes.

5 Click directly above or below existing notes to create a chord.

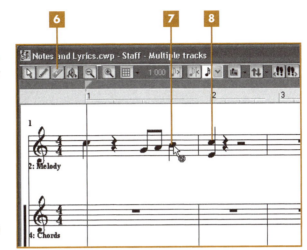

6 Click on the Erase Tool button. The mouse pointer will appear as an arrow with a slashed circle.

7 Click on a note. The note will be erased, and rests will fill the space it occupied.

8 Click on a chord note. The selected note will be erased, but the other notes will remain unaffected.

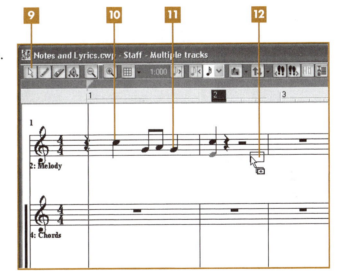

9 Click on the Select Tool button. The mouse pointer will return to its default arrow.

10 Drag a note left or right. The note will be repositioned in time.

11 Drag a note up or down. The note will be transposed.

12 Ctrl+drag a note. The note will be copied.

❁ Blend or Replace

Depending on how your Drag and Drop Options are set, you might be prompted to choose how the edit is performed when you drag notes. If you choose Blend Old and New, you can actually build chords by dragging notes on top of each other.

Changing How Notes Are Displayed

When you work with notes in SONAR's Staff view, it's essential to understand the difference between what's being displayed and what's being played. In general, the rhythms you see in the Staff view are being played as you would expect, but the timing resolution of the notation and the actual MIDI notes is very different. Imagine a series of eighth notes played staccato (short)—if you wrote the figure literally, it would be something like a series of thirty-second notes with rests between them, but that would be too difficult to read. Because the MIDI data must perform the phrase accurately, it retains such fine detail, but the Staff view can optionally round up the notes to eighth notes for a more appropriate appearance.

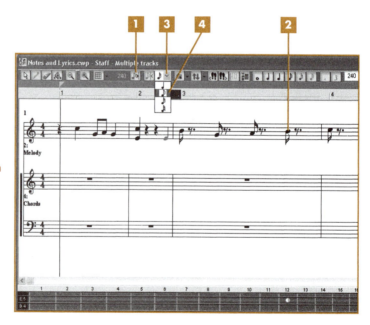

1. Click on the Fill Durations button. The button will be deselected.

2. Use the Draw tool to enter a series of sixteenth notes.

3. Click on the Display Resolution drop-down list.

4. Click on the eighth note. The notes will be displayed as eighth notes.

❋ Looking Better

The Display Resolution setting allows you to minimize the number of rests shown in the Staff view. This changes only the display of the notes; it does not change the actual MIDI data.

5 Click on the Fill Durations button. The notes will be displayed as quarter notes.

❋ **Fewer Rests**

The Fill Durations setting rounds up the value of notes (in this case to quarter notes) to minimize extraneous rests even further. The big difference between the Fill Durations and Display Resolution settings is that you can't enter rhythmic values smaller than the display resolution in the Display Resolution settings, while Fill Duration doesn't restrict your choice of rhythms.

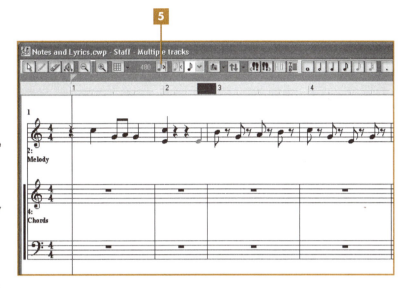

Using the Fret View

The Fret view shows you exactly what's happening when a guitarist plays your music. Each note appears as a note name icon placed on the correct fret. It even supports alternate tunings.

1 If necessary, click on the Fret View button to display the Fret view.

2 Click on the Draw Tool button and choose a note duration.

3 Click in the Time Ruler to set the Now time.

4 Click on a string in the Fret view. A note will appear both on the string and in the staff.

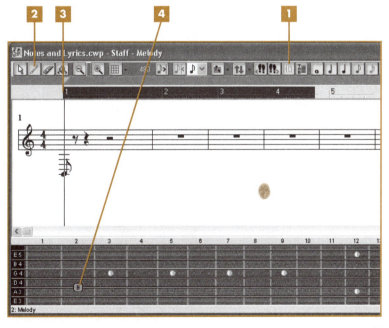

5 Click on the Erase Tool button.

6 Click on a note icon in the Fret view. The note will be deleted.

7 Right-click on the Fretboard.

8 Click on Layout. The Staff View Layout dialog box will open.

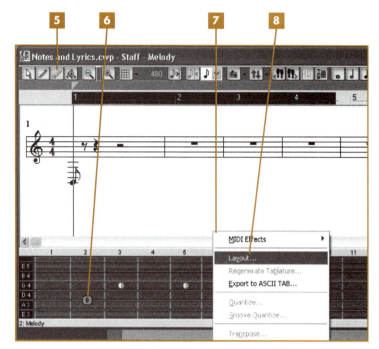

9 Click on the Clef drop-down list.

10 Click on Octave-treble.

11 Click on the Define button. The Tablature Settings dialog box will open.

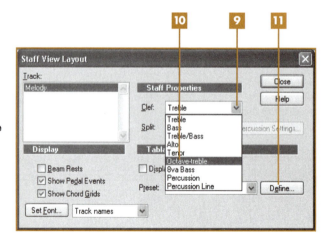

❋ Guitar Clef

Octave-treble is the standard clef for guitar notation. This causes all pitches to be written one octave higher than they actually sound, which keeps guitarists from having to switch between bass and treble clefs all the time.

12 Click on the String Tuning drop-down list.

13 Click on the desired tuning.

14 Click on OK.

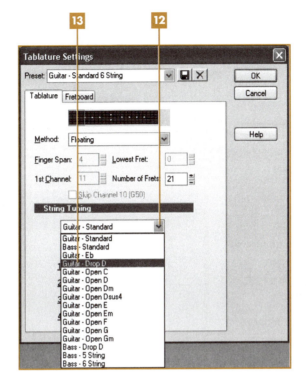

15 Click on Close. The clef and string tuning will be changed to reflect your choices.

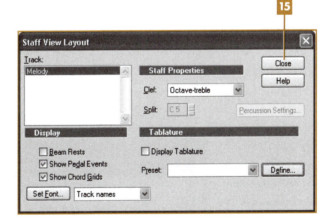

❋ **Tuning**

The notes on the staff will not change as a result of the new string tuning, but the position of the note icons on the frets will change accordingly.

Adding Expression Marks

SONAR lets you add certain types of expression marks, such as dynamics and hairpins, which are displayed and printed but have no audible effect. Pedal markings can also be added, and they do transmit MIDI events that emulate the behavior of a piano's sustain pedal.

1 Click on the Draw Tool button.

2 Click on the Expression Tool button. The mouse pointer will be a pencil only when you position it about two leger lines below the staff.

3 Click below the note or rest at which you want the expression mark to appear. A text box will appear.

4 Type in the text box.

5 Press Enter. The text box will close and the expression mark will appear.

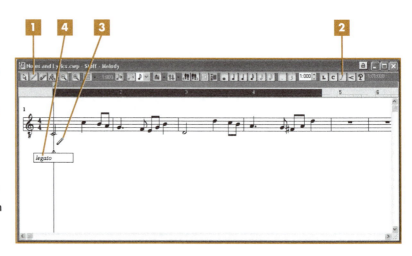

❋ Text and Dynamics

SONAR will display whatever you type as a text marking unless it is a standard dynamic marking, such as *mp* or *f*, in which case the corresponding dynamic symbol will be used.

6 Click on the Hairpin Tool button. The mouse pointer will change to a pencil only when you position it about two leger lines below the staff.

7 Click below the note or rest at which you want the hairpin to begin.

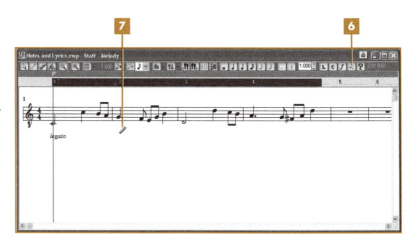

❋ ❋ ❋

1234567890

8 Right-click on the hairpin. The Hairpin Properties dialog box will open.

9 Click on the desired options or type values in number boxes to set the hairpin's parameters.

10 Click on OK. The hairpin will be updated according to your specifications.

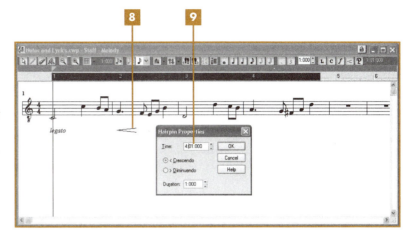

❀ Hairpin Memory

The next time you click to create a hairpin, the Hairpin Properties dialog box will use the most-recently specified parameters.

11 Click on the Pedal Tool button. The mouse pointer will change to a pencil only when you position it about two leger lines below the staff.

12 Click below the note or rest at which you want the pedal marking to begin. A pair of symbols (down and up) will appear.

13 Optionally, drag one or both of the pedal markings to a new location. The pedal events will be relocated.

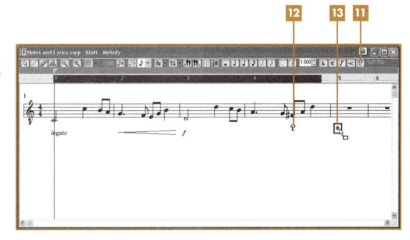

❀ Pedals in Order

Because the pedal markings have meaning as MIDI events, it's important to keep them in order. The P must always be followed by the * or you will not get the desired effect.

Using Lyrics

Lyrics will make absolutely no difference to the sound of your song, but SONAR gives songwriters the power to keep track of their lyrics, print them, and use them as a guide when recording vocals.

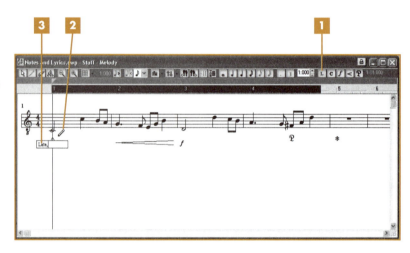

1 Click on the Lyrics Tool button. The mouse pointer will change to a pencil only when you position it directly below a note.

2 Click below the note at which you want the lyrics to begin. A text box will appear.

3 Type your lyrics in the text box.

4 Press Enter. The box will close, and your lyrics will appear below the notes.

❄ Typing Tips

The text box will advance to the next note whenever you type a space or a hyphen, so you can type as many lyrics as you have notes. You can type multiple hyphens for syllables that last over several notes.

5 Click on the Lyrics view button. The Lyrics view will open.

6 If necessary, click on the Pick Tracks button and use the dialog box that appears to choose the correct track.

7 Type lyrics in the text box. The lyrics will be updated in the Staff view as you type them.

8 Optionally, click on the Select font B button. The lyrics will be displayed in a much larger font designed to be visible from a distance (as when recording the vocal part).

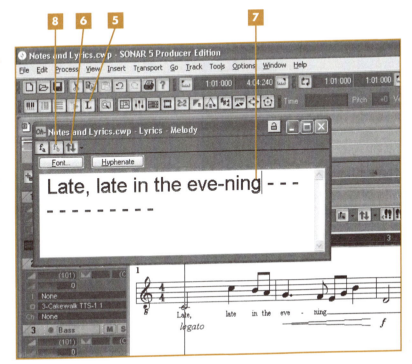

❋ Printing Parts and Scores

By Cakewalk's own admission, SONAR's Staff view is not intended to replace high-end music notation programs. It does, however, let you make decent reference parts and lead sheets for getting your ideas across quickly and clearly to your fellow musicians. Layout options are found in the Print Preview dialog box.

21 Using Drum Maps and the Drum Grid

Face it, drums are just different from most instruments. (Drummers are different, too, but that's another book!) Most drum sounds don't have pitches in the usual sense, and the duration of their tones is usually short and/or fixed. As a result, synthesizers deal with drums differently, and so does SONAR. Two tools—drum maps and the Drum Grid—let you manage MIDI drum information in ways uniquely suited to percussive instruments. In this chapter, you'll learn how to:

✳ Assign a MIDI drum track to a drum map
✳ View and customize the Drum Grid
✳ Use the Drum Grid's editing tools
✳ Customize a drum map

Assigning a Track to a Drum Map

A SONAR drum map is a special way of viewing MIDI drum tones. Synthesizers ordinarily assign drum sounds to a single patch, with snare assigned to one note, kick to another, and so on. SONAR lets you organize these tones into a manageable set, ignoring sounds you don't need and even reassigning note numbers for ease of playing or displaying your drum kit. Before you can use the Drum Grid, you need to assign a track to a drum map.

1 Click on the MIDI Output down arrow.

2 Point to New Drum Map.

3 Click on the name of the desired drum map. The chosen drum map will be displayed as the track's MIDI output.

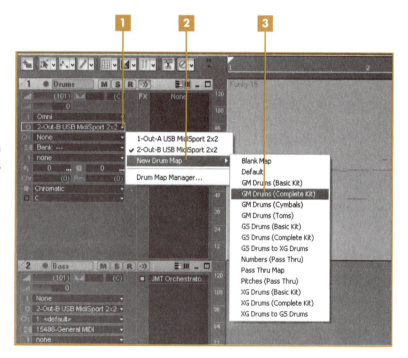

❄ Channel, Bank, Patch

Once you have assigned a track to a drum map, its Channel, Bank, and Patch fields will be inactive. This is because the drum map takes care of those assignments automatically.

Viewing the Drum Grid

The Drum Grid is really just a special case of the Piano Roll view whose display has been customized for dealing with drums. As with any SONAR editing view, you can control how the Drum Grid appears, allowing you to see information in the way that is most efficient and useful.

1 If necessary, assign a MIDI track to a drum map, as described in the preceding section.

2 Right-click anywhere on the track.

3 Point to View.

4 Click on Piano Roll. The Drum Grid will open.

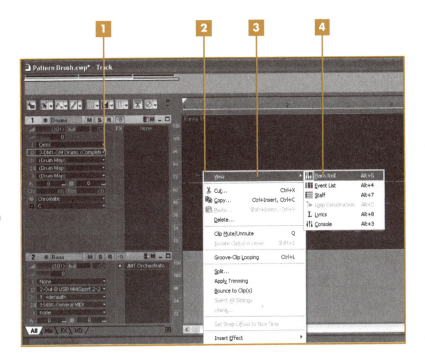

5 If necessary, click on the Show Velocity Tails button. Each note will display a small ladder that indicates its velocity.

6 If necessary, click on the Show Durations button to turn the display of note durations off.

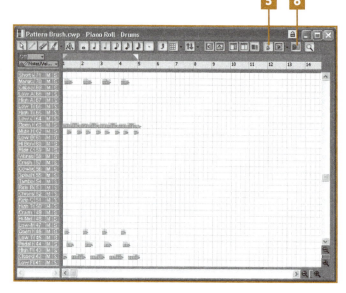

❄ Drum Durations

Showing note durations is unnecessary when working with drums, because when you hit a drum it rings and stops, unlike a clarinet tone that is sustained by the player. In fact, most MIDI drum patches completely ignore Note Off messages! Showing durations in SONAR's Drum Grid will ordinarily just make the view more cluttered, so leave durations off.

7 If necessary, click on the Show/Hide Grid button. A rhythmic grid will be displayed in the Notes pane.

8 Click on the Show/Hide Grid down arrow.

9 Click on the desired grid resolution.

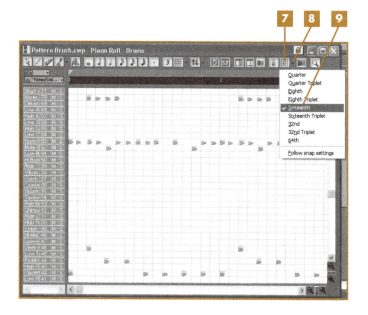

Editing in the Drum Grid

Editing in the Drum Grid is similar to editing in the Piano Roll view, but you have a couple of drum-specific functions at your disposal now. You will also find the Pattern Brush to be more interesting in this view.

1 Click on the Draw Tool button.

2 Click on a desired rhythmic value button.

3 Optionally, click on the Snap to Grid button. Drawing and editing will be rhythmically constrained to the grid.

4 Click in the Notes pane to create a new note.

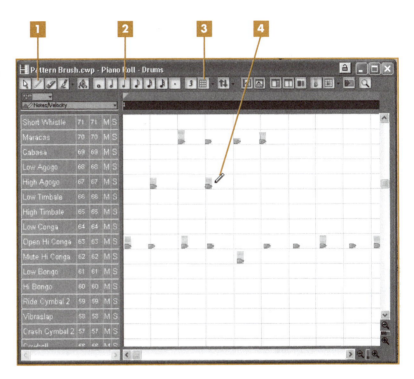

❄ **Familiar Techniques**

Other editing functions you remember from working in the Piano Roll view apply here as well, such as dragging notes with the Select tool, Ctrl+dragging to copy, and lassoing notes to move, copy, or delete them as a unit.

5 Point to a note's velocity tail. The mouse pointer will sprout a velocity tail of its own, indicating that it is ready to edit the note's velocity.

6 Click and drag the velocity tail up or down. The note's velocity tail will grow longer or shorter, indicating increased or decreased velocity, respectively.

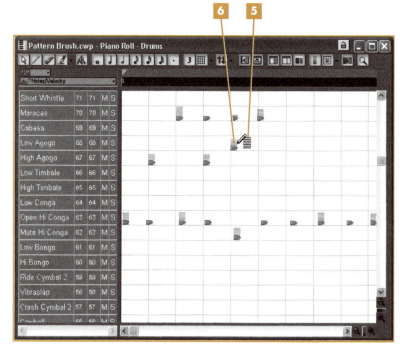

❋ Perfect View

Now you see the power of the Drum Grid. Everything is laid out according to a visible rhythmic grid, notes are identified by name instead of their equivalent keyboard pitch, irrelevant duration information is hidden, and velocity is easily edited right at the note level. Getting familiar with this view will definitely help you produce better drum tracks more quickly.

Painting MIDI Note Patterns

Okay, so the idea of painting music takes the whole graphic-editing thing a bit far, but SONAR has a very cool Pattern Brush tool that can speed the process of building authentic drum tracks. Although the Pattern Brush will work on any MIDI track, it's designed for drum tracks, so here's how to put it to work.

1 Click on the Pattern Brush down arrow. The Pattern Brush menu will appear.

2 Point to a pattern category and then click on a pattern.

3 Open the Pattern Brush menu again and click on Use Pattern Velocities.

4 Open the Pattern Brush menu again and click on Use Pattern Polyphony.

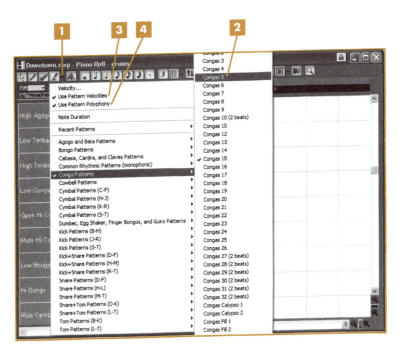

❊ Better Brushing

These two options tell SONAR to use the built-in pattern of accents and to use different notes when applicable, such as low and high agogo. You can overrule the built-in characteristics by choosing the Velocity and Note Duration options, which allow you to specify the default values.

5 Click on the Pattern Brush button. The mouse pointer will appear as a paintbrush.

6 Drag the mouse pointer from left to right across the grid. The chosen pattern will appear in the grid.

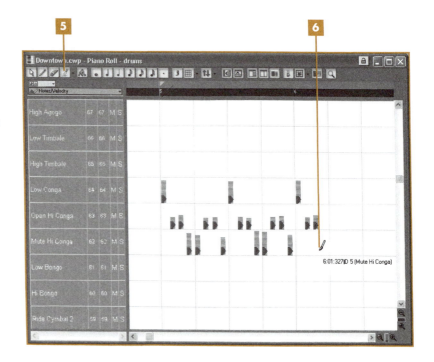

Pattern Polyphony

Because you told SONAR to use the pattern polyphony, you don't even need to drag anywhere near the pattern's assigned notes! SONAR puts the notes in the right place no matter where you drag vertically.

Editing Drum Maps

The drum map is responsible for how those notes are displayed along the left edge of the Drum Grid. SONAR allows you to customize a drum map in almost infinite ways, from limiting what notes get displayed to changing their order regardless of pitch. You can even build a drum map that triggers different hardware and software synthesizers on different notes—the ultimate drum kit! It's a deep and powerful tool, and these steps will get you started.

1 Right-click on the note you wish to modify in the Drum Map pane.

2 Click on Map Properties. The Map Properties dialog box will open.

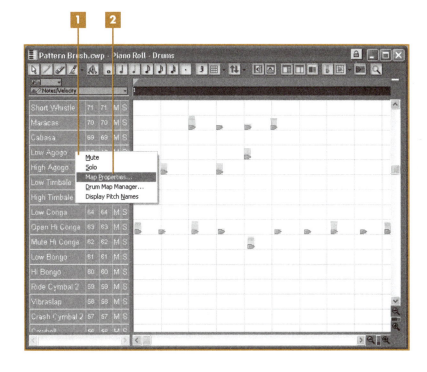

3 Edit the note's parameters as desired. Key parameters include:

❋ In Note. This is the pitch you will play to trigger this note.

❋ Out Note. This is the pitch SONAR will send to the synthesizer when this note is triggered.

❋ **So Far, So Good**

If this remapping of notes were the *only* thing SONAR's drum maps did for you, it would still be extremely cool. This allows you to reassign the various notes of a drum kit to notes that are easy to play from your master keyboard or to make a Kurzweil drum patch respond to the General MIDI arrangement of drum tones.

※ **Destination. These settings specify which synthesizer will be triggered when you play this note.**

※ Output Ports

Theoretically, each note of a drum map can trigger a different synthesizer. In this dialog box, the Out Port setting lists instruments as assigned in the Assign Instruments dialog box. (Refer to the section "Assigning Instruments" in Chapter 15 for details.)

4a Click on the Close button.

OR

4b Click on the Map Mgr. button. The Drum Map Manager dialog box will open.

5 Select **one or more** notes.

6 Click **on the** Delete button **to remove the notes from the drum map.**

7 Double-click **on any** note parameter**. The parameter will be highlighted for editing.**

8 Type **a** value **and** press Enter**. The parameter will be changed.**

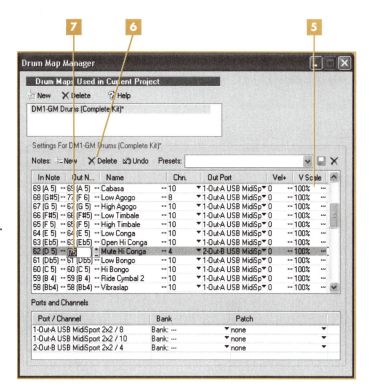

※ **All Access**

The parameters available in the Drum Map Manager are the same as those in the Map Properties dialog box, except that the Drum Map Manager gives you access to all notes in the map simultaneously. The Out Port field lists MIDI outputs rather than instruments, but it's referring to the same thing as the Map Properties dialog box.

9 Drag a note to a new location to change the order of notes.

10 Type a name in the Presets field.

11 Click on the Save button to save the current drum map for future use.

Roll Your Own

Take the time to configure a drum map that uses only the notes you regularly use. Arrange them in an order that is easy to read, and assign input notes that make it easy to play. Choose output ports that take advantage of the best sounds you have on your various synthesizers, and then save your new drum map as a preset so you can recall it whenever you are creating drum parts.

22 } Getting More Efficient

Having made it this far, you've got a good idea of how SONAR 5 works and how to do almost anything you want. The next thing for you to do is to become so efficient at operating SONAR that you can focus on your creativity rather than all this cool technology. SONAR includes a number of features that are designed to help you do just that. You can create custom templates that have all the tracks and buses you need for the way you work, and you can assign virtually any function to a keyboard command to save time fumbling through menus. In this chapter, you'll learn how to:

* Create and use custom project templates
* Use and customize key bindings
* Use the Patch Browser
* Use the Track/Bus Inspector
* Use the Track menu to assign inputs and outputs

Using Templates

Every time you create a new SONAR project, you choose from a list of templates. Each template holds a particular arrangement of tracks, I/O configurations, tempo, meter, key, metronome settings, and more information designed to save you time and effort in setting up a project. You should definitely spend some time exploring the existing templates to see which of them are appropriate for your needs. Some of them even provide good object lessons in SONAR signal flow, such as the various mixer templates at the top of the list.

Creating Your Own Templates

Sooner or later, you'll want to create one or more templates that are customized to your needs. It's as simple as saving a project—if you save it the right way and in the right folder, it will appear in your list of templates every time you start a new project.

1 Create a new project and customize it using one or more of the following steps.

2 Set the tempo, meter, and key.

3 Create audio and MIDI tracks.

4 Assign inputs, outputs, ports, channels, banks, and patches.

5 Assign effects.

6 Create buses and sends.

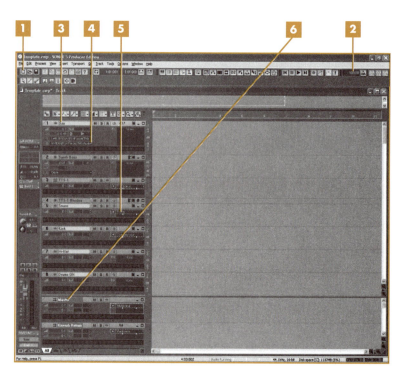

7 Click on File.

8 Click on Save As. The Save As dialog box will open.

9 Click on the Go to Folder down arrow.

10 Click on Template files (CWT, TPL). The window will display the contents of the Templates folder.

❋ **Where Are They?**

By default, the Templates folder is C:\Program Files\Cakewalk\SONAR 5 Producer Edition\Sample Content. (If you have SONAR 5 Studio Edition, the path will reflect that instead of Producer.) You can change the folder for storing templates from the Global Options dialog box.

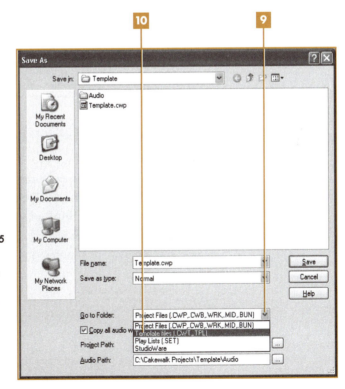

11 Type a name for your template in the File name field. SONAR will add the appropriate file extension.

12 Click on the Save as type down arrow.

13 Click on Template.

14 Click on Save. Your project will be saved as a template.

❄ **A Running Start**

The next time you create a new project, your template will be listed alphabetically among the available templates. When you base a new project on this template, you will start with all of the tracks and other settings you just configured, saving you valuable time.

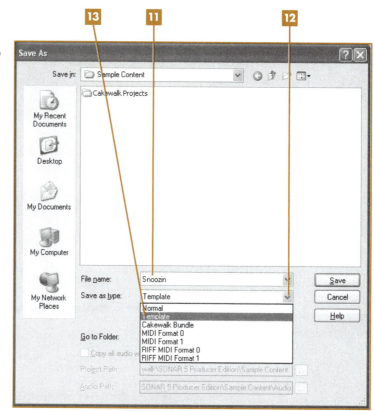

Creating a New Default Template

The default template is the one called "Normal" that is already highlighted every time you create a new project. It is also the file that opens if you bypass the Quick Start dialog box that greets you each time you start SONAR or use Ctrl+N to create a new project. It is a regular template, so making one of your templates the default is as easy as renaming it.

1 Open a template or configure a project as you want the default template to appear, then follow steps 7–10 from the preceding section.

2 Click on the Save as type down arrow.

3 Click on Template. The window will display template files.

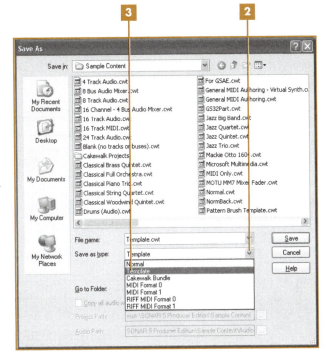

4 Right-click on the file Normal.cwt.

5 Click on Rename. The file name will be highlighted and outlined.

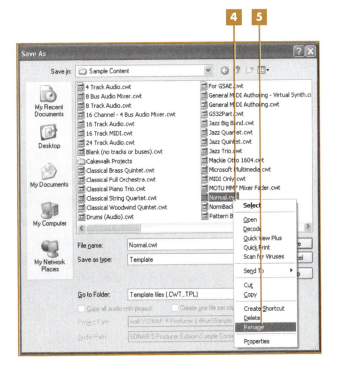

6 Type a new name for the old default template.

7 Press Enter. The old default template will be renamed, creating a backup should you wish to use it or reassign it as the default at a later date.

8 Type the name Normal in the File name field. SONAR will add the appropriate file extension.

9 Click on Save. Your project will be saved as the default template.

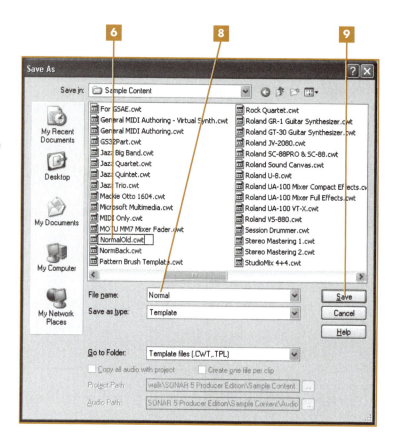

Using Key Bindings

SONAR's key bindings allow you to assign virtually any SONAR command to a key on your computer or MIDI keyboard. For example, you could open the Drag and Drop Options dialog box or turn the metronome on or off with a single keystroke and never have to delve into the menus. SONAR lets you use the Shift, Alt, and Ctrl modifier keys as well as the F1–F12 keys for hundreds of possible key bindings! For most of us, that's many more than we'll ever need, but any time you find yourself menu-diving for a function more than occasionally, you can save time by creating a key binding for that function.

1 Click on Options.

2 Click on Key Bindings. The Key Bindings dialog box will open.

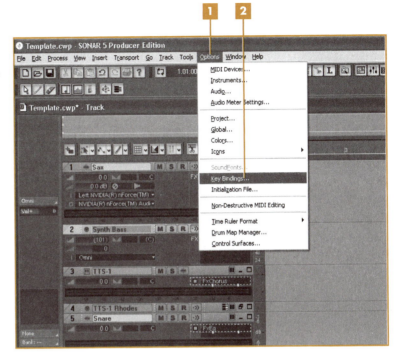

3 Click on the desired Type of Keys option.

4 Click on Enabled to make key bindings active.

❊ What Note Is Shift?

The MIDI Shift option alerts SONAR that you're no longer sending MIDI note and controller data, but instead you want to trigger a key binding. Good choices include the highest or lowest note on your keyboard or an unused pedal.

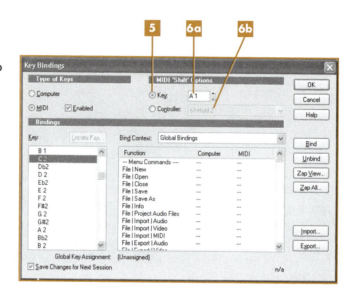

5 If you chose MIDI keys in step 3, click to use a Key or a Controller as MIDI Shift.

6a Type a MIDI note in the Key field.

OR

6b Choose a controller from the drop-down list.

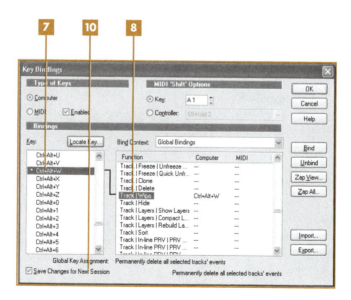

7 Click on a MIDI note or computer key in the Key list.

8 Double-click on a function to bind the key to that function. The binding will be indicated by a line connecting the key and function.

9 Repeat this process for other keys and functions.

10 Click on Save Changes for Next Session. Your key bindings will be remembered for future projects.

✳ One at a Time

You can create both MIDI and computer-keyboard key bindings, but you can only use one set at a time. SONAR will remember each set of bindings, so you can switch back and forth whenever you want without losing any bindings.

Using the Patch Browser

Instead of choosing a MIDI track's sound by using the Bank and Patch settings, SONAR's Patch Browser lets you choose from a comprehensive list of all patches in all banks. When you choose this way, the Patch Browser assigns the bank and patch automatically. It also lets you sort and do simple text searches.

1 Right-click on a MIDI track's Bank or Patch field. The Patch Browser dialog box will open.

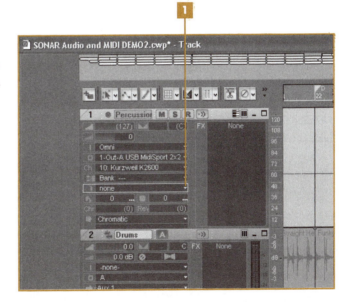

✳ This Way or That

You can also open the Patch Browser from the Bank/Patch Change dialog box (Insert, Bank/Patch Change), but that will create a bank/patch change event at the current Now time rather than as the default bank/patch for the track.

2 Click on Name to sort the list of patches by patch name in alphabetical order. Click again to reverse the order.

3 Click on Bank or Patch to sort the list by bank number or patch number.

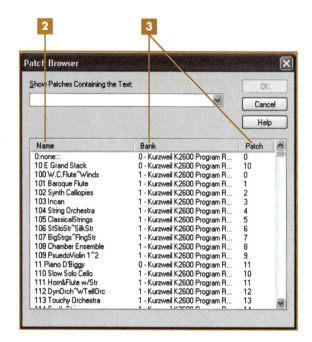

4 Type a whole or partial word in the Show Patches Containing the Text field. The list will be filtered to show only those patches with names that contain the text you typed.

5 Clear the Show Patches Containing the Text field to display the complete list.

6 Click on a patch name.

7 Click on OK. The patch you chose will be assigned to that track.

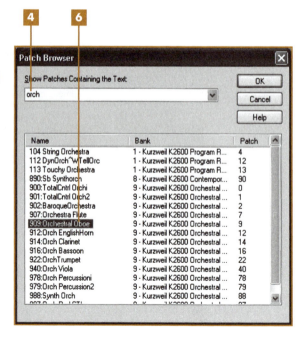

Using the Track/Bus Inspector

The Track/Bus Inspector provides an exploded view of a track's or bus's parameters in the Track view. The Inspector allows you to keep your track height small so you can fit more tracks onscreen and still be able to adjust volume, pan, and other settings.

1 If necessary, click on the Show/Hide Inspector button.

2 Click on any part of a track or bus. The Inspector will display parameters for that track/bus.

3 Click on the display buttons to change the display of sends, effects, volume, and EQ.

4 Adjust the desired parameters.

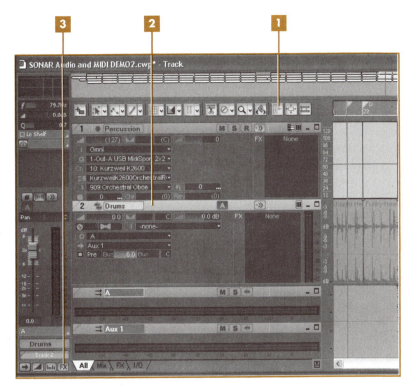

❋ **Think About It...**

It's so simple that you might overlook just how powerful the Inspector really is. Without the Inspector, you would constantly be resizing tracks so you could see their parameters and make adjustments. Think of the Inspector as a tiny window into the Console view that lets you see one selected track at a time.

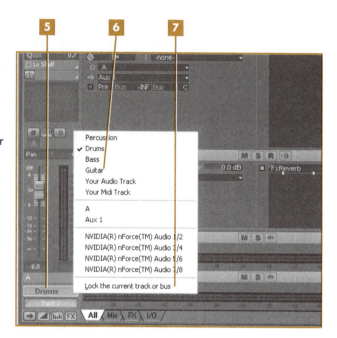

5 Click on the track name within the Inspector. The Track/Bus menu will appear.

6 Click on the desired track, bus, or main out. The Inspector will reflect that element's parameters.

❋ The Only Way

This is the only way you can display main outs in the Track view.

7 Optionally, click on Lock the current track or bus. The Inspector will continue to display the current track or bus even if you select a different track or bus in the Track view.

Assigning I/O from the Track Menu

The Track menu enables you to assign inputs and outputs on multiple audio and MIDI tracks at once. It's not very efficient for making changes to a track or two, but for setting up numerous tracks quickly it's just the ticket.

1 Select multiple tracks. The tracks will be highlighted.

2 Click on Track.

3 Point to Property.

4 Click on Inputs. The Track Inputs dialog box will open.

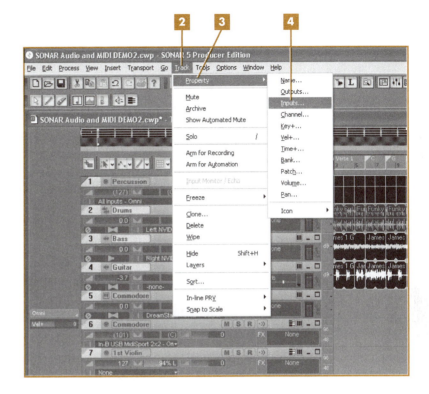

5 Click on a track name.

6 Click on the relevant Input drop-down list.

7 Click on the desired input.

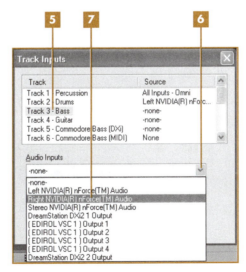

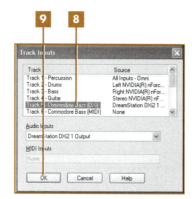

8 Repeat the process for other tracks.

9 Click on OK. The track inputs will be assigned according to your specifications.

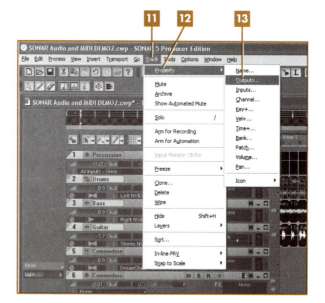

10 Select one or more audio or MIDI tracks.

11 Click on Track.

12 Point to Property.

13 Click on Outputs. The Track Outputs dialog box will open.

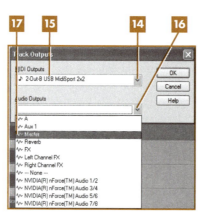

14 Click on the MIDI Outputs drop-down list.

15 Click on the desired output.

16 Click on the Audio Outputs drop-down list.

17 Click on the desired output.

18 Click on OK. The output assignments of all selected tracks will be updated.

PART VII

Appendixes

Appendix A: Setup and Troubleshooting

Appendix B: Understanding Audio and MIDI

Appendix C: Managing Your CPU Resources

A } Setup and Troubleshooting

SONAR works with many different types of audio hardware, from stock soundcards to professional-caliber audio interfaces. This appendix will guide you through the general aspects of getting SONAR and your interface to work together, as well as some preferred settings for best performance. If you have severe problems getting your system running properly, contact the tech-support folks at Cakewalk and at the manufacturer of your audio interface.

Audio Drivers

A *driver* is a piece of software that manages the interaction between software and hardware. In the case of your audio interface, the driver tells SONAR what resolutions are possible, how many channels are available, and how the interface is configured. Follow these steps to choose and configure your drivers under SONAR.

1 Click on Options.

2 Click on Audio. The Audio Options dialog box will open.

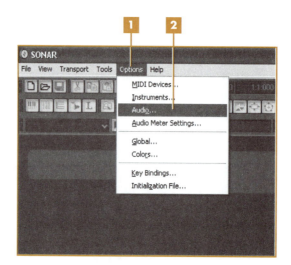

3 Click on the Drivers tab.

4 Click on one or more drivers. The highlighted driver(s) will be active.

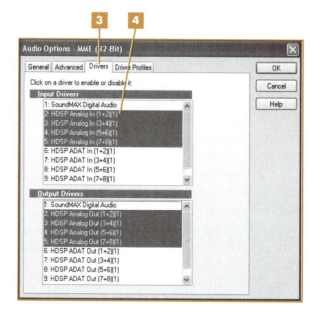

5 Click on the Advanced tab.

6 Click on the Driver Mode down arrow.

7 Click on the desired driver mode.

❋ **WDM or ASIO?**

Either WDM/KS or ASIO drivers are preferred to MME drivers, but which should you use? It depends on your soundcard or audio interface. Some work better with ASIO, and some work better with WDM. If the interface's manufacturer doesn't provide any guidance, try both and see which one behaves better.

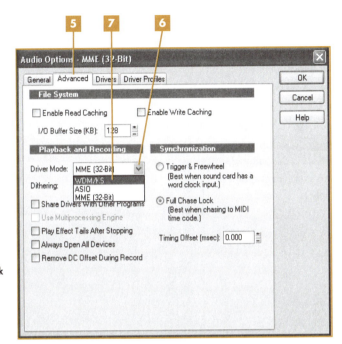

8 Click on the General tab.

9 Choose the desired options. The most important options are:

❋ Playback Timing Master. If you have both a soundcard and a high-quality audio interface, this should be set to your audio interface.

❋ Record Timing Master. If you have both a soundcard and a high-quality audio interface, this should be set to your audio interface.

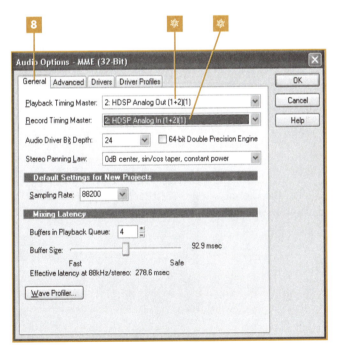

* **Audio Driver Bit Depth.** This should be set to 24 (bits) if your interface supports it.

* **Sampling Rate.** This should be set to 44,100 or higher. If your interface supports it, you should consider using a 96,000-Hz sample rate for higher fidelity.

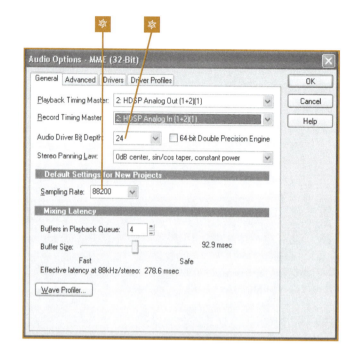

❄ Restarting

Many of the audio options require quitting and restarting SONAR before changes will take effect, and sometimes changing multiple settings requires more than one restart. Fortunately, once you get everything set correctly you won't have to fuss with the settings anymore.

1 Click on Options.

2 Click on Global. The Global Options dialog box will open.

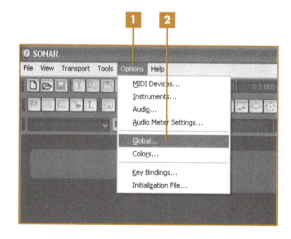

3 Click on the Audio Data tab.

4 Choose the desired Record Bit Depth from the drop-down list. This determines the quality of your audio recordings and should be set to 24 (bits) if your interface supports it.

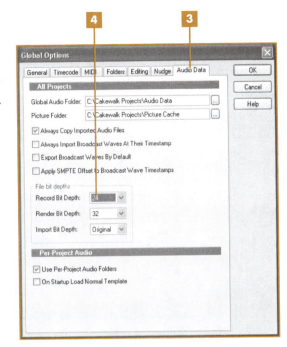

Wave Profiler

Unless you are using ASIO drivers, SONAR needs to profile audio hardware before it can use it properly. Ordinarily this only has to be done when you install SONAR or a new audio interface, but if your settings get corrupted you can restore them by forcing SONAR to run the Wave Profiler.

1 Click on Options.

2 Click on Audio. The Audio Options dialog box will open.

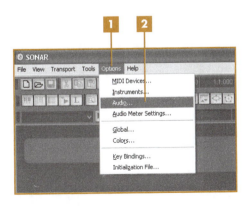

3 Click on the General tab.

4 Click on the Wave Profiler button. The Wave Profiler confirmation window will open.

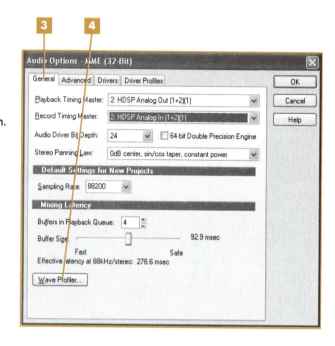

5 Click on Yes. The Wave Profiler progress window will open.

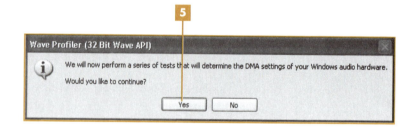

6 When the Wave Profiler has finished, click on Close. The window will close and you will return to the Audio Options dialog box.

7 Click on OK to close the Audio Options dialog box.

Managing Audio Latency

It takes a finite amount of time for audio to be digitized, travel through your computer, and be converted back to an analog sound so you can hear it. This is called *latency*, and if it's longer than a few milliseconds it can become a serious obstacle to getting any work done. Too much latency can also make the response of virtual instruments sluggish.

Latency is a result of the way audio is buffered at the CPU. Therefore, you can control latency by using the smallest buffer size and the fewest buffers you can get away with. With good drivers and a fast computer, you can set the buffer size and number so low that you don't notice the latency at all.

As you experiment with these settings, listen carefully for any distortion or dropouts. Such sonic mayhem is an indication that your buffers are not large enough or numerous enough for smooth and consistent audio recording and playback. Once you reach that point, reset your buffer settings to the last known distortion-free setting.

1 Click on the plus (+) or minus (−) buttons on the Buffers in Playback Queue number box in the Audio Options dialog box. The lower the number, the less the latency. Low numbers also increase the likelihood of distortion and dropouts, however.

2 Drag the Buffer Size slider. The further left, the smaller the buffer and the lower the latency. Click on OK to confirm the new settings.

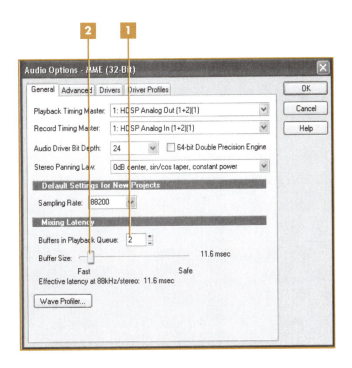

❅ Control Panel

If you are running in ASIO mode, these settings will have no effect. You must control the buffer size from the ASIO control panel.

To achieve the lowest latency with WDM or MME drivers, you will likely need to open your audio interface's control panel and set its buffer size to the smallest practical value. This buffer size is related to, but independent of, SONAR's Buffer Size setting. Once you have changed the interface's buffer size you will need to run the Wave Profiler again before SONAR will recognize the change.

❅ Situational Latency

The more plug-ins and virtual instruments you are running, the harder your computer has to work to maintain low latency. It's common practice for engineers to use a very low latency setting while *tracking* (recording) and a higher latency while mixing.

❅ The Direct Way

Most audio interfaces also feature a "direct monitor" or "hardware monitor" mode that effectively eliminates latency by bypassing the software. Audio coming in a record-armed input is immediately funneled back to the monitor outputs, so there is no delay. You should be able to enable this mode from your interface's control panel. Be sure you don't use SONAR's Input Echo when you are using direct-monitor mode, or you will hear an annoying echo or possibly even dangerous feedback.

B ♩ Understanding Audio and MIDI

SONAR 5 provides a unified environment for working with MIDI and audio. This makes it very easy to deal with the two types of musical material, but it also invites confusion between the two. This appendix provides general information about what makes each unique.

What Is MIDI?

MIDI is a language designed to control synthesizers. The term is an acronym for *Musical Instrument Digital Interface*, and it is pronounced *MIH-dee*. MIDI uses 8-bit digital messages to turn notes on and off, to set volume and pan, and to modify patch parameters. Most MIDI messages have 128 possible values: 128 patches per bank, 128 note numbers, volume values from 0–127, and so forth. These messages can be recorded, edited, and played back from within SONAR to control external hardware synthesizers or software-based virtual instruments, such as the TTS-1 DXi.

Because MIDI is simply a set of control messages, it's very easy to edit a MIDI performance in ways that you simply can't with traditional audio recording. For example, if you speed up a tape recording of someone speaking or singing, you get the classic "chipmunk" effect. This is, in fact, exactly how the voices of a number of famous cartoon characters were created. When you speed up the playback of MIDI notes, however, you get the same notes but at a faster tempo. Conversely, you can easily transpose a MIDI performance by telling SONAR to redefine which notes are to be triggered, and when you play the transposed performance it will sound as though it were recorded that way.

MIDI uses *channels* to organize its messages. As you've seen, SONAR requires that you specify a MIDI channel for each track output. Each channel has its own patch—although you can change a patch in the middle of a track using the Insert Bank/Patch Change command, you can only have one patch per channel at any given time. Similarly, pan and volume information are channel-specific. Each MIDI device can have up to 16 channels with which to work. The TTS-1, for example, lets you play 16 different instruments, each one on a different channel. This is called *multitimbral* operation. The DreamStation DXi, by contrast, is not multitimbral and can only play one patch at a time. Fortunately, you can run multiple DreamStations (or TTS-1s!) simultaneously to achieve multiple timbres.

What Is Digital Audio?

Sound is simply a variation in air pressure within a range of frequencies and amplitude our ears can perceive. Digital audio is a method of describing that variation numerically. The most common type of digital audio, *pulse code modulation (PCM)*, measures the air pressure many times each second and assigns a binary number to each of those measurements. On playback, these measurements describe the variation of air pressure over time that recreates the sound. There's more to the process, of course—the air pressure needs to be converted to voltage first, and then the measurements really describe a voltage pattern that moves a speaker that moves the air—but this translation of air pressure to binary numbers is the essence of PCM digital audio.

Digital audio can capture and reproduce sounds quite realistically if the measurements are taken often enough and accurately enough. The speed of measurement is called the *sample rate*, and it is expressed in *kilohertz (kHz)*—or thousands of samples per second. Typical sample rates for professional audio production are 44.1 kHz (the sample rate of CDs), 48 kHz, 88.2 kHz, and 96 kHz. The accuracy of measurement is determined by the *bit depth*, which determines how many units are available to measure the amplitude.

Professional recording is done at 16 bits (the bit depth of CDs) or 24 bits. In general, the higher the sample rate and bit depth the more realistic the reproduction.

The down side of recording at high sample rates and bit depths is that it takes up a lot of space on your hard disk. Recording at CD-quality resolution (16 bits, 44.1 kHz, stereo) requires 10 megabytes per minute of audio. If you record eight stereo tracks at that resolution, your three-minute song eats up 240 megabytes. The same song at 24 bits and 96 kHz devours almost 800 megabytes. Clearly, you're going to need a big hard disk for recording and lots of CDs or DVDs to back up your songs!

Comparing MIDI and Digital Audio

Of course, there's a good reason that SONAR lets you use both MIDI and digital audio in your projects. Each one has its strengths, so you'll use MIDI for some things and digital audio for others. The two factors that you want to consider in deciding which to use are file size and flexibility.

MIDI can pack a lot of instructions into a tiny amount of space. That same three-minute song would take up only a few dozen *kilobytes* if it were all MIDI data. For this reason, it's common for electronic musicians to keep their MIDI tracks as MIDI tracks for as long as possible and commit them to audio tracks (remember "Recording External Synth Parts" from Chapter 19?) only when they're ready for a final mix and export.

MIDI also beats digital audio for flexibility. If you get to the final stage of a project and suddenly discover that you misjudged your lead vocalist's highest notes, wouldn't you want to be able to use Process, Transpose to lower the key? If you had recorded all of your synthesizer parts straight to audio tracks, you would have a much harder time. Similarly, a last-minute tempo change would be much easier to accomplish with MIDI tracks than digital audio tracks.

However, once you've recorded an audio track it will sound the same every time in any studio because it precisely captured the sound of the original performance. A MIDI track is dependent on the quality of an available synthesizer, so if you don't have exactly the instrument you want you will not get the results you're after. A fantastic MIDI performance played back through a cheap synthesizer is a big let-down.

Most projects end up being a combination of audio and MIDI tracks. For example, you might have a MIDI drum track playing through the TTS-1, a MIDI bass track playing through the DreamStation DXi, and audio tracks with vocals and guitars. SONAR integrates all these elements seamlessly.

Managing Your CPU Resources

Your computer's CPU has to calculate the sound of a virtual instrument while calculating velocity offsets and equalization effects, all while drawing waveforms and controls on the screen. Sooner or later, even the fastest computer hits the wall. This appendix shows you how to keep the wall at bay a bit longer and what to do when you run out of gas.

The CPU and Disk Meters

In the lower-right corner of the SONAR window, there are two meters that have absolutely nothing to do with audio amplitude. The CPU meter tells you how much of your CPU's attention is currently being utilized, and the Disk meter tells you how much of your hard disk's read and write capacity is currently being utilized. If either meter hits 100%, SONAR will stop. Once that happens, you need to do something to free up resources.

Every virtual instrument and plug-in effect you assign will cause the CPU meter to increase. Every audio track you record or play will send the Disk meter higher. Use these meters as a guide to managing your resources. If your CPU meter is almost maxed out, you're not going to have any luck firing up another soft synth, and if your Disk meter is close to 100%, you're going to want to do something to fix that before you try to record a six-piece horn section and end up crashing every few measures.

Lightening the Load

There are several tricks you can use to free up CPU resources. One of the biggest is to make sure that when you run SONAR you *only* run SONAR. Other open applications consume processor cycles and memory that SONAR could be using on your music, so close them all. In particular, anti-virus programs, especially the ones that continually scan for harmful activity, tend to distract the hard disk and wreck great performances, so turn them off before starting SONAR. Look at your System Tray at the right end of your Windows Taskbar—if you've got more than a couple of icons there, you're wasting valuable system resources that SONAR needs. Disable as many of them as you can.

Using Group Effects

Reverb plug-ins tend to eat up more CPU resources than any other effect plug-ins. Because of this—and because of historical and aesthetic reasons—reverbs are ordinarily applied to groups of tracks by using buses. For example, if you wanted to add reverb to your background vocals you *could* insert a Lexicon Pantheon on each track. You could, but you shouldn't. Even if your system has the CPU resources to do that, it probably won't give you quite the sound you're after.

Instead, create a new bus and then create sends on all of your background vocal tracks that point to this new bus. Insert a Lexicon Pantheon or other reverb on the bus. Now a copy of each vocal track is being routed through the bus with the reverb, and you can balance the reverberated bus against the original audio tracks. Be sure to set the reverb to 100% wet. This is the standard way of routing reverb (as you learned in Chapter 19), and it only uses one instance of the plug-in, rather than needlessly eating up CPU resources with a reverb on every track.

Submixing Audio Tracks

In the heyday of the ADAT and other eight-track recorders, it was a common practice to *bounce* six tracks of drums to two tracks and then reuse those original tracks for recording additional parts. This *ping-ponging* of tracks allowed engineers to get a lot more than eight tracks of music onto a tape with only eight tracks. In SONAR, submixing tracks this way will not only free up CPU cycles from any effects that had been on the tracks originally, but it will also enable you to get more tracks of playback and recording out of your hard-working hard disk.

The Edit, Bounce to Track(s) command is similar to the File, Export Audio command, except that it automatically brings the bounced audio into an audio track. A typical application would be to solo all of your drum tracks, select them through the entire song, and bounce them to a new track. Once you've got the new track, select and archive the original drum tracks. All of their settings will be saved for future reference, but they will no longer use disk and CPU resources. Note that simply muting a track does not stop it from consuming disk and CPU resources.

Freezing Tracks and Synths

SONAR's Freeze function is a powerful way to maximize your CPU cycles. Freezing a track or synth (virtual instrument) is equivalent to bouncing the output of the track with effects and then deactivating the original. This effectively substitutes a processed audio clip for the original unprocessed audio plus effects, allowing you to use your CPU for something new.

I covered the process for freezing a track in Chapter 16—the process for synths is virtually identical. Select the track or tracks you want to freeze, and then choose Freeze Synth from the track's context menu. If you decide to tweak the track some more, you can unfreeze it to get the original back.

} Index

A

Absolute Time option (Snap to Grid dialog box), 105

Advanced option (Paste dialog box), 33

Align to Measures option

    Global Options dialog box, 29

    Paste dialog box, 33

Angle option, Surround Panner, 235

appearance of Console view, changing, 247–249

Apply Trimming command (Edit menu), 125–126

archived tracks, 120, 254

Ask Every Time option (Global Options dialog box), 29–30

Assign Instruments dialog box, 190–191, 194

Attack option, Sonitus:fx Compressor controls, 210

audio. See also songs

    clips

        backward masking, 115

        copying and pasting, 30–34

        deleting, 34–35

        drag and drop options, setting, 27–29

        fades, 110–113

        linked clips, 36–39

        moving, 29–30

        normalizing, 114–115

        reversing, 115

        selecting, 26–27

        selecting partial, 108

        silent parts between, removing, 116–117

        slip-editing, 109

        splitting, 106–107

        trimming, 125–126

exporting

    MP3 files, 257–260

    as WAV file, 254–257

folders

    cleaning, 126–128

    consolidating, 124

importing into projects, 7–8

latency, 311–312

recording

    Audio Engine, starting and stopping, 94

    distortion noises, 94

    feedback, 90, 94

    input echo, enabling, 95

    input name selection, 91–92

    loop recording, 100–102

    output options, 92

    punch recording, 97–99

    record-arming, 93

    signal flow, 90

    tracks, naming, 96

    Undo Recording button, 97

Audio command (Options menu), 306

Audio Driver Bit Depth option (Audio Options dialog box), 308

audio effects. See effects

Audio Engine, starting/stopping, 94

Audio Options dialog box, 306–308

Audio Track command (Insert menu), 44

auditioning loops, 58

auto-punch recording

    audio clips, 97–99

    MIDI clips, 169–171

B

B3 slicing marker, 85
B4 slicing marker, 85
backward masking, 115
banks and patches, 137–140
Beats in Clip value, 78
Begin value (Scale Velocity dialog box), 183
bit depth, 314
bit rates, exporting audio, 258
blank canvas, new project creation, 4–5
Blend Old and New option (Global Options dialog box), 28
bounce presets, 257
Bounce to Clip(s) command (Edit menu), 174
Bounce to Track(s) command (Edit menu), 319
Bus pane, 218–221
bus sends, 223–224
buses
    Console view, 243–244
    surround mixing, 233–236
buttons
    Draw Tool, 266, 269, 272
    Enable/Disable Automatic Crossfades, 112–113
    Enable Looping, 78–79
    Enable Slice Auto-preview, 81
    Enable Stretching, 79
    Erase Tool, 267, 270
    Eraser, 141
    Expression Tool, 272
    Fill Durations, 268–269
    Follow Project Pitch, 76, 80
    Fret View, 264
    Go to end, 17
    Hairpin Tool, 272
    Input Echo, 95
    Insert a New Tempo option, 69
    Insert Tempo, 69
    Layout, 265
    Loop On/Off, 22
    Map Mgr., 286
    Meter Options, 248
    Mute, 23, 253
    Mute Tool, 102

Narrow/Widen All Strips, 247
Next/Previous, 137
Pedal Tool, 273
Pick Tracks, 264, 275
Play, 16
Record Arm, 253
Rewind, 17, 253
Select Tool, 267
Set Loop to Selection (Time Ruler), 22
Show/Hide All Meters, 248
Show/Hide Bus Pane, 133, 219
Show/Hide EQ, 245
Show/Hide Grid, 280
Show/Hide Inspector, 50, 299
Show/Hide Pitch Envelope, 81
Show/Hide Plot, 245
Show/Hide Sends, 243
Show/Hide Volume, 242
Show Velocity Tails, 280
Snap to Grid, 281
Solo, 23, 252–253
Staff View, 264
Stop, 16
Track Layers, 102
Undo Recording, 97
bypassing effects, 212

C

Cakewalk
    MIDI track output options, 136
    Synth Rack feature, 134–135
    TTS-1 synthesizer, starting, 134–135
    tutorial project
        opening, 132–133
        playing, 137
channel 10, drum sounds, 191
chorus effects, 204–206
Clean Audio Folder dialog box, 127–128
cleaning audio folders, 126–128
Clef option (Staff View Layout dialog box), 270
clip-based effects, 214–215
Clip Boundaries option (Snap to Grid dialog box), 105

Clip View Options dialog box, 48–49

clips. *See also* tracks

  audio

    backward masking, 115

    copying and pasting, 30–34

    deleting, 34–35

    drag and drop options, 27–29

    fades, 110–113

    linked clips, 36–39

    moving, 29–30

    normalizing, 114–115

    reversing, 115

    selecting, 26–27

    selecting partial, 108

    silent parts between, removing, 116–117

    slip-editing, 109

    splitting, 106–107

    trimming, 125–126

  groove clips

    copying and pasting, 67

    creating, 76–79

    importing, 67

    looping, enabling, 77–78

    overview, 66

    pitch markers, 70–72, 75–76

    playback, 67

    root notes, 80

    samples, 66

    slices, 81

    sound of, changing, 81

    stretching, 79

    tempo, timing adjustments, 81–85

    tempo settings, 68–69

  loops as, 62–63

  MIDI

    controllers, 155–157

    events, 155–157

    input devices, 160–161, 163–165

    Key Offset (Key+) value, 187–188

    logical process, 182–184

    note length, changing, 148–149, 152

    note velocity, editing, 154

    notes, adding, 153

    notes, copying, 150–151

    notes, deleting, 153

    notes, lasso option, 151

    notes, moving, 150–151

    output devices, 160–161, 163–165

    recording, 168–174

    reversing, 147–148

    sliding, 183–184

    slip-editing, 144–145

    Time Offset (Time+) value, 186

    transposing, 146–147

    velocity, 182–183

    Velocity Trim (Vel+) value, 185

cloning tracks, 121–122

Close command (File menu), 12

closing projects, 12

commands

  Edit menu

    Apply Trimming, 125–126

    Bounce to Clip(s), 174

    Bounce to Track(s), 319

    Copy, 31

    Cut, 32

    Paste, 32, 36

    Select, 255

  File menu

    Close, 12

    Export, 255

    File Info, 9

    Import, 8

    New, 4, 218

    Open, 6

    Save, 11

    Save As, 11, 291

  Insert menu

    Audio Track, 44

    MIDI Track, 44

    Multiple Tracks, 44

  Options menu

    Audio, 306

    Global, 28, 166, 198, 308

    Icons, 50

    Instruments, 190, 194

    Key Bindings, 295

    Project, 232

commands *(continued)*

  Process menu

    Groove Quantize, 180

    Length, 148

    Quantize, 177

    Retrograde, 148

    Transpose, 146

  Tools menu, Clean Audio Folder, 127

  View menu

    Loop Explorer, 56

    Toolbars, 42

compressor effects, 210

Console view

  appearance of, changing, 247–249

  buses, 243–244

  inputs and outputs, assigning, 240–241

  pan slider, 242

  sends, 243–244

Consolidate Project Audio dialog box, 124–125

controllers

  MIDI clips, 155–157

  speed counts, 157

Copy dialog box, 31

copying

  copying and pasting audio clips, 30–34

  copying and pasting groove clips, 67

  loops, 61

  notes, 150–151

CPU meter, 317

crescendo, 182

crossfades, 112

Cut command (Edit menu), 32

D

decrescendo, 182

default templates, 292–294

Define Instruments and Names dialog box, 194–196

Delete button (Drum Map Manager dialog box), 287

Delete Whole Measures option (Global Options dialog box), 28

deleting

  audio clips, 34–35

  folders, 127

  loops, 61

  notes, 153

  silent parts between phrases, 116–117

  tracks, 46

Destination option (Map Properties dialog box), 286

Details option (Loop Explorer view), 57

dialog boxes

  Assign Instruments, 190–191, 194

  Audio Options, 306–308

  Clean Audio Folder, 127–128

  Clip View Options, 48–49

  Clone Track(s), 121–122

  Consolidate Project Audio, 124–125

  Copy, 31

  Define Instruments and Names, 194–196

  Drum Map Manager, 286–287, 289

  Export Audio, 255–256

  Export Options, 258

  File Info, 9–10

  Global Options, 28–29, 166, 198–199, 308

  Groove Quantize, 180

  Import Audio, 8

  Insert Tempo, 69

  Key Bindings, 295

  Length, 148–149

  Map Properties, 285

  Marker, 71

  MIDI Devices, 160–161

  New Project, 4–5

  New Project File, 218–219

  Open, 6

  Paste, 32–33, 36

  Pick Tracks, 264

  Project Options, 162–163, 232

  Quantize, 177–178

  Record Options, 98, 100–101, 170, 172

  Save As, 291

  Scale Velocity, 182–183

  Slide, 184

Snap to Grid, 104–106

Sort Tracks, 46

Staff View Layout, 265, 270

Tabulator Settings, 270–271

Toolbars, 42–43

Track Inputs, 301–302

Track Manager, 248–249

Track Outputs, 302

Transpose, 146–147

Unlink Clips, 38–39

digital audio and MIDI comparison, 315–316

Disk meter, 317

Display Clip Contents option (Clip View Options dialog box), 49

Display Clip Names option (Clip View Options dialog box), 49

Display Vertical Rules option (Clip View Options dialog box), 49

distortion noises, audio recording, 94

drag and drop options, audio clips, 27–29

Draw Tool button, 266, 269, 272

driver configuration, 306–309

Drum Grid

durations, 280

editing in, 281–284

viewing, 279–280

Drum Map Manager dialog box, 286–287, 289

drum maps

assigning tracks to, 278

editing, 284–288

drum sounds, 191

dry mix balance, 227

Durations option (Length dialog box), 149

E

echo, 95

Edit menu commands

Apply Trimming, 125–126

Bounce to Clip(s), 174

Bounce to Track(s), 319

Copy, 31

Cut, 32

Paste, 32, 36

Select, 255

editing

in Drum Grid, 281–284

drum maps, 284–288

slip-editing

audio clips, 109

MIDI clips, 144–145

Editing tab (Global Options dialog box), 28

effects

bypassing, 212

chorus, 204–206

clip-based, 214–215

compressor, 210

equalization, 207–209

freezing tracks, 216

FXChorus, 204–206

group, 318

LFE (Low-Frequency Effects), 233

order of, changing, 213

presets, 211

real-time, 204–210

reverb, 224–226

Sonitus:fx Compressor, 210

Sonitus:fx Equalizer, 207–209

sorting, 213

surround, 236–238

Eighth Notes slices value, 84

Enable/Disable Automatic Crossfades button, 112–113

Enable Looping button, 78–79

Enable Slice Auto-preview button, 81

Enable Stretching button, 79

End value (Scale Velocity dialog box), 183

equalization

effects, 207–209

four bands mode, 245

hidden mode, 245

one band mode, 245

Show/Hide EQ button, 245

Erase Tool button, 267, 270

Eraser button, 141

erasing notes, 267

events, MIDI clips, 155–157

Events in Tracks option
    Copy dialog box, 31
    Slide dialog box, 184
Export Audio dialog box, 255–256
Export command (File menu), 255
Export Options dialog box, 258
exporting audio
    MP3 files, 257–260
    as WAV file, 254–257
expression marks, 272–273
Expression Tool button, 272

F

fades
    crossfades, 112
    default fade curves, 113
    fading in/out, 110–111
    fast curves, 111
    linear fade, 111
    slow curve, 111
fast curve fades, 111
fast forwarding, 17
feedback, audio recording, 90, 94
File Info dialog box, 9–10
File menu commands
    Close, 12
    Export, 255
    File Info, 9
    Import, 8
    New, 4, 218
    Open, 6
    Save, 11
    Save As, 11, 291
File name field (Export Audio dialog box), 256
files, consolidating, 124
Fill Durations button, 268–269
filtering inputs, MIDI, 198–199
Focus option, Surround Panner, 236
folders
    cleaning, 126–128
    consolidating, 124

Folders option (Loop Explorer view), 57
Follow Project Pitch button, 76, 80
formats, surround mixing, 231–233
four bands mode, EQ display, 245
freezing tracks, 216, 319
Fret view, 269–271
Fret View button, 264
fretboard, 270
Front/Rear Balance, Surround Panner, 236
FXChorus effect, 204–206

G

General tab (Global Options dialog box), 167
Global Options dialog box, 28–29, 166, 198–199, 308
Go to end button, 17
green rectangle, Project Navigator feature, 19–20
groove clips
    copying and pasting, 67
    creating, 76–79
    importing, 67
    looping, 77–78
    overview, 66
    pitch markers, 70–72, 75–76
    playback, 67
    root notes, 80
    samples, 66
    slices, 81
    sound of, changing, 81
    stretching, 79
    tempo, timing adjustments, 81–85
    tempo settings, 68–69
Groove Quantize feature, 179–181
group effects, 318
group velocities, 154
guitar notation, octave-treble clef, 270

H

hairpins, 272–273
headphone mix, 221–224

hidden mode, EQ display, 245
hiding toolbars, 42–43

I

icons
    speaker, 14–15
    track icons, showing, 50–51
Icons command (Options menu), 50
Import Audio dialog box, 8
Import command (File menu), 8
importing
    audio into projects, 7–8
    groove clips, 67
    loops into projects, 59–60
In Note option (Map Properties dialog box), 285
Independent, Not Linked At All option (Unlink Clips dialog box), 39
input assignment, Track menu, 301–302
input devices, MIDI clips, 160–161, 163–165
input echo, enabling, 95
input name selection, audio recording, 91–92
inputs
    Console view, 240–241
    MIDI
        filtering, 198–199
        recording multiple, 197
Insert a New Tempo option button, 69
Insert Tempo dialog box, 69
instruments
    assigning, 190–193
    definitions, importing, 193–196
    drum sounds, 191
interface sends, 221–222
Interval option (Paste dialog box), 33

K

key bindings, 294–296
Key+ (Key Offset) value, 187–188

L

lasso option, notes, 151
latency, 167, 311–312
Layout button, 265
Length dialog box, 148–149
length of MIDI notes, changing, 148–149, 152
LFE (Low-Frequency Effects), 233
linear fades, 111
linear PCM files, 254
Link to Original Clip(s) option (Clone Tracks dialog box), 122
linked audio clips
    pasting clips as, 36–37
    selecting, 38
    unlinking, 38–39
logical process, MIDI clips, 182–184
Loop Construction view, 74
Loop Explorer view
    Details option, 57
    Folders option, 57
    opening, 56
    Preview Bus drop-drown list, 58
    Status Bar, 58
Loop On/Off button, 22
loops
    auditioning, 58
    Beats in Clip value, 78
    as clips, 62–63
    copying, 61
    defined, 56
    deleting, 61
    enabling, groove clip creation, 77–78
    importing into projects, 59–60
    locating, 58
    loop recording, MIDI clips, 171–174
    moving, 60–61
    playback, 21–22
    repeating, 61
    sample, 59
    status of, viewing, 58
Low-Frequency Effects (LFE), 233
lyrics, 274–275

M

Map Mgr. button, 286
Map Properties dialog box, 285
Marker dialog box, 71
markers, slicing, 82–85
merging takes, recording options, 174
Meter Options button, 248
metronome, configuring, 161–163
MIDI
    banks and patches, 137–140
    controllers, 155–157
    defined, 313–314
    digital audio comparisons, 315–316
    events, 155–157
    input devices, 160–161, 163–165
    inputs
        filtering, 198–199
        recording multiple, 197
    instruments
        assigning, 190–193
        definitions, importing, 193–196
    Key Offset (Key+) value, 187–188
    logical process, 182–184
    multitimbral operation, 314
    notes
        adding, 153
        copying, 150–151
        deleting, 153
        lasso option, 151
        length of, changing, 148–149, 152
        moving, 150–151
        velocities, editing, 154
    output devices, 160–161, 163–165
    output options, 136
    recording
        loop recording, 171–174
        punch-recording, 169–171
        tempo selection, 168–174
    reversing, 147–148
    sliding, 183–184
    slip-editing, 144–145
    tempo changes, 140–141
    Time Offset (Time+) value, 186
    transposing, 146–147
    velocity, 182–183
    Velocity Trim (Vel+) value, 185
MIDI Devices dialog box, 160–161
MIDI Event Type dialog box, 155–157
MIDI tab (Global Options dialog box), 199
MIDI Track command (Insert menu), 44
mixing
    dry mix, 227
    rock/pop, 230
    stem creation, 229–230
    subgroup creation, 227–228
    submix creation, 229–230
    surround mixing
        effects, 236–238
        formats, setting, 231–233
        pan controls, 234–235
        tracks and buses, 233–236
    wet mix, 227
Mode option (Snap to Grid dialog box), 105
Move By option (Snap to Grid dialog box), 106
Move To option (Snap to Grid dialog box), 105
moving
    audio clips, 29–30
    loops, 60–61
    notes, 150–151
MP3 files, exporting, 257–260
Multiple Tracks command (Insert menu), 44
multitimbral operation, 314
Musical Time option (Snap to Grid dialog box), 105
Mute button, 23, 253
Mute Tool button, 102

N

Name field, New Project File dialog box, 219
naming
    projects, 5
    templates, 292
    tracks, 43–44, 96
Narrow/Widen All Strips button, 247
New command (File menu), 4, 218

New Linked Group option (Unlink Clips dialog box), 39
New Project File dialog box, 4–5, 218–219
Next/Previous Marker buttons, 137
No Slicing option, 83
normalizing audio clips, 114–115
Note Durations option (Quantize dialog box), 178
notes
    deleting from drum map, 287
    display options, 268
    drawing, 266
    erasing, 267
    MIDI notes
        adding, 153
        copying, 150–151
        deleting, 153
        lasso option, 151
        length, changing, 148–149, 152
        moving, 150–151
        velocities, changing, 154
    moving, 267
    patterns, painting, 283–284
Now time, setting, 18, 32

O

octave-treble clef, 270
Offset option (Quantize dialog box), 178
one band mode, EQ display, 245
Only Notes, Lyrics, and Audio option (Quantize dialog box), 178
Open command (File menu), 6
Open dialog box, 6
opening
    Cakewalk tutorial project, 132–133
    Loop Construction view, 74
    Loop Explorer view, 56
    projects, 6–7
Options menu commands
    Audio, 306
    Global, 28, 166, 198, 308
    Icons, 50
    Instruments, 190, 194
    Key Bindings, 295
    Project, 232
order of effects, changing, 213

order of tracks, changing, 45–47
Out Note option (Map Properties dialog box), 285
output assignment, Track menu, 301–302
Output/Channel option, Assign Instruments dialog box, 191
output devices, MIDI clips, 160–161, 163–165
outputs
    audio recording, 92
    Console view, 240–241
    MIDI tracks, 136
Overwrite option (Record Options dialog box), 101, 170

P

panning
    Console view, 242
    surround mixing, 234–235
parts and scores, printing, 275
passages in songs, repeating, 21–22
Paste as New Clips option (Paste dialog box), 34
Paste dialog box, 32–33, 36
Paste into Existing Clips option (Paste dialog box), 34
pasting
    clips and linked clips, 36–37
    copying and pasting audio clips, 30–34
    copying and pasting groove clips, 67
Patch Browser feature, 297–298
patches and banks, 137–140
Pattern Brush options, 283–284
PCM (pulse code modulation), 314
pedal markings, 272–273
Pedal Tool button, 273
Piano Roll view, 279–280
Pick Tracks dialog box, 264
pitch markers, 70–72, 75–76
Play button, 16
playback
    groove clips, 67
    looping, 21–22
    volume adjustment, 14–15
Playback Timing Master option (Audio Options dialog box), 307
playing
    songs, 15–16
    tutorial project, 137
pop/rock mix, 230

Position toolbar, 43
presets
  bounce, 257
  effects, 211
Preview Bus drop-down list, Loop Explorer view, 58
printing parts and scores, 275
Process menu commands
  Groove Quantize, 180
  Length, 148
  Quantize, 177
  Retrograde, 148
  Transpose, 146
Project Navigator feature, 19–21
Project Options dialog box, 162–163, 232
projects
  closing, 12
  creating new, 4–5
  importing audio into, 7–8
  importing loops into, 59–60
  information, documenting, 9–10
  naming, 5
  opening, 6–7
  saving, 10–11
pulse code modulation (PCM), 314
punch recording
  audio clips, 97–99
  MIDI clips, 169–171

Q

quantization
  Groove Quantize feature, 179–181
  timing adjustments, 176–179
Quantize dialog box, 177–178
Quarter Notes slices value, 84

R

Ratio option, Sonitus:fx Compressor controls, 210
real-time effects, 204–210
Record Arm button, 253

Record Options dialog box, 98, 100–101, 170, 172
Record Timing Master option (Audio Options dialog box), 307
recording
  audio clips
    Audio Engine, starting and stopping, 94
    distortion noises, 94
    feedback, 90, 94
    input echo, enabling, 95
    input name selection, 91–92
    loop recording, 100–102
    output options, 92
    punch recording, 97–99
    record-arming, 93
    signal flow, 90
    tracks, naming, 96
    Undo Recording button, 97
  merging takes, 174
  MIDI clips
    loop recording, 171–174
    punch-recording, 169–171
  multiple inputs, MIDI, 197
  synth parts, 252–253
Recurse option (Clean Audio Folder dialog box), 127
Release option, Sonitus:fx Compressor controls, 210
repeating
  loops, 61
  song passages, 21–22
Replace Old with New option (Global Options dialog box), 28
resizing tracks, 49–50
resolution, 257
Retrograde command (Process menu), 148
reverb effects, 224–226
reversing
  audio clips, 115
  MIDI clips, 147–148
Rewind button, 17, 253
rewinding, 17
rock/pop mix, 230
root notes, groove clips, 80

S

sample rates, 314

Sampling Rate option (Audio Options dialog box), 308

Save As command (File menu), 11, 291

saving projects, 10–11

Scale Velocity dialog box, 182–183

scores, printing, 275

Select command (Edit menu), 255

Select Tool button, 267

selecting

    audio clips, 26–27

    audio clips, partial, 108

    linked audio clips, 38

sends

    bus, 223–224

    Console view, 243–244

    interface send, 221–222

Set Loop to Selection button (Time Ruler), 22

Set Punch Points (Time Ruler), 98

shortcuts

    fast forwarding, 17

    loops, enabling, 63

    Now time option, 18

    rewinding, 17

Show/Hide All Meters button, 248

Show/Hide Bus Pane button, 133, 219

Show/Hide EQ button, 245

Show/Hide Grid button, 280

Show/Hide Inspector button, 50, 299

Show/Hide Pitch Envelope button, 81

Show/Hide Plot button, 245

Show/Hide Sends button, 243

Show/Hide Volume button, 242

Show Velocity Tails button, 280

signal flow, audio recording, 90

silent parts between phrases, removing, 116–117

situational latency, 312

slicing markers, 82–85

Slide dialog box, 184

Slide Over Old to Make Room option (Global Options dialog box), 29

sliding MIDI data, 183–184

slip-editing

    audio clips, 109

    MIDI clips, 144–145

slow curve fades, 111

Snap to Audio Zero Crossings option (Snap to Grid dialog box), 106

Snap to Grid button, 281

Snap to Grid dialog box, 104–106

Solo button, 23, 252–253

songs. *See also* audio

    current location within, selecting, 18

    passages in, repeating, 21–22

    playing, 15–16

    stopping, 16

Sonitus:fx Compressor effects, 210

Sonitus:fx Equalizer effects, 207–209

Sort Tracks dialog box, 46

sorting

    effects, 213

    tracks, 45–47

speaker icon, volume control, 14–15

speed counts, controllers, 157

splitting audio clips, 106–107

Staff view

    configuring, 264–266

    expression marks, 272–273

    lyrics, 274–275

    notes

        display options, 268

        drawing, 266

        erasing, 267

        moving, 267

    parts and scores, printing, 275

    staves size, changing, 265

Staff View Layout dialog box, 265, 270

Standard toolbar, 43

Start Times option

    Length dialog box, 149

    Quantize dialog box, 178

Starting at Time field (Paste dialog box), 33

Status Bar (Loop Explorer view), 58

staves size, changing, 265

stem creation, 229–230

stereo bus, 220

Stop button, 16

Strength option (Quantize dialog box), 178

stretching clips, 79

String Tuning option (Tablature Settings dialog box), 271

subgroup creation, 227–228

submix creation, 229–230

surround mixing

    effects, 236–238

    formats, setting, 231–233

    pan controls, 234–235

    tracks and buses, 233–236

Surround tab (Project Options dialog box), 232

Swing option (Quantize dialog box), 178

synth parts, recording, 252–253

Synth Rack feature, 134–135

synthesizers, banks and patches, 137–140

System Tray, speaker icon, 14–15

T

Tablature Settings dialog box, 270–271

tabs

    Editing (Global Options dialog box), 28

    MIDI (Global Options dialog box), 199

    Surround (Project Options dialog box), 232

templates

    default, 292–294

    naming, 292

    new project creation, 5, 290–292

tempo

    gradual changes, 140–141

    groove clips, 68–69

    MIDI clip recordings, 168

    MIDI tracks, 140–141

    timing adjustments, 81–85

Threshold option, Sonitus:fx Compressor controls, 210

Time Offset (Time+) value, 186

Time Ruler

    Insert Tempo button, 69

    Now time settings, 18, 32

    Set Loop Points, 172

    Set Loop to Selection button, 22

    Set Punch Points, 98

Time+ (Time Offset) value, 186

timing adjustments

    Groove Quantize feature, 179–181

    quantization, 176–179

    tempo, 81–85

Tool menu commands, Clean Audio Folder, 127

toolbars

    hiding, 42–43

    Position, 43

    showing, 42–43

    Standard, 43

    Transport, 43

    Views, 19, 43

Toolbars dialog box, 42–43

Track/Bus Inspector feature, 299–300

Track Inputs dialog box, 301–302

Track Layers button, 102

Track Manager dialog box, 248–249

Track Outputs dialog box, 302

tracks. See also clips

    archiving, 120, 254

    arranging, 45–47

    assigning to drum maps, 278

    cloning, 121–122

    creating, 43–44

    deleting, 46

    fitting to window, 47–48

    freezing, 216, 319

    icons, showing, 50–51

    Mute button, 23

    naming, 43–44, 96

    order of, changing, 45–47

    resizing, 49–50

    Solo button, 23

    sorting, 45–47

    surround mixing, 233–236

    track numbers, 46

    unfreezing, 216

    view options, setting, 48–49

    wiping, 123

Transient Detection option, 83

Transport toolbar, 43

Transpose dialog box, 146–147

transposing MIDI clips, 146–147
trimming audio clips, 125–126
TTS-1 synthesizer, starting, 134–135
tutorial project, Cakewalk
	opening, 132–133
	playing, 137
Type of Keys option (Key Bindings dialog box), 295

U

Undo Recording button, 97
unfreezing tracks, 216
Unlink Clips dialog box, 38–39

V

Vel+ (Velocity Trim) value, 185
velocity
	notes, editing, 154
	scaling, 182–183
Velocity Trim (Vel+) value, 185
View menu commands
	Loop Explorer, 56
	Toolbars, 42
view options, tracks, 48–49
Views toolbar, 19, 43
voice settings, chorus effects, 205–206
volume
	adjustment, 14–15
	headphone mix, 224

W

WAV file, exporting audio as, 254–257
Wave Profiler feature, 309–310
wet mix balance, 227
What to do with existing material option (Paste dialog box), 33
Width option, Surround Panner, 235
Window option (Quantize dialog box), 178
wiping tracks, 123

Y

yellow loop marker, 22

Z

zoom controls
	discussed, 51
	previous zoom levels, 52
	tracks, fitting to window, 47–48

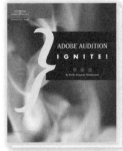